D1230691

# BOOKS WRITTEN BY DAVID L. EDGELL, SR.

1. International Tourism Policy (1990)
2. (Co-author) Selected Readings in International Tourism Policy (1991)
3. (Co-author) Coopetition: Global Tourism Beyond the Millennium (1995)
4. Tourism Policy: The Next Millennium (1999)
5. Best Practices Guidebook for International Tourism and Attractions Development for Rural Communities (2002)
6. (Co-author) Eco-Travel and Sustainable Tourism (2003)
7. Managing Sustainable Tourism: A Legacy for the Future (2006)
8. (Co-author) Tourism Policy and Planning: Yesterday, Today, and Tomorrow (2008)
9. (Co-author) Tourism Policy and Planning: Yesterday, Today, and Tomorrow (second edition – 2012)
10. Managing Sustainable Tourism: A Legacy for the Future (second edition – 2016)
11. (Co-author) Tourism Policy and Planning: Yesterday, Today, and Tomorrow (third edition - 2019)
12. Managing Sustainable Tourism: A Legacy for the Future (third edition – 2020)

# BOOKS WRITTEN BY BONNIE KOGOS

1. Manitoulin Adventures: I Was Mistaken For a Rich, Red, Ripe Tomato (2001)
2. Manhattan Manitoulin, A Novel of Manitoulin (2012)
3. The Boat That Brings You Home: Set in the Sultry Caribbean Sea (2019)
4. Newspaper Columnist for The Sudbury Star, Northern Ontario for 31 years
5. In collaboration: The African Cookbook, by Bea Sandler (1970). Accompanied Bea Sandler to eleven African countries and Zanzibar collecting recipes and menus for this award-winning cookbook of 300 recipes and tips for elegant preparation.
6. Editor & Publisher of The Zenith Traveler Newsletter, twenty years, in New York.

# THE WORLDLY TRAVELERS

These Lives and Journeys Changed the World

To appreciate the magnitude of their impact on our world, we happily immerse ourselves in their thoughts, lives and travels.

Herodotus, Marco Polo, Ibn Battuta, Zheng He, Christopher Columbus, Jeanne Baret, Charles Darwin, Mark Twain, Nain Singh, Charles Lindbergh, Amelia Earhart, and Yuri Gagarin

Experience the excitement, the romance and danger in their journeys!

Where did they go, what did they do, and how did their journeys change our lives?
Why we get that CHILL when we learn what each has done!

by

## David L. Edgell, Sr.
## and
## Bonnie Kogos

**author**HOUSE

*AuthorHouse™*
*1663 Liberty Drive*
*Bloomington, IN 47403*
*www.authorhouse.com*
*Phone: 833-262-8899*

*Published by AuthorHouse   06/30/2023*

*ISBN: 979-8-8230-0198-4 (sc)*
*ISBN: 979-8-8230-0197-7 (hc)*
*ISBN: 979-8-8230-0196-0 (e)*

*Library of Congress Control Number: 2023903548*

*Print information available on the last page.*

*Any people depicted in stock imagery provided by Getty Images are models, and such images are being used for illustrative purposes only.*
*Certain stock imagery © Getty Images.*

*This book is printed on acid-free paper.*

*Because of the dynamic nature of the Internet, any web addresses or links contained in this book may have changed since publication and may no longer be valid. The views expressed in this work are solely those of the author and do not necessarily reflect the views of the publisher, and the publisher hereby disclaims any responsibility for them.*

# REMEMBRANCE

*Remembering these worldly travelers of yesteryear as they changed the world in which we live today.*

**In memory of:**

John C. Anema Jr., a wilderness traveler and a contributing member of the Audubon Society, as well as a strong supporter of sustainable travel.

Chuck Gee, a good friend and long-time Dean of the School of Travel Industry Management at the University of Hawaii, and a champion of sustainable tourism research and development.

Alexander Harris, our dear friend and colleague, a worldly traveler who kept inspiring us all throughout his life.

Fred Kogos, author and publisher, born in Ukraine, who immigrated to Boston with his family as a youngster. He attended Boys Latin, graduated from Harvard College and built his own publishing company; the Apparel Manufacturer Magazine, and created sixty textbooks for the apparel needles trade around the world. With joy, he studied, researched, curated and continued the growth and fun of learning and speaking the Yiddish language, with five popular books published.

David N. Parker, a twenty-first century worldly traveler, a strong supporter of global tourism policies, and a major advocate of national parks throughout the world.

George A. Baumgarten, a world traveler, travel agency owner and journalist at the United Nations, who inspired us with his knowledge and stories.

**We dedicate this book in honor of our children, future worldly travelers.**

Phoenix Rose Gust, Starla Ray Gust,
and Nathan Lee Edgell
Grandchildren of David L. Edgell, Sr.

Scarlett and Audrey Beckman
Grandnieces of Bonnie Kogos

# CONTENTS

# INTRODUCTION

"The world is a book and those who
do not travel read only a page."
-St. Augustine, *City of God* (413 C.E.)

*The Worldly Travelers* offers amazing stories that we know will delight
and inspire you. These fascinating accounts are the true events of real
people who traveled, changed and shaped the world in which we live.

These few men and two women changed the course of human history
resulting from their curiosity, courage, and their extraordinary travels,
risking their lives and livelihoods in pursuit of their dreams. Of
every nationality, every walk of life, and of every determination, each
lived remarkable lives. Each had a formidable character connected to
powerful historic and cultural events. These gypsy souls ably and eagerly
wandered from one place to another to see how the unknown excited
them.

*The Worldly Travelers* journeyed and made discoveries that have
significantly altered humankind's understanding of history, geography,
the environment, and social-cultural development. These travels have
added special insights and knowledge about new global destinations,
geographical structures, and about how the inhabitants' cultural values
have forever impacted the way in which future generations might live
and view the universe. Many of them wrote books, providing us with
basic principles, practices and philosophies of travel which continue to
drive the travel and tourism industry in our modern world.

*The Worldly Travelers* weren't emperors or kings. In different times,
they might have gone unnoticed, except that each was able to shape and

change humanity forever. Their views of the world were as varied as their journeys. Like most people, they had virtues, sins, good days and bad, yet they survived the questions of kings and queens, tests and skepticisms of great leaders, and jealousies of contemporaries and detractors, to pursue unusual travels and leave behind vivid descriptions of where they had been and what they had learned. Their backgrounds and personalities are colorful and distinctive, and their stories exhilarate us, shaping and affecting the world in which we live.

Some stories may be familiar, yet forgotten in the annals of time, or not considered important enough in our educational institutions to merit attention. Yet their legacies continue to affect present day interests in historic events, ancestral behavior, geographical pursuits, and cultural-heritage travel and tourism. They are certainly worth knowing.

In writing **The Worldly Travelers,** attempts were made to identify the sources of research examined, which may be found at the end of the book in the two sections titled: "A Guide to Further Reading" and "General References".

We do not pretend to claim the mantle of historians; we're dedicated storytellers, perusing with care what others have written. We've sought information from the Internet, used our imagination and teased out stories that fit the characters and time periods. In portraying these fascinating lives, fact and fiction merge frequently in the stories. If mistakes of facts were made, or information discredited, we apologize in advance.

Please note the use of B.C.E. (Before the Common Era) and C.E. (Common Era) instead of B.C. and A.D. Such abbreviations are used in scholarly literature and in historic references to time periods. This usage is simply an effort by the authors to follow recent trends in identifying historical timelines. After the chapter about Herodotus, C.E. is used sparingly; the remaining characters were in the C.E. time period.

Where information was scarce, some material in the chapters seek to fill in the gaps, and to offer suppositions. This is based on reasoned judgment in what may have happened during certain time periods, or what the traveler may have encountered along the way. While we haven't deliberately fictionalized the basic information of the life of each traveler available to us, we've taken certain licenses in explaining certain circumstances of each of the worldly travelers, based on reasoned conjecture.

Enjoy these amazing, incredible journeys. As we so enjoy sharing these with you.

# PROLOGUE

*"Sing in Muse, and through me tell
the story...the wanderer..."*
-Homer, *the Odyssey*, 800 B.C.E.

*A deep powerful voice boomed across the quiet room: "The Father of the universe has, indeed, provided for earthly beings to travel in some form or another since the beginning of time."*

*The storytelling prophet faced the crowd before him with a mesmeric gaze, knowing he captured their attention. His audience was riveted, focused on his profile. A hushed silence fell as they eagerly listened for more. With a mystifying smile, he knew they were struck with roused curiosity. What would this oracle say about travel?*

*"The sights and sounds of travel stretch the mind," the prophet said slowly, "as to the peculiar movements into the unknown. The further one travels along newly found paths, the more glorious the journey. A traveler may see only what he wants to see, or find secret destinations that only exist in the mind."*

*The sage quietly walked among the circle of people to search the expressions on each face staring back at him. His entire audience trembled with suspense, keen to the point of excitement, waiting....*

*"We're all wanderers in the wilderness of the world. And we learn from the great travelers of other centuries about the mysteries of life. Travel teaches us to tolerate the ideas and customs of societies that we are unaccustomed to in our daily lives. When we travel, we strive to reach other dimensions, to venture beyond the next horizon for fulfillment. A*

*destination is never a place; it's a search for knowledge and adventure. This is the essence of human spirit."*

*Murmurs of approval reached his ears. This seer of the future began his story, the likes of which had never been told, of the epic adventures of the worldly travelers who, as a result of their travels, have changed the world in which we live. Come along with us.*

# CHAPTER ONE

# THE ORIGIN OF TRAVEL

"For three million years we were hunter-gatherers,
and it was through the evolutionary pressures
of that way of life that a brain so adaptable
and so creative eventually emerged…"
-Richard E. Leakey-

*The hunter-gatherers, these twenty cave dwellers, sat dejectedly near the fire to keep warm and to contemplate how best to find food for their clan. Consistent with time, a million years ago, men were the hunters of animals, and women were the gatherers of nuts, berries, and edible plants. It had been too long a depressing time for the tribe, with little to eat. Game was disappearing; the clan had not eaten meat, their main staple, for over a week. The few fish they managed to spear in the nearby stream were almost gone. Wild onions and dandelions were the only vegetables they could find near the edge of the forest. Frightened to venture farther into the dark woods to search for nuts, berries, or small game, they thought of their dear clan member who had recently been killed by a large saber tooth tiger. The food situation was getting worse.*

*The eldest member of the clan was on the verge of death by starvation. The Clan Code dictated that, when there was a food shortage, the best hunters must be fed first. If their strength waned, the entire tribe could starve. Next in the survival group were the young women of child-bearing age. Without them, the clan would disappear. Children followed in the critical flow pattern of the food distribution, with the elderly being last to be fed.*

*The children had no more than a few berries to eat. With the specter of starvation staring at them, decisions had to be made. One young hunter, more adventurous than his fellow tribesmen, had ventured farther from the cave than his fellow hunters. He noted that more animals and plants existed in the valley below. But to move the clan from the cave near the mountain presented many problems. The cave provided them with security from wild beasts of prey, a place to retreat for safety. A few months earlier, members from another tribe had wandered into the area, horrifying them while they were hunting, and challenged the clan for dominance over their hunting domain.*

*Yet, the enemy dared not enter the cave, seeing several tall spear-and-club wielding hunters staring back at them.*

*After much grunting, the clan chief, a prolific hunter-leader, convinced the group that the best strategy was for him to travel to the valley with the young hunters to seek possible new locations for shelter and availability of food sources.*

*Early the next morning, the sun broke through the clouds, allowing the mountain to shimmer with golden light as the barefoot travelers began their adventure. Uncertain of what they might find, their travel was difficult and dangerous, and they felt frightened about the unknown. Yet they were curious and excited about what they might find moving forward.*

\* \* \*

I nitially, early travel was motivated by the simple desire to survive from day to day, to find food and water, and secure a protective place for the tribe to live. Movement to a new location was tedious, primitive, and risky. Yet as we evolved, not only were our survival instincts important, the desire to search for new surroundings and a basic curiosity of what might be over the next hill began.

Our ancestors who journeyed to far-flung destinations eventually changed present day societies. From the dawn of the human race, man has been on the move as he crisscrossed the planet earth, seeking an improved way of life and good fortune in one form or another. Words from the Bible portended the future of mankind venturing into unknown destinations, and passing the knowledge learned from such travels to the next generation.

Read *Daniel 12:4*: "Many shall run to and fro, and knowledge shall be increased..."

Archaeologists, paleontologists, paleoanthropologists, ethologists, anthropologists, and palynologists have each provided us with evidence of ancient time periods. Our ancestral species *Homo erectus,* meaning upright human, evolved in Africa two million years ago, having the modern long - legged body type and walking upright with long strides, as we do today. They stood erect and had the ability to walk and run long distances. While they had small brains, they were capable of building fires for warmth and cooking meat, organizing hunts for food, and fashioning crude tools and weapons.

The next step in the evolutionary process was for *Homo erectus* to travel beyond their accustomed habitats to new environments. Gradually, as a result of changing environmental and climate conditions and for purposes of obtaining more food, *Homo erectus* migrated from Africa to western Asia and beyond.

**Living and travel in the earliest of times**
(All Non-Africans Are Part Neanderthals, 2012)

As early as 600,000 years ago, *Homo erectus* evolved into our more advanced ancestors, the *Homo sapiens*. With this evolution, they developed bigger skulls, larger brains, and greater curiosity, and were able to travel even greater distances. Eventually, about 200,000 years ago, archaic man developed a language to communicate with individuals within their local area, allowing them to pass on to future generations what they experienced or had seen in their limited travels. Then, 100,000 years ago, with many evolutionary changes in-between, antediluvian man eventually migrated from the Rift Valley in East Africa into the Middle East, Asia, Europe, and finally to the Americas and beyond.

Gradually, early man became increasingly more curious to know what was beyond the next hill. Primitive men initially journeyed in search of food, water, shelter from the weather, and safety from wild beasts and hostile tribes. Later, 10-20,000 years or so ago, some of the clans possibly followed steppe bison, woolly mammoths, reindeer, or caribou from Siberia across the northern frozen tundra of the Bering Strait into the Americas, eventually reaching the tip of South America.

Wherever our early predecessors went, they made changes and developed new knowledge to deal with the circumstances and environment surrounding them. Primarily, techniques were designed to find better ways of killing animals and to develop protective weapons against intruders; hence, bows, arrows, arrowheads, spearheads, wood clubs, and stone axes were developed. As knowledge increased, man wandered to areas beyond his immediate vicinity, not only for necessities of life, but for the pure enjoyment of exploring new environments and even encountering unfamiliar people.

As they journeyed beyond customary haunts, they appreciated the excitement of new locations, recognized the beauty of a sacred sunrise or sunset as it glistened off the earth's bodies of water, and were awed by the towering snowcapped majestic mountains. They noticed dancing shadows over the flowering meadows at sunset, and listened to the whispering of the wildlife as the silver moon appeared in the sky. In this recognition of the earth's magnificence was the true origin of travel that has been celebrated by humanity for centuries to come.

While the records of man's early treks are limited, enigmatic cave drawings of primitive man's movement exist. In this early era, fishing, hunting, and food gathering were the prime motivators of most short trips. Later, family bonding and socialization with other clans became important reasons to journey to a new area. Movement by our ancestors was not only difficult by foot, but strewn with natural and contrived obstacles. Travel was perilous, often requiring the traveler to face marauding fierce tribes, large carnivorous animals, and challenging wild terrain. However, if there appeared to be better opportunities for food and shelter elsewhere, the clan simply gathered their belongings and moved to a new location.

A wanderer in primitive times had little information to guide him on his movements to new areas. Stories about travel were verbally passed on to each generation. Yet such information only hinted at motives, means, and methods of peregrinating to other destinations. People, afraid of the unknown, conjured up images of monsters waiting to pounce on the traveler. Superstitious, they were concerned that demons existed everywhere beyond their home. To ensure a safe trip, the journeyer paid homage to "the gods", however they were defined, asking for protection.

These immortals included gods of the moon, sun, lightning, thunder, winds, love, knowledge, war, seas, or other. This was the reality of travel in ancient times.

Early travel was by foot, over rough trails where little of the landscape was known. In modern times, walking is still the preferred method of serious travelers who want to know about the environment, people, and places they visit. Present-day travelers, us, with many choices of transport, fondly talk about walking tours to visit the treasured structures of yesteryear, hiking into the wilderness to revel in the flora and fauna of the area or trekking up some magnificent mountain. But primitive wanderers had no choice; they moved by foot. We guess that ancient man may have ridden a log down a river or swum across a stream, but, essentially, movement over land was by walking long distances, the primary mode of travel for thousands of years.

As humankind gradually progressed to becoming an agrarian society, as early as 8,000 B.C.E., there was a constant search for better lands on which to cultivate crops and for grazing animals. This phenomenon caused the exploration of new destinations and the move to areas where the land was more fertile, and water readily available. Gradually, small villages appeared, and an exchange of products became a reason to travel beyond one's small settlement.

Later, it became important for farmers to trade their agricultural produce for products made or mined by more distant civilizations; thus, this trade provided unprecedented new opportunities. Such journeys for commercial purposes evolved slowly at first, because the trader-traveler, traveling by foot, could only carry a limited number of goods. Some societies began to utilize slave labor for such activities, resulting in larger loads being transported. But the real breakthrough for business pursuits in transporting merchandise long distances resulted from the domestication of animals that could carry heavy burdens. This allowed for the organization of merchant trade caravans and other groupings of travelers for purposes of broadening merchandise exchanges, providing greater safety and security, as well as socialization amongst the traders and travelers.

Once animals were domesticated to transport cargo, it was easy to take the next step, to ride the beasts. Donkeys were early alternatives to foot travel and revolutionized the ability to move both individuals and larger amounts of goods longer distances. Eventually, traders found other animals that could travel faster and further and carry greater loads. Pack animals, as mules, camels, and even elephants began to be used in caravans to transport a variety of freight and the travelers' belongings. Yet, dusty and often muddy trails, stormy weather, insects, wild beasts, highwaymen, and marauders all tested the will and courage of our traveling merchants or curious wanderers along every step of their journey.

Determining where and when the oldest civilization began to develop is still being studied. Most researchers suggest the Mesopotamia Civilization as possibly the eldest. Around 5500 B.C.E., the Sumerian society, part of Mesopotamia, arose along a region between the Tigris and Euphrates rivers, which emptied into the Persian Gulf in what is now southern Iraq. This area, from north Jordon to southeastern Turkey and east to Iran, is often referred to as the "Cradle of Civilization." The area is also noted as the "Fertile Crescent" due to its rich soil. Later, the Greeks referred to this area as "Mesopotamia", which means, "The land between two rivers," which is now modern-day Iraq. This Sumerian civilization was advanced for its time period, way ahead of other more primitive civilizations. They developed a political structure of independent city-states and were the first to become organized socially, militarily, and economically. They provided each community with its own ruler throughout the region and they built a city they called Eridu, near the ancient city of Uruk.

This Sumerian city is generally thought to be one of the oldest cities in the world, although many scholars suggest that Uruk might be older. Uruk progressed into a large city of about 50,000 by 3,000 B.C.E. The Sumerians greatly improved farming techniques, including the invention of a crude plow and the development of better irrigation systems. These advancements allowed the farmers to produce a surplus of food for storage or trade.

Babylon is a famous ancient city-state within the region of the Sumerian cities, and well-known in history throughout most of the world. While developed later than the Sumerian society, about 2300 B.C.E., Babylon became a major cultural center and possibly the first ancient city to reach a population of 200,000 residents. Babylon became famous as a destination for Greek travelers who wanted to visit the *Hanging Gardens of Babylon,* described by the Greeks as one of the "Seven Wonders of the Ancient World."

Our first Worldly Traveler, the well-known Greek respected historian, Herodotus, gives a vivid description of the gardens in his book, *The Histories.*

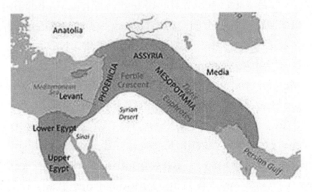

**Map of the Fertile Crescent**
(Majid, 2013)

The Sumerians are credited with inventing the wheel, one of the most significant advances devised by man. With innovation in the use of the wheel, these highly intelligent people were able to fashion a crude vehicle, initially pulled by donkeys, for transport, travel, and trade. They improved their roads, which led to more travel over greater land distances, and, at the same time, they built boats that could be used for hauling goods, transporting travelers, and for trading with other societies.

With respect to the impact of the wheel on the advancement of travel, further improvements were made over the next several hundred years. More sophisticated wheeled carts, and wagons, forerunners of the more versatile covered wagons dating to sometime around 2500 B.C.E., became available. These vehicles were pulled by an ox or an onager, an ass-or horse-like animal. Transportation became more functional, revolutionizing movements of people and goods, especially from long distances, such as the exotic locations of Egypt and India. This gave merchants the opportunity to increase the amount of goods for trading. The invention of the wheel allowed more productive movements of products, and laid the groundwork for a future global trade economy.

In addition, the Sumerians further revolutionized the ability to travel and increase trade by developing "cuneiform" script writing. Reed pens, and writing on clay tablets made it easier to record written communication and to give travel directions. They developed a system for recording units of time, dividing a day into 24 hours and one hour into 60 minutes.

Some historians also give the Sumerians credit for inventing money. The Sumner "shekel" was used around 5000 B.C.E. Herodotus, our Greek historian and worldly traveler anointed the Lydians with this honor, because they were the first to advance the making of coins. Lydia was an ancient country of West Central Asia Minor on the Aegean Sea.

The achievements of the Sumerians contributed to the possibilities for travelers to move longer distances and to transport larger amounts of trade goods. Having money allowed travelers a choice to either barter or pay for their travel. Travelers now had options for transport, forms of payment, and, sometimes, written directions or guides to advise them in their journeying. The Sumerians, as leaders of the civilized world during this era, undoubtedly left an impressive legacy of travel and trade advances for future generations to build on.

While the Sumerians made impressive advancements in travel, they left a tarnished record on society in the process. While they invented an easy form of writing, only a small percentage of Sumerians became literate. And they were the first society to develop schools.

Initially, the Sumerian society treated men and women mostly equal. Yet, as the system of power expanded, with governmental bureaucracies evolved, these changes led to the development of a government of city-states ruled by male kings or monarchs who claimed their power came from the gods. These claims made by the Sumerian kings allowed them to rule in whatever way suited them. According to their ordinances and rulings, they wrote the laws, dictating the power of men over women, leading to a male-only dominated travel society. Greedy kings, anxious to increase their power and wealth, made war on other communities, with the victors enslaving the vanquished. Like later societies, the Sumerian kings justified their actions through their religion, which declared, the *gods would not have given them victory if they were not a superior people.*

The Sumerian society, existing from 5000-1750 B.C.E. was infiltrated by Semites from the north, which led to the downfall of the Sumerian society in about 2000 B.C.E. Yet, in the annals of trade and tourism, the Sumerian society's early contributions set the stage for future generations to build from and make dramatic new advancements in travel.

Other advanced societies also contributed to improvements; the ancient Egyptian civilization basically evolved as a result of the rich soil, plant and animal life along the Nile River. Organized agrarian pursuits and small communities along the Nile River burgeoned around 5000 B.C.E.

Later, about 3100 B.C.E., ancient Egypt became an advanced society, introducing laws of government, arts, science, agriculture, culture, and religion. Egyptian society, and the large cities of Memphis and Thebes, far outclassed the earlier Sumerian communities, one way by developing great monuments and other structures that attracted travelers and traders throughout the ancient world. The pyramid at Giza, built 4500 years ago as the resting place of the Egyptian pharaoh Khufu, still stands as an amazing tribute to the unbelievable knowledge of science, engineering, and architecture developed by ancient Egypt. For four centuries, it was the world's tallest building. Nearby, the pyramid, and possibly constructed shortly thereafter, is the great symbol of Egypt, the Sphinx, having the body of a lion with a pharaoh's head, another of the great achievements of early Egyptian engineering, architecture, and craftsmanship. The Egyptians certainly set a firm foundation for modern-day travel and leisure.

With the political unification of Upper and Lower Egypt leading to the age of the godlike pharaohs, a strong, powerful society developed. Under an elaborate system of religious beliefs, wealthy Egyptians were able to travel for religious activities, curiosity, trade, and pleasure. Yet the early Egyptians had many gods to placate. Appeasement included lavish festivals and events, which led to the popularity of today's tourist festivals and events. And the development of professional event planning and its impact on tourism; a legacy to us from our early Egyptian travel organizers.

The Egyptians enjoyed traveling the beautiful four thousand miles of the Nile River to celebrate the changing of the seasons, good harvests, and thanking the gods for their rich life. While visiting Egypt, Herodotus, wrote in his famous book, *Histories*: "...The Nile is the Gift of Osiris, an important Egyptian god; Egypt is the gift of the Nile..."

The Egyptians went further, building impressive river vessels to be used for well-organized cruises on the Nile River, that we think may have been as exciting and entertaining thousands of years ago as our super cruise ships and travel itineraries are today.

By 2700 B.C.E., the Egyptians' increasingly improved boats were used to transport huge rocks, weighing thousands of pounds, from the rock quarries along the Nile. These stones, under the guidance of intelligent builders utilizing unique construction techniques, were used to build the pyramids, temples, obelisks, and other famous historic structures that became important travel sites and destinations. This transportation was also used for trading with other societies along the Nile River.

Say hello to the Nubians, another society making its appearance at the same time as Egypt, in their ancient settlements south of Upper Egypt. Today, known as modern day Sudan, it was referred to by the Egyptians as "Yam." There were many similarities between the Nubian society and ancient Egypt. Nubians, like Egyptians, lived in stone houses. Nubians buried their dead in a similar fashion to that of the Egyptians, burying bodies facing west and leaving materials with the dead that might be useful in the afterlife. Both Nubian and ancient Egyptian religions viewed the important goddess, Isis, goddess of the moon in the same way. With many similarities between Egypt and Nubia, it was clear that travel and trade were taking place.

Ancient, or "Old Kingdom Egypt" shows records of major travelers and traders journeying on their missions, which occurred during 2287-2278 B.C.E.

Harkhuf was an Egyptian official and caravan leader who made four trips to Yam, each one taking eight months. His primary business was trade with the people of Nubia. He wrote that his first travel took place when he was a youngster, with his father who'd been requested by King Merenre of Egypt to explore Yam.

Harkhuf had grown and was living on Elephantine Island in the Nile River, opposite Aswan city in Upper Egypt. On his second expedition, he traveled alone to Yam. Curious, inventive and eager, he brought back exotic gifts that mesmerized the court officials at court. So well did he do, bringing these gifts and information that King Merenre asked Harkhuf on his third journey to investigate data, rumors, evidence, facts and figures about the ruler of Yam and to note what ambitions the ruler might have, especially his military campaigns against the southern Libyans. The King also wanted Harkhuf to assess Nubia's military might in case Egypt might wish to invade Nubia.

By Harkhuf's s fourth trip, Egypt had a young King named Pepi II, and Harkhuf brought him many gifts from Yam; incense, ebony, skins, ivory, animals, and even a talented pygmy who could do exotic dances, which delighted King Pepi II. At this time, few Egyptians could write, and those who were able to write did so on papyrus "paper" that, unless preserved under special conditions, eventually crumbled. As a result, we depend on Harkhuf's writings to learn about Nubia. Wishing to be remembered by future generations, Harkhuf scratched and carved a brief *autobiography* of his life, local customs, and travels to Nubia on his tomb. His writings have survived, providing us much early information about ancient Egypt and Nubia.

**Pyramids of Giza**
Alnoaim, 2019

By 1500 B.C.E., the Egyptians traveled regularly for official celebrations, trade, and pleasure. One remarkable story of Egyptian travel; Queen Hatshepsut, after ruling Egypt for six years on behalf of a stepchild, took a bold step and declared herself to be the pharaoh. She went so far as to wear traditional male clothing and wore a fake beard like the ones worn by previous males who sat upon the throne of Egypt. One of her great accomplishments was beginning the construction of the *Mortuary Temple of Hatshepsut*, also known as the *Djeser-Djeseru* in Upper Egypt on the cliffs of Deir-el-Bahari on the west bank of the Nile River.

In 1480 B.C.E., Queen Hatshepsut journeyed upon the Nile River, a highly organized trip to see the finished temple, near Luxor. This temple is still considered to be one of the most important ancient structures in Egypt. Her major tourism venture is described by scratches on the walls of the temple. It was common for Egyptian travelers to scratch their names and other information on soft stone with a knife or other sharp objects. Later, other societies, as the Romans, left their marks on ancient structures giving rise to the term "graffiti", which is Italian for "scratching".

By 1400 B.C.E., Egyptians were sophisticated, desiring to travel and experience the arts, historic structures and cultures in other communities outside their own. Prosperous trade and travel took place between the official kingdom of the Pharaohs and the Levantine kings. The exchange dealt in gold and precious goods, while war chariots were exchanged for slaves and horses. Traveling Egyptians also sought to find and purchase unique gifts for their friends and relatives; thus, the basis for shopping emerged, so important to many of today's tourists.

Egyptian government couriers, officials with their entourages, business travelers with their goods, and tourists were often seen on the roads, near the rivers and in the local communities seeking hospitality. They learned through word of mouth from other travelers the locations which lodgings and food would be available. Today, this form of learning about hospitable destinations from talking with friends and relatives is a major source of information in modern tourism.

The Greek society became interested in the Egyptian culture and religion. The greatest of the early Greek travelers and the ancient world's first travel writer, our Herodotus, noted all this in a section of his famous book *The Histories*. His details of an itinerary down the Nile River pertaining to one of the Egyptian religious events that took place in the formative years of travel fascinated us: "The Egyptians have religious gatherings not once a year but frequently, especially, and most enthusiastically, in the city of Bubastis in honor of Artemis, the Goddess of the Hunt, Forests and Hills, the Moon," he wrote. "Their second-favorite city is Busiris..., third is Sais..., fourth is Heliopolis..., fifth is the city of Bluto..., sixth is Papremis... This is what they do when they travel to Busiris: men travel together with women, and large numbers of both travel in each boat. Some of the women have rattles, which they shake, while some men play the flute during the whole voyage. The rest of the men and women sing and clap their hands. Whenever they sail near any other city, they bring their barge close to shore and do this: some of the women do as I have just said, while others jeer and shout at the women in the city. Some dance; while, still others stand up and hoist their skirts. They do these things along the riverfront of every city. When they arrive at Busiris, they celebrate huge sacrifices and have a feast. They drink more grape wine during this feast than in all the rest of the year..."

We loved reading this, respecting that his description is familiar with respect to events of today, such as the religiously related Mardi Gras and Carnival season, celebrated with its festivities, merrymaking, feasting, and drinking.

About the same time, as the Sumerians and Egyptians were moving from an agrarian society toward more advanced civilizations, there were less developed areas throughout the world that were inhabited by Neolithic settlers, who began the practice of farming. One area was the settlement in the Boyne Valley in ancient Ireland, where possibly the world's oldest surviving substantial monument was built, known as the Newgrange. While the Newgrange is possibly older than the great pyramid of Giza in Egypt, it has not received much attention in the history of ancient civilizations. The Neolithic farmers of ancient Ireland learned to build larger dwellings over time. Advancing in their ability to build such structures, they built what came to be known as passage tombs; the most famous was the Newgrange passage tomb.

Built over 4500 years ago, this amazing edifice is older than the more famous Stonehenge structure of England. The Newgrange structure was decorated with eye-motifs offering a rare look at Neolithic Age art. It was built of stone with a circular wall 280 feet in diameter and 45 feet high and covered an area of one acre. Above the entrance to the inside of the edifice was a roof box that narrowly let sunlight shine perfectly down the passageway of the structure only during the period of the winter solstice sun starting on or about December 21st. Researchers still suggest this impressive structure was more than a "passage tomb" and was, more likely, a religious temple.

Everywhere, early transportation, whether by land or sea, demanded a comprehensive understanding of craftsmanship and the intelligent use of animals for carrying burdens. The horse was put into service about 2300 B.C.E. pulling light carts and wagons. Around 1600 B.C.E., the horse-drawn chariot was developed and became the travel vehicle of choice for emperors, kings, princes, generals, and dignitaries. The chariot was popular for racing, for use in war, and was a comfortable conveyance for leisure travel.

We did not find a definite date regarding the riding of horses for simple enjoyment. General horseback riding must have happened sometime about 1000 B.C.E. because, by 875 B.C.E., the Assyrians had developed a cavalry. Such a military use of the horse required certain equestrian knowledge, gained from persons riding a horse for pleasure or, possibly, by messenger express riders in the service of the government. The Persians developed a sophisticated messaging system that utilized several horse riders, with stops along the way for obtaining fresh horses, to carry messages long distances from city to city. This effective communication system was copied by other societies, and used extensively in Asia. Much later, it was popularized as the famous Pony Express system for delivering mail in the western part of the United States of America.

The horse certainly revolutionized business travel, adding greatly to improved communications beyond the immediate environment, and becoming an important part of early military transport and battle strategy. The use of the horse also allowed for personal relaxation; the rider could visit new areas comfortably and return home the same day or move to a new destination. Initially, the riding of horses was exclusively used by men for travel. Women probably rode draft horses on the farms, yet it was a long time before the equestrienne would appear on the scene in her elegant riding outfit.

Prior to the use of domesticated animals for transportation, another revolution in travel was taking place. Primitive man learned he could ride a log down a stream for faster transport. . Rudely constructed boats were developed for use in fishing, transport to hunting grounds, for warring on hostile tribes, and for short exploratory trips to nearby areas. Some early societies simply dug or burned out the centers of logs to form canoes, or put logs together to construct rafts. Later, innovative craftsmen constructed coracles and skin-floats that enabled and simplified movement across streams. Later, reed boats were built, but had severe limitations for traveling long distances, actually only functioning well in small streams and rivers.

Gradually, innovative boat builders designed vessels that could sail upon the seas safely for long distances. One of the earliest seafaring societies, according to Herodotus, were the Phoenicians, highly intelligent people who had settled in an area that includes modern day Lebanon, around 2300 B.C.E. The Phoenicians were Canaanites, but the Greeks referred to them as Phoenicians, or as master shipwrights. By 1550 B.C.E., the Phoenicians had fabricated large sophisticated sea-worthy merchant vessels used for trade, travel, and transport throughout the Mediterranean Sea. The Phoenicians constructed the best warships of the era and had the capability to produce cruise vessels for pleasure travel. A gracious result of the long reign of the Phoenician society; movement of people and goods were dramatically improved. The Phoenicians occupy a very special place in the history of travel.

As famed shipwrights and bold navigators of this period, the Phoenicians became the world's most successful merchants, renowned for trading in silks, frankincense, myrrh, ebony wood, and precious metals that included copper, lead, and gold. They transported these from far destinations in Asia to communities throughout the Mediterranean Sea, and were the first to utilize the Strait of Gibraltar as passage into the Atlantic Ocean, transporting timber, silver, tin, and amber from Europe. They mapped trade routes, increased the knowledge of waterways and coastlines, and developed travel patterns that were made easier to follow by using the stars to navigate. Establishing trading centers along the coasts of North Africa, Sicily, and Spain, they spread their culture and knowledge among less advanced peoples.

In addition to seamanship, the Phoenicians excelled in literature, arts, architecture, and engineering. They invented our alphabet and they taught it to the Greeks and Mediterranean communities. The Greeks sometimes referred to the Phoenicians as "The Purple People," due to the Greek word "Phoenix", which refers to the purple-dyed goods from the ancient Phoenician capital, Tyre. This reddish-purple dye was made from the difficult-to-obtain glands of murex mollusks. The complicated process to produce the purple dye made it expensive. Thus it was a service only available to the rich or to royalty. Today, the expression "born to purple" refers to a person who is born into a noble family or someone who is a monarch, a king, or someone who is exceedingly wealthy. This dye process was another one of the great legacies left to us by the seafaring travelers, the Phoenicians.

Due to further explorations by Phoenicians, later generations were provided with important maps and useful information for their journeys to new areas. There are theories that Phoenicians were the first explorers to travel to South America. Additional accounts written by Herodotus implied that Phoenicians may also have circumnavigated Africa. The Phoenicians sailed the best boats of the era, which by today's standards were not safe, yet they explored unknown continents, mingled with the natives, confronted the dangers of extreme heat and cold, and risked their lives, all as a result of their pure love of travel, trade, and adventure. We're amazed they even loaded their ships with cedar logs from Lebanon to sell to the Egyptians for the scaffolding to help construct special Egyptian structures and pyramids.

As shipbuilders, navigators, merchants, miners, dyers of cloth, engravers of hard stones, inventors of an alphabet and as engineers, mathematicians, and philosophers, the Phoenicians exceeded all who preceded them. Their inventions and innovations lasted for many generations.

The Phoenicians also believed that travel was important for one's happiness. More important, they believed in the equal rights of the sexes, a belief unheard of by earlier societies. The Phoenicians deemed it acceptable for women to travel and trade with men, another revolutionary concept of the day.

As artists, ideas and materials for their art depended on travel; the Phoenicians journeyed to new destinations to learn about better equipment for art, and sought new subjects in faraway locations to paint. The creation of beautiful artwork included using materials as metal, glass, ivory, terra cotta, wood, and stone. Their ivory carvings had family seals and names engraved on the object. They were, as well, advanced in music, and musicians often performed before large groups and developed special religious hymns that were dedicated to their Gods. And, as the great pioneers of travel, they introduced the true art of business travel, with a sophisticated system of barter that was used for generations throughout the world. They brought the world beyond to their doorstep.

Another great society that relished opportunities to travel were the Greeks. The Greek culture, and later in a different format, the Roman society, as well, were particularly attuned to pleasure and sports travel. Great sporting events as the Olympic Games weren't just athletic events, but embodied strong religious and cultural overtones. The early Greek society revered the body, with respect to performances in sporting events. They embraced in their pleasures of life a strong affinity to worshiping their many gods. As outlets for their athletic prowess and cultural interests, as well as to appease the gods, they developed a series of athletic-cultural events and contests. The popular ones became known as the Olympic Games, Pythian Games, Isthmian Games, and Nemean Games. These athletic events and cultural festivals attracted the leisure class from near and far. Since traveling was difficult, those of the higher class who had the means to travel not only visited the sporting events, but took part in cultural activities, including visiting historic sites, art exhibits, storytelling events, plays, and famous buildings.

First held in 776 B.C.E., the Olympic Games were the oldest and most popular of the four great Games. The Olympic Games were held every four years in honor of the Greek God Zeus at Olympia. The celebration of the Olympics, lasting for five days, drew foreigners as well as thousands of visitors from areas throughout Greece. With different national societies interested in the Games, some of which were warring nations with each other, safety and security was a major concern for spectators, and it was resolved in the guise of political cooperation known as the Olympic Truce. In effect, nations in conflict with each other decided to cease all warfare for a month during the Games, thus, sending forward a message of peace. During the Truce, athletes, artists, families, and even ordinary visitors to the Games could travel in safety to participate in or attend the Games. The Truce also granted protection to all as they returned to their respective cities and countries after the Games.

The Olympic Games included, in addition to athletic events, contests of dance and choral poetry. The athletes were all males. Each of the athletes trained their bodies with great care, as such athletic contests were performed in the nude. In addition, the Games promoted special attention to art, music, sculpture, plays, storytelling, public speaking, food, drink, and other cultural-related activities. Greeks and neighboring societies participated with great passion in the festivities, including visits to temples, coliseums, amphitheaters, concert halls, galleries, and other locations, some of which still exist today. Every form of accommodation was in use during the games, including tents or simple pallets for sleeping under the stars.

Although the religious tones and nude performances are long gone from the Olympic Games, the Games still take place every four years. The Olympics, then and now, truly represent tourism in all its many varieties and vagaries.

\* \* \*

We begin to learn about Herodotus, who became known as the Father of History. Born in Halicarnassus in Iona in the 5th Century B.C., he wrote "The Histories," in which are found his "inquiries" which later became, to mean to modern scholars, to mean the facts of history.

Herodotus, and others, made suggestions to travelers of popular places to visit. Their lists have not survived, but they were certainly known at the time of the Greek writer, Antipater of Sidon, who compiled the first known list of the "seven wonders" of the world as described in a poem around 140 B.C.E. His list contained:

1. The Great Pyramid of Giza (Egypt)
2. The Hanging Gardens of Babylon (Iraq)
3. The Temple of Artemis at Ephesus (Turkey)
4. The Statue of Zeus at Olympia (Greece)
5. The Mausoleum of Maussollos at Halicarnassus (Turkey)
6. The Colossus of Rhodes (Greece), and the Lighthouse of Alexandria (Egypt)
7. The Lighthouse of Alexandria

The only one still standing is the Great Pyramid of Giza. The "New Seven Wonders of the World" (2022) include the Great Wall of China, Petra (Jordan), Christ the Redeemer-statue (Brazil), Machu Picchu (Peru), Chichen Itza (Mexico), Roman Coliseum (Italy), and the Taj Mahal (India). Most modern chroniclers, however, will add to their lists an "honorary" eighth wonder, the Great Pyramid of Giza.

While earlier societies developed rudimentary travel guides, it was the Greek native Pausanias who published the first comprehensive travel publication in 170 C.E. His ten-volume travel guide, *A Guide to Greece*, described opportunities for travel throughout Greece, with descriptions and detailed information that promoted and marketed travel. Such a guide was an early equivalent of the use of the Internet by travelers of the twenty-first century.

As noted earlier, most of the historic and cultural sites visited were in Egypt and Greece. The pyramids of Egypt near Cairo and the lighthouse of Alexandria were important sites to be visited by the leisure traveler, as were the hanging gardens of Babylon. However, Athens became the best known and most popular travel destination. This was the result of the country's impressive culture, arts, music, architecture, and religious artifacts, and because of Pausanias' travel guide. The popularity of Greece was also enhanced by the fact that the Greeks traveled more for leisure than any other society in that early time period.

The legacy that the early Greek travelers left behind would not be eclipsed for many generations. Today, travelers seek to travel to Greece to enjoy the Greek heritage and history, as well as the scenic Greek islands. Each time the Olympics take place, no matter in which part of the world, its origin in Greece comes to mind.

Another society revered in ancient times were the Persians, whose perpetual war with Greece was well-known. In 539 B.C.E., Cyrus the Great of Persia conquered Phoenicia and utilized the Phoenician ships and new road construction techniques to expand his own empire and to support his armies. Under Cyrus the Great and his son, Darius the Great, the Persian Empire was the paramount empire in this time period, with its vast coverage extending from India to the Mediterranean. King Darius reorganized and rebuilt the ancient highway system of the empire into what became known as the Persian Royal Road, greatly improving transportation and communications within his vast empire. He organized a system whereby mounted couriers could travel the empire within a matter of days.

"There is nothing in the world that travels faster than these Persian couriers," wrote Herodotus. Persian travelers and long-distance traders were able to travel great distances, improving not only their ability to move more quickly, but led to increased communications to regions outside the Persian Empire. Later, during the Roman Empire, the Romans improved parts of the Persian Royal Road by using hard-packed gravel surfaces, thus, opening a new era of travel which allowed worldly travelers such as Marco Polo and Ibn Battuta to employ animals for faster travel.

As vehicles for transportation became more sophisticated, it was necessary to improve road building. The walking traveler simply needed a path. Travel by donkey required only a slightly wider track. Now, with carts, wagons, and chariots in use for transportation, as well as increases in caravan travel, roads needed to be constructed. The Greeks, Mycenaean people, Indians, Persians, and other early societies began to build to transport large numbers of people.

The Romans, largely for military purposes, not only facilitated travel by means of the building of good roads, many of which were paved with stones, but also constructed rest stops, inns, eating establishments, and recreation centers throughout their empire. Of extreme importance to early travel was the Roman emphasis on security; keeping the roads safe from terrorists, bandits, and marauding enemies, while also safeguarding the high seas from attacks by pirates. Attention to safety and security has always played a key role throughout history. For us in today's world, safety and security issues are a prime determinate of whether we decide to travel at all.

Early Roman travel was initially related to military conquests. Once the armies had established good roads and provided safeguards, food services, and accommodations along the roads, the number of civilians traveling increased. Now, advanced guidebooks, maps, and improved means of transportation for traveling longer distances were available to a growing proportion of Roman leisure travelers. Visiting historic Egyptian and Greek monuments and touring the countryside were an important part of Roman travel. In addition, many wealthy Romans had summer homes outside Rome, enjoying fresh air, good food and wine, and receiving friends and relatives into their homes. Such visits represented another precursor to modern tourism; visitation with friends and relatives as a prime reason for traveling.

While remains of hostels date as far back to 1500 B.C.E., the origin of lodging facilities and inns were available much earlier. Even though the rich and powerful often took their comforts with them; tents, linens, utensils, good food and wine, and servants or slaves were available to accommodate their needs.

Public places also became available to travelers, first to accommodate government officials but, gradually, for any visitor. Ordinary travelers, other than rich merchants and government officials, might have stayed in rat-and-bug-infested inns eating bad food and drinking poor wine. Whatever the circumstances, food, rest, and entertainment have always been important to the traveler. Hospitality on the early travelers' itinerary included supplying drinks and women. In most towns, it was the women who served the food and drink, which many times also led to sexual favors and companionship. Such forms of prostitution had come into early existence in the world's society, but not as a direct result of travel. Down through the ages, travelers certainly used such services; this aspect of travel remains in today's travel world as well.

*   *   *

Story telling has an ancient pedigree. Herodotus, our first great worldly traveler, led all others in the ancient world in understanding the exotic splendors of the universe and the pleasures of leisure travel. He left an impressive legacy to the world of travel and written history. During his lifetime, and for generations to come, the result of his travels have forever changed the world in which we live. *The Histories* presents an embodiment of ancient political history. No ancient worldly traveler fulfilled that philosophy more completely than Herodotus. His curiosity about the world, travels under difficult circumstances, laid the groundwork for future generations to better understand the ancient world. Recording what he learned from his travels, his written descriptions became a valuable guide for future travelers. Who was this bold adventurer? It's time to find out.

# CHAPTER TWO

# HERODOTUS, THE ORIGINAL WORLDLY TRAVELER

"A guest never forgets the host who
has treated him kindly."
-Homer, *The Odyssey*, 9<sup>th</sup> Century B.C. E.-

*Catching his breath, young Herodotus paused for a moment to rest. This was one of his first trips and he was only halfway up the circuitous road to **The Acropolis**, the old, walled religious center, which was the towering glory of the city-state of Athens. Winded and perspiring heavily, he knew this was certainly worth the climb. Above him loomed the lustrous Pentelic marble temple named the Parthenon, which was dedicated to the Greek warrior goddess Pallas Athena, the daughter of Zeus and namesake of Athens, protector of Athens. Climbing further, he paused to reflect on the proportions of this magnificent edifice. Oh yes, the beauty of Athens was a perfect anodyne for this difficult climb.*

*Nearby were the temples of Poseidon, Nike, and the Proplyaea, their fluted columns standing gracefully up against the dense blue Grecian sky. Ah, the elegance in the architectural virtuosity of these amazing structures! Below spread the city of Athens, which, for Herodotus, represented the center of civilization. He looked at the*

*broad sweep of the Agora below bustling markets which
sold goods and produce and provided a political forum
for speakers; here were quiet corners for scholars to meet
and instruct their students. As far as he could see from
this high position on the hill, the world below inspired
him. What an eclectic mosaic of the arts and culture of
the great city of Athens! How lucky he was to be there
He wondered if there were any other cities of the world
as beautiful as Athens. This moment of reflection set in
motion for young Herodotus a passionate desire to travel
and to see the world, and to find out!*

*    *    *

Herodotus lived in an era when the multi-lingual Persian Empire dominated the world. Through his studies and growing up, he knew the world was divided, split into Persia in the Middle East, and Greece in Europe in the West; both parts constantly at war. Like many young thinkers, he wanted to know why these great nations could not live in peace with each other.

He felt the primary aim of a country was its self-preservation, and also that a military victory should be a step towards obtaining positive socio-economic goals by the leader, rather than an end in itself. His answer lay in understanding the histories of Persia, Greece, Egypt, and other important societies. This deep need for understanding kept at him, as he longed to write about important and remarkable achievements produced by both Greeks and non-Greeks. His philosophy was basic; when you come to a country's border, *just cross it,* and learn about its people, history, and culture. He began to devote his life to this love and learning through the medium of his travels and he worked to express his passion in his writings.

Something we certainly understand and cherish.

The Persian king, Cambyses, had conquered the great civilization of Egypt in 525 B.C.E. at the Battle of Pelusium, making it a province of Persia. Through a series of wars in the fifth and sixth centuries, Persia ruled most of the Middle East and areas beyond, a much larger territory than the great Roman Empire established many years later. Greek colonies bordering Persia had paid homage and taxes to the Persian kings to keep the Persian civilization and military at bay so that they could live a relatively peaceful life.

Based on Herodotus' early education and place of birth, he initially had a negative viewpoint with respect to Persian dominance and subjugation of non-Persian subjects. After he was able to travel to parts of Persia, he learned more. Surprised to find them to be courteous, respectful, effective administrators, and, mostly, truthful and helpful, he was impressed that Persians tolerated all religions throughout their kingdoms.

So when he wrote *The Histories*, he gave a mostly fair, balanced picture of the Persian wars with Greece, which began in 490 B.C.E. and lasted for twenty years. His interest in visiting the battle sites enabled him to learn more about the history of the wars.

Persia had long been in a struggle to dominate the Greek city-states which had been organized as independent nations, particularly Athens and Sparta. The multi-national Persian army, led by Darius the Great, was larger and more powerful than that of the Greek military. The Persians also had a state-of-the-art fleet of ships, most of which had been inherited from their victories over the best shipwrights in ancient history, the Phoenicians.

Early Greece was a piecemeal of *city-states*, each with its sovereign government, dialect, religion, culture, education systems and economic life. These differences among early Greek city-states often complicated travel, communication, and cooperation. In addition to being revered for its advanced development and great wealth, Athens was the largest of the independent communities with a more democratic system of government, and maintained an impressive port, Piraeus, supported by a large navy.

In contrast to Athens, Sparta was small, yet known to have a well-trained army and excellent education system that included programs for both young men and women. This was rare at a time when education was not usually provided for women.

When the advent of the Persian invasion of Athens was about to begin, many of the Greek city-states recognized the need to at least organize alliances. The Greeks knew it would take a large and highly trained army to defeat the Persian military machine. Athens, as a single city-state, wasn't able to raise a substantial army, so they requested and received commitments of military support from Sparta, Thespiae, Thebes, Corinth, and a few small Greek city-states. Sparta, while not as large as Athens, had the best trained soldiers in Greece.

These allies tactically strategized that, if Athens fell, they might be the next target, thus they decided to act in unison with Athens against the Persians. Fighting on their own soil, the Greeks knew the landscape, the strengths, and weaknesses of their surroundings, giving them a strategic and tactical military advantage.

Initially, the strong Persian army destroyed the limited resistance they encountered along the way moving toward Athens until they got to Marathon, Greece. Athens was no match for such an army, and, according to Herodotus, the leaders of Athens sent a message to Sparta declaring, "Men of Sparta, the Athenians ask you to help them and not stand by while the most ancient city of Greece is crushed and enslaved by a foreign invader."

Sparta did not respond to this cry for help. Meanwhile, realizing Athens had no help, Darius the Great divided his forces so that half his army was put on ships to attack Athens, while the other half continued marching toward Athens by land. At Marathon, near Athens, a great battle took place in which Darius was defeated by the Athenians, a major blow to his ego and a stumbling block in his intention to add Greece to his empire. He returned his armies to Persia to fight another day.

Herodotus noted in *The Histories* that Darius died before he had another opportunity to pursue his quest to conquer Greece. He was succeeded by his son Xerxes, a highly charged leader with an unwavering desire to expand the Persian Empire and, most importantly, to conquer the Greeks. Xerxes the Great was ardent about avenging his father's defeat in Greece, and organized a large well-trained military force to invade Greece in 480 B.C.E.

It was not until Xerxes' advancing army arrived at the city of Thermopylae in 480 B.C.E. in northern Greece that he received serious opposition. At Thermopylae, an important strategic pass, a famous historic battle took place under the impressive military leadership of King Leonidas of Sparta. With a small but brave contingent of Spartans under his control, these allies fought bravely against Xerxes the Great.

Prior to the last battle at Thermopylae, according to Herodotus, King Leonidas knew his forces would be defeated by the Persians. To save many of the allied soldiers, King Leonidas ordered the greater part of the allied army to leave the battle site and flee for their safety. This left the King with 300 Spartans, 700 Thespians, 400 Thebans, 400 Corinthians, and a few hundred other allies to fight the 80,000 or so Persians. While the vastly outnumbered Sparta military allies were able to do battle, doggedly standing their ground against the imponderable opposition of the superior Persian force, they were totally defeated. King Leonidas and every individual in his small army were slaughtered. Herodotus wrote that Xerxes the Great ordered King Leonidas' head cut off, put on a stake, and his body crucified.

When word of this defeat reached Athens, the Athenians panicked, packed up their possessions and evacuated the city. The Greek military removed to the port city of Salamis. Xerxes, in his revenge, burned and destroyed Athens, including the religious temples of *The Acropolis*. Later, the Greeks defeated the Persians at Salamis and drove them from most Greek provinces. Athens, including the Parthenon temple honoring the goddess Athena in *The Acropolis*, was rebuilt, allowing the Greek society to become strong and vibrant again.

The Persian invasion had one positive impact on Greece. For the next 50 years, it led to a partial uniting of the city-states of Athens, Sparta, Corinth, Thebes, and the surrounding smaller communities. With this alliance and general peace existing throughout most of Greece, the entire area grew and prospered. Athens was fortunate in having a strong charismatic leader in General Pericles, whose leadership allowed Athens to become the dominant Greek city-state for many years. Again, Athens progressed to become the center for architecture, trade, art, literature, education, travel, and philosophy. It was into this political and social environment throughout Greece and the city of Athens in which our *Herodotus* entered.

*   *   *

Traveling during the fifth century B.C.E. was, of course, dangerous and difficult. The challenge of geography, transportation and accommodations made it all slow and uncomfortable. Often, conflicts took place throughout the regions where early Greek travelers attempted to explore. Greeks traveling through Persian territory were not always welcomed. Travelers were always confronted by the possibility of encountering thieves. What normal person, not required to do so, would care to travel under such dreadfully difficult and dangerous conditions? But military personnel, merchant traders, religious pilgrims, all of whom felt obligated to travel, did.

Yet when Herodotus stepped forward to explore and write, he became a unique traveler, observing every aspect of life in the countries he visited. He wrote about the histories of the places where he traveled, the cultures of the various communities, and noted the geography of each region. Yes, Herodotus was easily the first cultural tourist and geotourist in the history of global travel and tourism.

**Herodotus carries pages of the manuscript
of his masterful book *The Histories*.**

\*   \*   \*

Herodotus was not a typical fifth century B.C.E. traveler. Most Greeks traveled only within Greece for the purposes of visiting friends at country estates or possibly traveling for sporting and cultural events, such as the Olympics. Yet, intent on learning about the history and culture of other lands, Herodotus became a rare exception within the Greek's traveling society.

Since childhood, Herodotus' memory was a major asset throughout his life. He was intelligent, inquisitive, strong, and healthy enough to endure the hardships of travel. Generally recognized as the world's first travel writer, he used his imagination, his genius and ability to interact with people of other countries. He developed a fascinating ability to tell stories that attracted listeners. The written accounts of what he saw and heard to change the world for future generations of travelers, is still our gift.

According to most accounts, Herodotus was born in 484 B.C.E. during *The Classical Period in Greece*. This period, known as the "Golden Age", was a time of great change and enlightenment throughout Greece. He grew up in Halicarnassus, formerly part of Caria, and the name of the Greek colony under the subjugation of Xerxes the Great. The Greeks of Halicarnassus were vassals, entitled to protection provided by the Persian rulers, but expected to accept onerous burdens and tyranny imposed on them by their sovereign. Its location, a substantial travel distance from Athens and Sparta, meant that it could not be readily defended by Greece and, therefore, the city had to pay homage to Persia.

The father of Herodotus was Lynxes who belonged to the native population referred to as Carians. His mother, Dryo, was thought to be Greek but was not from Athens. The fact that neither parent was born in Athens later upset Herodotus who tried, but was unsuccessful, to become a citizen of Athens.

In fifth century B.C.E., Athenians were quite snobbish and racist and wanted to keep their *purity of race*. Athens law stated that to be a citizen of the city-state of Athens, one or both parents had to be born in the Attica region of east central Greece in which Athens was the principal city. Not being able to be a subject of Athens and take up residence initially bothered Herodotus, yet he learned early in life to adjust to whatever the circumstances the city or destination offered and to blend in with the nuances of that society.

There's no indication if his parents were well-educated or if they directly influenced Herodotus to become a writer or traveler. Yet the family was comfortable, and lived well. His uncle, Panyassis, was a popular, renowned Greek epic poet and perhaps he had an influence on young Herodotus in terms of his education and his interest in storytelling and history. Other family members provided valuable insights for our young, curious, and adventurous lad.

Herodotus was strongly influenced in his boyhood reading by the best-known storyteller and poet of the era, Homer, who wrote The *Iliad* and

*Odyssey.* We think the wanderings of Odysseus in the *Iliad* and *Odyssey* influenced Herodotus and his interest in traveling. Possibly, Homer was a role model for Herodotus. Many scholars who've analyzed Herodotus' writings arrive at the conclusion that Herodotus is "most Homeric." A great compliment. Yet Herodotus' real education took place when he physically traveled, saw places, and met with the local citizens in the various countries and communities he visited.

During Herodotus' youth, the city of Halicarnassus was governed by a woman, Artemisia, whose principal responsibility appeared to have been to supply money and troops for the Persian military. In a highly unusual move, the Persian king allowed her to command several vessels in the Persian-Greek wars. Artemisia had proven to be a very able and brave sachem during the war and was given, as a reward, the charge to rule Halicarnassus.

Herodotus didn't say much about his early childhood or growing up, which makes us sad, as we know little about his character or his personal life. Also, ancient classical writers simply did not write about their own lives. So there's no firsthand information about our lad, including whether he was ever married or if he fathered children. What we do know is that he was reasonably well-educated and a reader of the limited literature available to him. In addition, he was blessed since childhood with an eidetic memory, an intellectual asset he relied on throughout his worldly travels.

The family of Herodotus was wealthy enough to provide their son with an environment for learning and later allowed him to indulge in his wanderlust of the world. His father may have been a merchant or sea trader, which would be common enough in a port town such as Halicarnassus. Persian military and merchant ships as well as Phoenician, Greek, and Egyptian trade vessels all docked in the harbor of Halicarnassus at some point. Successful traders and merchants were usually worldlier than most of the local population. They were often in the higher echelons of income and often culturally involved in the local community. It was common for such families of greater wealth to have slaves. This luxury allowed wealthier families time for the more leisure pursuits of life such as education, cultural events, and interactions with peoples outside the local area.

We believe Herodotus spent much of his early childhood watching the boats from many different nations coming into the harbor. The salt air from the ocean would have permeated throughout the community. He knew the boats were from exotic places on the earth and imagined the strange people inhabiting those far off places. He dreamed of these locations and imagined what it might be like to meet strange people, see different plants, animals, and structures of a world different from his own.

As a young man, Herodotus was keenly aware of the politics of the area in which he lived. His father and his uncle Panyassis were part of a rebellious group opposed to the repressive Persian rule in Halicarnassus. During a terrible confrontation with the Persian rulers of Halicarnassus, his dear uncle Panyassis was killed. While the rebellion was unsuccessful, it caused Herodotus' family to get out of the city and flee to the mountainous island of Samos, a Greek island off the west coast of present-day Turkey.

The island of Samos was a member of the Ionian League of Greek settlements, considered to be beautiful, wealthy, powerful, and lusciously green, located in the eastern Aegean Sea, and known for its culture and luxury. It had a reputation of being full of mystery and legends. Even the Greeks on Samos saw the supernatural gods having a hand in one's daily life. Legend has it, according to Herodotus that the mythical god Hera, the wife of Zeus, queen of the ancient Greek gods, and goddess of marriage and family, was from Samos. Herodotus also noted that the largest temple in Greece was dedicated to Hera. At one time, these Greeks, as Pythagoras, the father of mathematics, Aristarchus, the astronomer, the philosopher Epicurus, and Aesop, the teller of fables, all lived on Samoa at one time or another. Yet, while Herodotus lived in Samos, he was frequently absent due to his many trips, especially travels to Athens and other Greek city-state destinations.

Traveling to Athens was the first major trip for Herodotus. The leadership in Athens wanted the city to become a major tourist destination and, hence, provided considerable hospitality to visitors. Here, everything would be inviting and magnificent. Later in life, he wrote about the legendary contest between the Greek gods, Poseidon and Athena.

Supposedly, according to Herodotus, Poseidon and Athena both requested that the city carry their name. Athena, of course, was the victor. One of the most important religious sites in ancient Athens was the Temple of Athena, known today as the Parthenon.

Athens was a powerful city-state with its own government, laws, military, and the best educational system in ancient Greece. Early in Greek history, prior to the rise in power by Athens, the military city-state of Sparta was the most known Greek community. Sparta's educational approach for young boys beginning at the age of seven was oriented solely toward teaching the student the art of war. While most ancient Greek communities focused on the education of males only, Sparta also educated young girls in military science that was less intense than that for males. Education in Athens, contrary to that of Sparta, was broader and included a concentration on reading, writing, music, art, literature, science, math, physical education, and politics for males through high school. After high school, the boys attended military school. In ancient Greece, except for Sparta, girls did not go to school, only learning to read and write from their mothers who might have such skills. Wanting to learn about the culture, politics, and education of Athens, traveling here was an experience about which Herodotus had long dreamed.

As a young man, not yet worldly, Herodotus went about the prospect of visiting Athens in 447 B.C.E. He was excited to leave by boat from the military harbor of Samos to travel to port Piraeus near Athens. Many of the boats used for travel at that time were not fit for sea travel. When Herodotus looked over the Greek bireme, with its shallow hull and lofty, open superstructure, he could hardly believe it was a seaworthy vessel.

We think he suppressed some laughter. However, the trip by boat on the Aegean Sea was uneventful with an opportunity for him to meet several fellow passengers who were knowledgeable about Athens and who were willing to help him with his travel arrangements.

After his arrival in Athens, Herodotus anxiously began his tour of the great city. We suggest that our young man was a true flaneur, enjoying the social life and appreciating wonderful architectural beauty and cosmopolitan culture of Athens. He was impressed by the religious temples of *The Acropolis*, which added to his lifelong interest in the religions of the world. He was thrilled to visit the Agora section of Athens, the heart of teeming activity, commerce, politics, culture, and important events of the city, which had a considerable influence on how he'd measure other destinations as he traveled the world. Possibly most important was to relish in the opportunity to hear in-person lectures given by the highly intellectual Athens community, home for many of the great worldly philosophers. For young Herodotus, Athens was the perfect paradigm of the ideal a civilized city-state should aspire to.

Athens was a stark contrast to his birthplace, the city of Halicarnassus. Not only did the superb Athenian architecture surpass anything he'd seen as a child in that distant Persian colony of Halicarnassus; the political life and social milieu were radically different. Athens was the epitome of democracy, a most important and cultured city-state in Greece.

Herodotus' view was that if the world could adopt the ideas and philosophies of Athens, it would certainly be a better place, a chimerical idea for the time period. He met noted Greek scholars and leaders such as Pericles, a general and great statesman. He met Sophocles, a famous playwright, and Socrates, a well-known philosopher. He met Hippocrates, the father of medicine, and Thucydides, a general and military historian.

If his inherited family circumstances could have provided the opportunity, he would have become a much-coveted citizen of the city-state of Athens. But as a non-citizen of Athens, he could only visit, or stay permanently. Later, as his fame increased as a historian, Herodotus was regularly invited as a special guest and scholar/lecturer on world history, culture, and travel within the intelligentsia community of Athens.

It was his curiosity about the world, and his immense imagination that set his traveling itinerary in motion, which allowed him to become the world's first globalist. He learned about distant civilizations, enamored in wanting to know about the histories and cultures of the known countries of the world of his era.

After Herodotus visited Athens, he returned home to prepare for a difficult, worldly trek. He decided to sail north from Samos to visit countries that were relatively unexplored and for which there was little information. He was aware there were a few Greek settlements along the Black Sea. And beyond that were the wilderness areas of Thrace and Scythia, which were subjugated under the control of Persia. These were places and cultures Herodotus knew nothing about, and he was determined to explore them. After sailing along the coast of Asia Minor, his vessel passed through the strait of Hellespont and he visited communities in Macedonia, Thrace, and Scythia. These areas included modern-day Bulgaria, Romania, Ukraine, Russia, Georgia, and Turkey. For a Greek to go beyond the Greek trade settlements along the Euxine Sea, now called the Black Sea, was fraught with danger. Of course, he was already aware of potential marauders and thieves to contend with, as well as traveling without good maps or directions, or the knowledge in locating food and lodging, but Herodotus was young, physically fit, and yearning for adventure.

Undaunted, he plunged ahead, praying his travels would not be seriously interrupted. Several times during this journey, he was helped by fellow travelers and was able to continue his adventure unabated.

In the province of Thrace, Herodotus encountered the Indo-European tribes, or Thracians, inhabiting a large area in southeastern Europe.

They were considered to be an inferior race by the Greek society in the fifth century B.C.E. During the time period of Xerxes the Great of Persia, according to Herodotus, the Persian army defeated the Thracians, and, thus, the Persians subjugated the Thracians to Persian rule. During this trip, Herodotus visited the city of Olbia within the Greek settlements along the Black sea. Here he learned about the Scythians of the central European Steppes, an area known at the time as Scythia. The Scythians were an ancient Iranian tribe known for their use of horses for transportation and for their nomadic lifestyle. They were also trading partners with the Greeks, which Herodotus also wrote about in *The Histories.*

While Herodotus had captivating experiences in Thrace and Scythia, which he recorded, he was not impressed with some of the culture and political organizations he encountered. After being in Athens, he found the Thracian way of life to be antiquated and he was anxious to leave to continue his travels to an area and civilization he had read and studied for many years.

Yes, to see the great kingdom of Egypt. Many Greeks had traveled there after receiving permission from the ruling Persian empire. Herodotus, as did most of the educated Greeks, learned much about Egypt and was impressed with the mysterious culture of Egypt. He knew in advance a journey to Egypt would be a serious challenge--- because of the formidable hardships of traveling such a long distance. Yet his burning desire to visit and learn about the magnificence of the Egyptian culture, its antiquities and structures trumped the enormous hardships for a traveler to overcome during this early age of travel. He knew, after arriving in Egypt, he would have an onerous overland trek if he were to see and learn all he wanted to know. Yet he felt undaunted by these potential difficulties.

He left Greece and sailed across the Mediterranean Sea for Egypt and while there were never comfortable accommodations on the vessel, and limited amounts of food available, he knew there were no alternatives to such rigors of travel.

Travel from ancient Greece to Egypt in the fifth century B.C.E. was a major feat of stamina, patience and luck. Travelers prayed for good weather and hoped the treacherous pirates on the high seas didn't attack. The trip was so perilous that many travelers made sacrifices and said prayers to their favorite gods before embarking on the journey, always wanting to be on the good side of the gods.

Once Herodotus arrived in Egypt, he journeyed on foot to find people willing to help arrange for his overland travels in Egypt. He sought out the services of a *Proxenos,* a Greek citizen appointed in a foreign country to act as consul or as hospitality ambassador for Greek visitors to strange nations or places. He wanted to visit far outposts of the country, requiring him to walk or ride a donkey, a mule, or, if he was fortunate, a horse for part of the journey over often unmarked paths.

Good prevailed, in that Herodotus often found comfort when he arrived at his destination or at temporary stopovers along the way in areas unknown to him. He interacted with local populations, fascinated by social mores and customs. Because of his accumulated family wealth, we learn he was able to have a slave to assist him on these difficult journeys. Having slave help was not uncommon for early Greek travelers. On segments of his trip, he was luckily able to join a caravan that included officials on government business and traders who had been to the destination before. Traveling in groups helped ward off thieves and highwaymen and provided welcomed companionship and information.

Herodotus' favorite travel destination, after Athens, became Egypt. As mentioned earlier, it was a province of Persia at the time. He was so excited to visit Egypt, a land of mysterious customs and architecture, he wrote, "I will lengthen my tale because Egypt has more wonders than all the entire world ..." He was so in awe at the advancements that Egypt had made in comparison with the rest of the world, that when he first saw the Egyptian pyramids, he, like many generations then and after, was amazed at the unbelievable engineering feats. The great pyramid at Giza was the apotheosis of the Egyptian advanced civilization in ancient times. Immediately, Herodotus began to inquire as to how they were built. The answers varied, and like today, they remain somewhat of a mystery.

One aspect of the geography of Egypt that fascinated Herodotus was the beauty and economic importance of the 4,000 mile Nile River. He recognized that without the Nile, Egypt would simply be a large desert. He called Egypt "the gift of the Nile." As we wrote in Chapter One, it was noted that Egyptians loved sailing down the Nile River for enjoyment and to commemorate religious celebrations.

While Herodotus was fascinated in the religion and cultural lives of the Egyptians, he was surprised that in Egypt women were highly respected. Equal to Egyptian men. Egyptian women could own land, trade without a male being present, have equal entitlement in inheritance, and could bequeath their possessions as they saw fit. We wonder if he fell in love!

In effect, Herodotus seemed to believe that almost everything Egyptian was different from the rest of the world. Present day scholars wrote "Sometimes he would elide facts that did not fit the occasion and, instead, make use of innuendo to convey his bizarre messages."

Elide means to omit or leave out of consideration…. As he described some of the Egyptian customs in these words: "For instance, women go out to the town square and sell retail goods; while men stay at home and do the weaving…Or again, men carry loads on their heads; while women do so on their shoulders. Women urinate standing up; while men do so squatting…Everywhere else in the world, priests have long hair, but in Egypt, they shave their heads…Other people, unless they have been influenced by the Egyptians, leave their genitals in their natural state, but the Egyptians practice circumcision…"

This makes us realize how human and curious Herodotus was.

We learn that Herodotus didn't actually "see" most of what he wrote about, but, rather, obtained it from travel guides and from talking, usually through interpreters, with local citizens. His pleasant countenance put whatever audience he encountered at ease. Yet, with respect to many of the comments and notes made by Herodotus, we also must rely on conjecture based on historic documents and known practices to fill in the details of his visit to Egypt. He patiently tried to verify the information he received from a variety of sources, but was handicapped because he only spoke Greek. Since he didn't speak Egyptian, it's likely some facts got twisted through translations. Also, information gleaned from contacts with Greeks living in Egypt, caused additional suspect with respect to accuracy of the descriptions. Hmm!

On occasion, some Greeks living in Egypt deliberately, for their own selfish reasons, attempted to mislead Herodotus. Most of the time, he was too perspicuous to fall for their hoaxes. But still, with all the difficulties of obtaining accurate information about Egypt, Herodotus, with typical panache, offered anecdotes that became bright pieces in a vibrant mosaic puzzle that revealed more clearly the customs and culture of Egypt. He knew much of his information likely came from myths and legends and old shibboleths handed down verbally from generation to generation, but, regardless of the source, the stories were entertaining. He accepted both the known facts and the remarks by local storytellers with equanimity.

As Herodotus grew in stature, he intuited that a connection between the religious practices and customs in the Greek society were based on Egyptian culture. He credited the Egyptians in naming twelve gods, and he conjectured that the Greeks simply borrowed them from Egypt. These kinds of remarks did not make him popular in Athens, and alienated him from many of the leaders in Greek city-states. Certainly, his ideas and comments challenged the religious and cultural dogmas of the time, but he did not back down from his comments, whether or not his fellow Greeks agreed with them. His arguments were generally cogent and, at times, elegantly expressed. His critics, full of animus, argued that Greek culture was at the center of world customs and civilization! It was the Greeks who passed on their great society to other countries and not the reverse, as might be suggested by Herodotus. Herodotus never backed down from his detractors and countered with suppositions based on his travels, such as: "…the Egyptians were the first people in the world to hold general festive assemblies, and religious processions and parades, and the Greeks learnt from the Egyptians."

Most of what we know of Herodotus' travels come from *The Histories*, his only book. It discussed the history of wars and provides fascinating country information on travel, culture, religion, flora, fauna, and geography of the ancient world. It absolutely enlightened the Greek population at the time and made future generations more aware of ancient civilizations and cultures and the difficulties of traveling in the fifth century B.C.E.

**Bust of Herodotus and fragment of the text from *The Histories VIII* on papyrus oxyrhynchus 2099, early 2nd century AD** (Hughes, 201)

An educated visitor to Greece during the period 450-435 B.C.E. would likely have heard of Herodotus. His efforts in reporting on history, based on his extensive travel and interactions with foreign cultures, made him a well-known figure. Herodotus' incredible memory of his many travels was the intellectual asset he relied on most during his many lectures. And his amazing friendships with Sophocles, local intellectuals, and artists, as well as with other brilliant writers, such as Aeschylus and Aristophanes in Athens, added to his notoriety.

Herodotus' stories also had a strong religious bent. His was the time period in Greece and in many countries of that era, when men and women saw the hands of the gods firmly involved with daily life. He wrote about the impact of the gods on almost every society he visited, and was particularly interested in the religious practices of Egypt. Fascinated by Egyptian religion and customs. He noted, for instance, the Egyptian deification of certain animals, such as the half-lion and half-man represented by the Sphinx.

Our worldly traveler often used trade terms and described trading customs in the areas he visited. These references suggest he was likely a merchant or trader of sorts, giving him the means and time for long distance travel. And he may have earned additional monies from his writings, although not many people could read. More probably, he received a speaker's fee as a professional storyteller and commentator-entertainer. This would be highly likely in such cities as Athens, Olympia, Corinth, and Thebes, since he had seen and known more about the world than his contemporaries or the general Greek population. Wealthy residents enjoyed festive gatherings, entertained not only by dancers and performers, but also by storytellers, poets, and intellectuals of the day. A good storyteller like Herodotus could earn a handsome fee at gatherings; whereby, he entertained the audience by his fascinating tales of his travels.

There is evidence suggesting that he was so popular that the Greeks of Athens voted to give him a very large sum of ten talents of gold from the Athenian Assembly.

It was the fact that Herodotus was the most traveled Greek citizen of his time and a skillful raconteur continued to endear him to the Athenian intelligentsia. While he began his travels throughout Greece, he also ventured to destinations around the lands along the Mediterranean Sea, Aegean Sea, and the Black Sea. He visited Caria, Lydia, Mysia - all provinces of present-day Turkey, as well as Rhodes, Pontus, and Euxinus, the southern islands of the Aegean Sea, between present day Greece and

Turkey. In addition, he visited Thrace, Macedonia, Sicily, Egypt, and Persia. While traveling on land was always difficult, he moved along well with caravans or government officials, avoiding, of course, potential thieves and marauders.

Travel on the seas during this time often proved to be far worse than land travel. Accommodations on board these ships were cramped; passengers often camped on the deck. Pirates roamed the seas preying on whatever boats moved on the water without protection. Many vessels were not seaworthy, and vulnerable to shipwrecks during stormy periods, making the voyages treacherous and frightening.

*The Histories,* offering major information about the Persian Wars, is largely based on the oral testimony of local citizens in the countries he visited, as well as observations he made during his travels. He relied heavily on translators and help from others who spoke Greek to obtain information. Yet, reliance on these translators and receiving most of his travel knowledge third hand made him vulnerable to innuendos and subterfuges by local falsifiers of history intent on misleading him for their own aggrandizement.

As we mentioned, this caused many readers to question Herodotus' veracity, especially his references to places he hadn't visited. Much of his intelligence gathering was based on unsubstantiated oral history recited to him by persons he met who may have learned about events through a chain of ancestors. There were probably a lot of myths, tales, and legends mixed in with the stories told to him. Not unexpected, many discrepancies and numerous contradictions in his writings cannot be substantiated. These conditions certainly challenged him in his quest to assemble the history of the Persian wars. It was not so much that his writing of *The Histories,* was accurate, but that his work translated antiquity for generations of scholars that would follow in his footsteps, still providing valuable information about the customs and geography of the areas he visited.

The personal interview techniques Herodotus used for gathering facts introduced a completely new style of reporting and recording history. He was clever, intelligent, with a strong memory, able to gain the confidence of the leaders and thinkers of the communities he visited, and to obtain and assimilate the knowledge he received. It wasn't that others had not written about history, but, rather, they had not been able to obtain the in-depth information with the same capacity as our Herodotus.

While analyzing important perceptions of the people and places he visited, Herodotus designed probing questions about events and happenings of early time periods in a way not earlier perceived. His clear-sightedness and interesting descriptions made history come alive. He believed his reporting was accurate, at least with the facts he had to work with. However, he was not opposed to spicing the literature with a bit of gossip! He was a voracious reader and determined to get to the destinations where great events of history had taken place. We believe he was the first internationalist and multi-cultural traveler; deeply interested in the geography and culture of the world at large. As a result of his travels and writing, cultural travel was born.

From Herodotus' picturesque descriptions of local customs, humor, heroes, tragedies, and historical events, the world gained much knowledge about the early societies outside Greece. Others in the upper strata of the Greek society were likewise curious, but they didn't seem to have the will or fortitude to undertake journeys as lengthy and difficult as he did.

Even though the educated population was particularly interested in military history, there was very little written about the wars and battle sites outside of Greece. Even less about the heritage and customs of people in other lands. Herodotus was able to listen, asked questions of the local citizens, visited sites, talked to guides, and then piece-by-piece put the puzzle of world history together.

His writing style was full of colorful commentaries about his extensive travels, which outpaced even the well-traveled of the Greeks. In addition to those places he actually experienced, he also described places he did not visit. As a result, he was not against accepting unproven rumors and reporting them as if they really happened with his picturesque fables enlivening the pages of his book.

He described one tribe called the Massagetan of Eastern Iran in these words: "If a Massagetan desires a woman, he bangs his quiver outside her wagon and has sex with her, with no fear of reprisal." While he seemed to have an interest in women and sex, he never let us know about his own personal views or experiences about these subjects.

We're also aware that Herodotus usually simply accepted the description of customs as told to him without comment, although, he was known to criticize, from time to time, certain behaviors he disagreed with. He was conservative, and if the custom seemed too far from the norm established in his mind, he would not hesitate to give his notions about the culture. The Babylonian custom which required every native woman to have sexual intercourse with a stranger once in her life was completely unacceptable to his way of thinking; he did not hesitate to make his opinions about this abnormal cultural trait known.

Herodotus died around the age of 60 in 425 B.C.E.

While historians claim him as the Father of History, his legacy as the father of world travel can be valid, as the first travel writer and major contributor to the study of ancient culture and geography. The understanding of the history of the ancient world expanded as Herodotus elucidated on many hidden treasures in countries he visited and provided, for us, knowledge of the primeval existence of early modes of travel.

**Statue of Herodotus in his hometown of Halicarnassus**
(Mingren, 2017)

Because of Herodotus' extensive travel journals, our generation has been given this great book of *The Histories*. We appreciate this epoch-making travel narrative that has given the world an opportunity to know and better understand what it was like to travel during the fifth century B.C.E. His explanations of his journeys during the time period in which he lived had a tremendous bearing on how the world was viewed. He was our first cultural tourist as well as our first geo-tourist.

At the time of his death, there was little recognition of the enormity of his travels and impact on society. Wealthy residents that heard him speak of his journeys at special forums accepted his stories mostly as entertainment. Few had read *The Histories*, as the general number of educated people was small, and reading ancient Greek was no easy task. In addition, not many copies of the book were available. Hand copying hundreds of rolls of papyrus accurately was a major challenge. Later generations and present-day readers have learned to appreciate his historic trips, to visit some of the places he describes, and to become fascinated by the history and heritage of the areas as he did.

Political leaders, military strategists, including such men as Caesar, and a few of the Greek elite read his book and were able to make important decisions based on his writings. Herodotus' contributions to the study of ancient history and his detailed accounts of early travel are important legacies for today's travelers. Travelers who followed in his footsteps were well served by his many insights and exciting descriptions.

We are indebted to him.

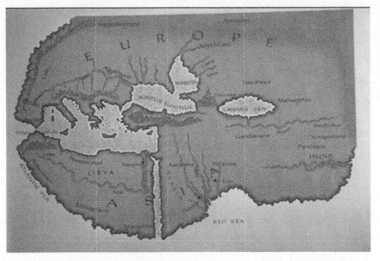

**Ancient map of the world in the era of Herodotus**
(Pinterest)

# CHAPTER THREE

# A JOURNEY WITH MARCO POLO

"The end is not apparent from the very outset."
-Herodotus, the *Histories*, 440 B.C.E.

*The place: the city-state maritime Republic of Venice, Italy, a leading nation for international trade. The year: 1266. The activity: a trade fair.*

*This morning, young Marco Polo was ecstatic, seeing the boats from abroad docked at the port on the edge of town. A sign that the annual trade fair was about to begin. The traveling merchants from distant lands had arrived with their armed guards and exotic products for sale. The gaily covered red, yellow, and blue striped tents were in place and the townsfolk rapidly moved along the twisting cobblestone streets to partake of the festivities. In addition to the international trade merchants, gypsies had arrived in town from far-flung locations. Adorned in their colorful dress, they made music, sang and danced, providing entertainment, as well as offering goods for sale.*

*Excitement filled the air as people celebrated! Meeting, greeting, and looking to see what they might buy at this popular festival. The merchants have already been trading among themselves and with the local folks. And oh, the variety of international merchandise for sale: damasks, silks, taffetas, spices, perfumes, balsam, hides, ivory, furs, benzoic, and, of course, exquisite jewelry. Even articles from nearby communities were marketed along with goods that had been transported from faraway places like India, China, and the Middle East.*

*Booths set up by local tradespeople offered their goods for sale as well as provided food and beverages for those in attendance. The functionaries of Venice promenaded in their best attire throughout the crowded streets, extolling the virtues of the city. Women, breaking away from daily life, preened, and immersed themselves in the activities and merriment associated with this festive event.*

*Young Marco fantasized about traveling to the destinations where these trade fair goods came from. Hearing about these distant places from family members who had traveled abroad as traders, he studied maps and read books to learn about other parts of the world, which only intensified his imagination to travel. He wondered how to make his wish come true as he visited each booth, and asked questions of the visiting merchants. After a full day, he returned home. That night, he dreamed he was one of those traders at the fair. In the dream he envisioned himself, in brightly colored attire, ready for any journey.*

**Marco Polo dressed in his traveling finery**

\*    \*    \*

During the *Middle Ages*, 476-1453 C.E., few Europeans traveled. Major exceptions were the Vikings, who traveled extensively. Leif Ericson is one of the best-known Vikings as well as the first known European explorer to the Americas. Others who traveled were merchants engaged in traveling fairs and a few adventurous explorers, as we've written about above. Most people in this era were ill-fed, illiterate peasants who oftentimes led wretched lives in bondage on a manor dependent on the whims of some suzerain who had little interest in their welfare. It was highly unusual if a man were to rise from such abhorrent conditions to become a respectable citizen with a successful trade, or to gain honors of sorts as a hero from participating in the Crusades that never seemed to end. Medical care was almost non-existent, and people died from polluted water, bacterial infections, untended wounds, broken bones, and worst of all, the black plague.

During these medieval times, the Middle Ages, women suffered far more than men and had very few rights. Girls married at age 13 or 14, and church canon law encouraged men to beat their wives *for their own good*. A typical noble lady was in the custody of her husband and was expected to obey him. Additionally, she was expected to accept that her husband would likely possess a concubine or two, and, if children resulted, the noble lady, as a wife, would see to the care of the concubine's children. If a woman of Europe hadn't married by her late teens, she might likely become a nun or a spinning-wheel operator, referred to in England as a spinster. To preserve their limited clean bedclothes, poor women gave birth on their dirty ones. About a fourth of all children born died within a year of birth.

Most people lived in small villages, fearing bears, wolves, and outlaws. They were terrified to travel more than short distances from their homes. The world for them was anywhere past the village boundary. If you, as an individual, dared go further, you were certainly in *God's hands* for protection from many perceived predators. Within a few miles of the village, local dialects in other small communities were confusing, and forms of communication were difficult at best. Village folk mostly lived without much hope for a better life. Perhaps eighteen out of every twenty people reached the ripe old age of forty, if they were lucky.

Little news was available in the villages about other societies and outside events such as wars, popes, kings, or natural disasters. The people knew almost nothing about the world outside their local community, and an occasional traveler who happened by such a village was looked on with surprise. And if the traveler was lucky, feted by the community. What little bounty available in the local village was often shared with the visitor?

Marco was fortunate, not to be born in a remote village. He was born in the progressive, wealthy, international trade city-state of Venice. The city-state maritime Republic of Venice in the thirteenth century, by comparison with most of the rest of Europe, was a cosmopolitan and advanced society with a major impact on international commerce. Venice was leading the way toward the Renaissance period in Europe, especially with respect to the arts and culture and shared some of its fame as a trading capital with such other mercantile republics of Italy as Pisa and Genoa. Despite this competition in trade and for leadership, Venice was considered the most important city-state in

Europe, a worldly, independent, self-governing community. Venice's monetary and fiscal policies preceded modern banking and as an early money lending nation, it accepted deposits and loaned money to many governments and nobles. Venice was a veritable crossroad where traders, travelers, and adventurers crossed paths, shared maps, and told tales of areas beyond the trade routes.

As the most democratic European country, the Republic of Venice, a Catholic nation, was also tolerant of other religions. The city attempted to keep religion devoid of its politics, yet had frequent conflicts with the Papacy. Also as a major maritime power, Venice was the epicenter of commerce, and a trade leader among the Byzantine Empire, a continuation of the Roman Empire, and the Islamic world. Its leaders also recognized the strength, power, and advanced society of the Mongol Empire of China, as well as the potential opportunities for trade with such a vast empire. Recognizing the commercial values of trade with the east early on, Venice strategically developed a trade relationship with the Mongol Empire.

In his book *The Travels of Marco Polo*, Marco Polo used the Anglicized word *Cathay* in referring to China. His book was so popular in Europe that Cathay became the most used name for China for many years.

In the middle of the thirteenth century, the Mongol Empire was ruled by a broad-minded, effective, and tolerant emperor, Kublai Khan, also called the *Great Khan*, or supreme ruler, and the wealthiest and most powerful ruler in the thirteen-century. Kublai Khan was the founder and ruler of the Yuan Dynasty in China.

By most standards, in 1298, the Chinese civilization was considerably more advanced than Europe and most of the rest of the world. At this time, the Chinese invented a wooden, movable type printing press. This invention long preceded the Gutenberg press, which was used in Europe in the 1450s. Additionally, gunpowder had been in use in China since the ninth century C.E. and was used in firearms and grenades by the twelfth century. China was in full use of guns and cannons by the thirteenth century, and through trade negotiations, such advances were copied and adopted by armies in the Middle East. By the fifteenth century, Europe was beginning to use gunpowder on a limited basis.

Back to Venice. While Venetian vessels did not yet have cannons, during the time of Marco Polo, the Republic of Venice protected its maritime power with more than 36,000 sailors and over 3,000 ships in her service. Her sailors were among the best in the world; her boats utilized the latest available navigation instruments, and her captains were well informed and had available to them up-to-date maps of Europe. Lesser known to most of the world, was Venice's military strategy of training all men from seventeen to sixty in the art of using the crossbow. If a Venetian ship were attacked, its soldiers, sailors, and even its trade merchants, were effective defenders using such weapons as crossbows, swords, and javelins.

*　　*　　*

A popular travel author, one of the most famous in history, Marco was born January 15, 1254 in the progressive city-state maritime Republic of Venice. His father, Niccolò Polo, did not witness the birth of his son, as he and his brother, Maffeo, were traveling on an extensive international trade mission that would last almost fifteen years. In essence, Marco's mother acted as a single parent in raising Marco for the first fourteen years of his life. She had considerable help from extended members of the highly successful trade merchant Polo family, yet sadly, she died before his fifteenth birthday, leaving Marco to be raised by an aunt and uncle.

Although Marco was well-educated, he did not learn Latin, the international language, which was deemed important in the thirteenth century. Latin was used extensively in important documents and was spoken during Catholic Church services in most countries of the world during Marco's era. It is likely that Marco's mother, being the wife of a highly successful trade merchant, must have imbued her son with tall tales of the adventures of the merchant class of Venice. In addition, the well-known Polo family of merchants helped him understand trade-related topics like foreign currency, details about cargo ships, geography, and other necessary skills for international trading.

Marco's education would have been supplemented by contact with the large trading community of Venice and by being exposed to the many churches, canals, quays, bridges, historic buildings, and the open squares of the city. Venetians were well-known for their cultural activities in art, music, and festivals, all of interest to our young lad. He had an astute ability for retrieving and retaining information, learning about the world from associations with trade merchants and explorers passing through Venice on their way to exotic destinations in the east.

Growing up, Marco recognized the importance of international trade for his family, who were aggressive commercial businessmen, having traveled and traded extensively in the Middle East and beyond, which established his family to reach a position of wealth, recognition, and prestige.

Before Marco was born, his father, Niccolò, and uncle, Maffeo, had left Venice to travel east toward Constantinople on a trade-commercial mission. Venice, already a major international trading capital, had supplanted the great Constantinople trading center before the Crusades began in 1095. Constantinople was considered one of the great intellectual, progressive, and prosperous business communities of the world prior to the thirteenth century.

Early in the thirteenth century, after the partial success of the Fourth Crusade, the Venetians governed a part of Constantinople. In 1260 political changes took place, wherein Constantinople began its downfall as a most powerful trading center. The Polo brothers, having considerable political savvy and commercial wisdom, realized Constantinople would not remain tangential to Venice for long. The city was losing its reputation as the world center for trade and culture, so they liquidated their property and commercial interests in Constantinople, invested it in jewels and other merchandise, and ventured east by ship to Sudak, located in present day Crimea, Ukraine, a peninsula of South Ukraine on the Black Sea west of the Sea of Azov.

At the time of the Polo brothers' visit to the city of Sudak, a principal community along the lucrative Silk Road trade route, the area was under the control of the Turco-Mongo Golden Horde, related to the Mongol Empire. Part of the Silk Road, Sudak was central to cultural interactions, commercial activities, and was the communication center connecting the West and East from the Mediterranean Sea to China.

A distinct advantage for the Polo brothers in Sudak was the existence of a colony of Venetians living in the area who had built a protective fortress around their city. Another Polo brother, Marco the Elder, a trading partner with Niccolò and Maffeo, owned a residence in Sudak that became their business headquarters. They decided to sell jewels in the Crimea and then return to Venice with their newly bought trade goods. When political upheavals and warring factions in the area prevented their return to Venice, they continued eastward to the city of Bukhara, located in modern day Uzbekistan.

Bukhara was one of the key outlying regions of the Mongol Empire, a neutral territory in the midst of warring inimical factions of the Tartar rulers. Conjecture is that the Polo brothers remained there for three years, conferred with other traders, learned the Tartar language, and became intrigued with the commercial opportunities for trade with China. They also obtained valuable knowledge about the Great Ruler, Kublai Khan (1214-1294 C.E.), Emperor of China, and grandson of the world's most famous Mongol warlord and military genius, Genghis Khan.

As a young man, Kublai Khan had fought side-by-side with his grandfather in the defeat of the Chinese, and earned the respect of his countrymen.

In Bukhara, the Polo brothers met one of Kublai Khan's important representatives who was on his way to see the Great Khan. The stories of the Great Khan, his already vast achievements since ascendancy as Emperor in 1259, and his great wealth fascinated the Polo brothers. They understood Kublai Kahn ruled over the greatest connected land empire the world had ever seen at that time, stretching from China to Iraq and including parts of Russia as well. Being curious and still unable to travel back to Venice because of warring conflicts, the Polos obtained an invitation to join the caravan of Kublai Khan's emissary to travel eastward to join his court. Eventually, the Polo brothers ended that part of their journey four years later in 1265, at the summer capital of Kublai Khan's empire in Shang-tu, two hundred miles northwest of what would be the new winter capital of Beijing in 1267.

Few Europeans had ever penetrated that far into Cathay. One such European who had made a visit to the Mongol Empire prior to the visit by the Polo brothers was Friar Giovanni of Plano Carpini, Italy. He had been sent by Pope Innocent IV to obtain information about this strange Mongol empire, and to find and meet with any of the Christian Mongols that might live here. As a result, Kublai Khan became curious about the intricacies of this Christian religion he learned about from Friar Giovanni.

Fortunately for the Polo brothers, Kublai Khan was also a man of immense curiosity and anxious to learn about the Republic of Venice, Europe, and especially about the Christian religion. His envoys into Persia, Turkey, and Arab lands spoke often of the great religions of Islam and Christianity, and provoked his interests in worldly affairs beyond his great empire.

Kublai Khan treated the Polos with great respect; an engaging and positive relationship developed. He, like his grandfather Genghis Khan, was interested in and fascinated by different religions. Genghis Khan, for instance, had included soldiers representing many different religions in his army: Muslims, Christians, Buddhists, and other religious sects as well.

Wanting to know more about Christianity and about the Catholic Pope, Clement IV, more than the Polo's could supply, Kublai Khan eventually sent them back to Europe as his ambassadors to the Pope! He also sent letters with them inviting the Pope to send one hundred Christian scholars to China to explain the Catholic religion. The Polo brothers had already informed Kublai Khan about the importance of Jerusalem in the Christian religion, which led Kublai Khan to request holy oil from that religious city. As a gesture of good will, he converted many of his subjects to Christianity. Imagine all this, as if you had been there.

As the Polo brothers left Kublai Khan's compound, he gave them a large gold tablet inscribed with the words: "By strength of the eternal Heaven, holy be the Khan's name. Let him that pays him not reverence be killed." This tablet was recognized throughout the Khan's empire and carried with it assurances of protection, safety, and security for the holder. When presented to local authorities, it commanded that they be provided with food, lodging, transportation, guide services, and hospitality available in the area.

**Kublai Khan presenting the inscribed gold
tablet to Niccolò Polo and Maffeo Polo**
(Marco Polo and Kublai Khan, 2016)

By the time the Polo brothers reached Acre, north of Jerusalem in present day Israel, the eastern outpost of Latin Christendom in 1269, Pope Clement IV had been dead for a year. The brothers decided to return to Venice to await the election of the new Pope. Arriving in Venice, Niccolò Polo found that his wife had died and that a son, Marco, had been born, who by then was 15 years old. It didn't take long for a father-son bonding; Marco was fascinated by the travel tales of his father and uncle and dreamed of adventures for himself.

Marco Polo's father and uncle felt a great moral obligation to deliver on the promises made to the Great Khan regarding his interests in Christianity. After all, they took their role as Khan's ambassadors to Europe seriously, and Kublai Khan had rewarded them with an impressive array of expensive gifts. So the Polo brothers waited patiently in Venice for a new pontiff to be elected, yet after two years, a successor had not yet been selected. It was not at all clear when a new Pope would be chosen. By then, their patience had worn thin and being the merchants they were, they surely did not want to lose such a lucrative market in China.

They decided it was important that they return to tell the great Kublai Khan the reason for their failure. On their journey, beginning in 1271, they took the young Marco, now 17, with them. This begins his fabulous written account of his adventurous 24-year odyssey with his father and uncle, which led to the publishing of *The Travels of Marco Polo.*

While Marco's father and uncle traveled almost exclusively for monetary gain through trade activities, his travel was part of his wish for adventure, new experiences, and an expansion of his education. He naturally developed a keen interest in the people, land, plants, animals, history, geography, languages, and culture of the areas he visited.

Marco Polo at the age of 17, sitting astride
between his father and his uncle as they
begin their epic journey in Venice.
(Kalan, 2014)

The first stop on their journey was the city of Acre, an important community to the Christian faithful. They explained the requests made by Kublai Khan to the papal legate in Acre, Theobald Visconti, who gave them permission to obtain holy oil from Jerusalem. Kublai Khan had made this request for his mother who was a Christian. But the Polo brothers were disappointed that no one from the religious order would join them on the trip to China. In view of their promises to the Great Khan, this situation became an intractable dilemma.

Shortly after leaving Jerusalem, they learned that Theobald Visconti had been elected Pope, taking the name Gregory X. They immediately returned to Acre again, hoping they could obtain the 100 Christian wise men, then required, to visit by the Khan. But they were able to convince only two Dominican friars to accompany them. Historians have speculated that had the Polo brothers been successful in their quest for 100 Christian wise men to accompany them, China might well have become a Christian nation. We speculate with them.

The party hadn't gone far when they were confronted by a major conflict that frightened the friars. The priests quailed in the face of unknown dangers, realizing with great fear the adversities of this long and arduous travel; it was too much for them. When their party happened upon a group of Templar Knights headed by the Grand Master of the Templar Knights, the friars fled from the Polo brothers and headed back to lands under Christian control and the protection of the Templar Knights. The Polos were also alarmed by the nearby hostilities, yet they decided to continue their journey, hopeful that Kublai Khan would understand their lack of obtaining religious leaders to explain Christendom. The two brothers always envisioned large profits to be made from trade within these distant parts of the world. And Marco was with them.

As they journeyed toward the East, they encountered countless obstacles; constantly changing weather conditions, dust and sandstorms, all frequent. Yet, they learned to adjust to enormous changes in temperatures from the lowlands to the mountains, coping with rain, snow, sleet and rampaging rivers. Roving bandits and marauding armies were a constant threat. Plus, communications with local people in numerous different languages and dialects was always strained, trying to understand a wide variety of cultures and customs as they passed through. Yet the Polos stoically moved forward, the brothers wanting to teach and instill Marco with hardiness. We find it fascinating to note in the thirteenth century, the etymology definition of the word "travel" came from the French word *"travail"*, which is defined as "...strenuous physical or mental exertion..." or semantically as reflecting the *difficulty of any journey in the Middle Ages.*

Of particular difficulty was the crossing of deserts; there was almost no food, and it usually took two days to get to the next watering hole. To be safe, the Polos more than likely were participants in a trade caravan crossing the desert. On occasion, it was reported that a number of caravan travelers often became delirious and saw mirages or other illusions with images of trees and water.

Marco described crossing the great Gobi Desert in a passage of his book this way: "The truth is this. When a man is riding by night through this desert and something happens to make him loiter and lose touch with his companions, by dropping asleep or for some other reason, and afterwards he wants to rejoin them, then he hears spirits talking in such a way that they seem to be his companions. Sometimes, indeed, they even hail him by name. Often these voices make him stray from the path so that he never finds it again. And in this way, many travelers have been lost and have perished. And sometimes in the night they are conscious of a noise like the clatter of a great cavalcade of riders away from the road, and, believing that these are some of their own companies, they go where they hear the noise and, when day breaks, find they are victims of an illusion and in an awkward plight. And there are some who, in crossing this desert, have seen a host of men coming towards them and, suspecting that they were robbers, have taken flight; so having left the beaten track and not knowing how to return to it, they have gone hopelessly astray. Yes, and even by daylight men hear these spirit voices, and often you fancy you are listening to the strains of many instruments, especially drums, and the clash of arms. For this reason, bands of travelers make a point of keeping very close together. Before they go to sleep, they set up a sign pointing in the direction in which they have to travel. And round the necks of all their beasts they fasten little bells, so that by listening to the sound they may prevent them from straying off the path."

Imagine yourself on crossing the endless desert on a moon-less night....

Marco, unlike his father and uncle who were basically interested in trade opportunities, was enthralled by the different customs, cultures, geography, flora, and fauna as they traveled east. He noticed diverse terrain and was fascinated with the different habits and manners of the people in the many villages they passed through in Central Asia.

In one village, Marco described Kamul in Central Asia within the Mongol empire, noting the differing sexual mores of the community. He wrote: "The villagers are a very gay folk, who give no thought to anything but making music, singing, and dancing, ...and taking great delight in the pleasures of the body...if a stranger comes to a house here to seek hospitality, he receives a very warm welcome. The host bids his wife do everything that the guest wishes. Then, he leaves the house and goes about his own business and stays away two or three days. Meanwhile, the guest stays with his wife in the house and does what he will with her, lying with her in one bed just as if she were his own wife; and they lead a gay life together. All the men of this city and province are thus cuckolded by their wives, but they are not the least shamed of it. And the women are beautiful and vivacious and always ready to oblige."

There are some historians who suggest this custom prevailed because it was believed that outsiders or travelers brought new blood to the family that would improve the offspring and lead to a better future. All righty!

Growing older and bolder, Marco took great interest in the opposite sex, and, while he never stated that he had sexual encounters with women along the way, it can be inferred that physical contact did take place. There are readers of his book who think he deliberately refrained from including any of his personal escapades that might be deemed inappropriate by the Catholic Church in order not to taint his character.

After they had traveled across the hazardous deserts of Persia, the Polo brothers and Marco reached the snowy mountain ranges of the Pamir Mountains in Central Asia. These mountains are over 15,000 feet high at the top, called the "Roof of the World."

Here, Marco had difficulty adjusting to such heights, becoming ill with acute mountain sickness, including a dangerous fever. The Polo party was also exhausted, deciding to remain a full year in Balkh, present day northern Afghanistan, to rest and nurse Marco back to health. During their stay, they studied the local languages and culture, including foods, dress, and religions. Knowing and understanding different cultures and languages helped the Polos everywhere, throughout their journey to China and during their return trip.

Once Marco recovered, they moved ahead to ascend to the plateau of Pamir; their major concern keeping their toes from frostbite and their hands from suffering chilblains. Again, travel was perilous, yet by now the Polos were seasoned travelers and experienced negotiators who knew how to obtain assistance from the locals, which allowed them to proceed, no matter what the circumstances.

As the Polo party moved east, they stopped in the city of Karakorum in Mongolia, once the capital of the Mongol Empire in the thirteenth century. Marco chose the stopover in Karakorum to explain in his writings about how Genghis Khan became so powerful.

"Now it happened in the year of Christ's incarnation, 1187," he wrote, "that the Tartars, these Mongolians, chose a king to reign over them whose name in the language was Chinghiz Khan, a man of great ability and wisdom as well as a gifted orator, a brilliant soldier and a leader. After his election, all the Tartars in the world, dispersed as they were among various foreign countries, came to him to acknowledge his sovereignty. When Chinghiz Khan saw what a following he had, he equipped them with bows and their other customary weapons and embarked on a career of conquest."

The matter of the Mongolian empire established by Genghis Khan was of great importance and concern to the Europeans just prior to Marco Polo's era. The European communities bordering on or near the empire were nervous that any day the Mongolian hordes might invade and destroy their villages; a major cause of distress and a real threat to their security. However, with a few isolated exceptions, Genghis Khan did not invade Europe, and, instead, the Europeans were the benefactors of new trade relations with the Mongol Empire controlled by Genghis Khan.

Two months before the Polos reached the court of Emperor Kublai Khan, his network of spies and military outposts informed him of their impending visit. He immediately sent emissaries to ensure their protection and to provide for their comfort.

Finally, after having traveled for three-and-a-half years and more than 7,500 miles, the ambassadors and Marco Polo arrived at the court of Kublai Kahn.

Marco was twenty-one years old, and Kublai Khan was 61. Kublai Khan was now the ruler of China, Mongolia, Tibet, and areas in the Middle East. Kublai Kahn's court was such that obsequious obedience to him by his people was the rule of the day.

The Polo brothers felt they had really let the Khan down. The little they had to give him were letters and a few personal gifts from the new Pope, and a small amount of sacred oil from the Holy Land. Although such presents were hardly fit for a leader such as Kublai Khan, he accepted these with patience and dignity.

While Kublai Khan was familiar with the Polo brothers, he became curious about the young man, the third member of their party. Niccolò Polo then introduced his son, Marco, saying to the Great Khan, "Marco is at your service."

It is speculated that Marco, during these travels, learned the Mongol language, and possibly a smattering of some of the Chinese and Persian languages. This allowed Marco to talk with Kublai Khan in his language, which would have greatly impressed the Great Khan. During the first meeting, and after, Marco became completely loyal to Kublai Khan and became a favorite friend of the Great Khan.

Immediately after arriving to the court of Kublai Khan, Marco applied himself to learn the written and spoken languages and cultures of the nearby areas, which also impressed and endeared him to the Emperor. Marco had known nothing about the politics of China and Mongolia, but through his august mentor, Kublai Khan, he learned about the Khan's grandfather, the great Genghis Khan, and about the current squabbles of relatives of Kublai Khan over territories that had been inherited from Genghis Khan.

Imagine this joy of learning and sharing!

But one problem was that Kublai Khan's first cousin, Kaidu, was constantly challenging the Great Kahn over territories throughout the empire. Kublai Khan was not worried that Kaidu could win a conflict with him, but he was concerned about the disruptions Kaidu was causing in his empire. Later, after Marco had the full story of the dispute, he took the liberty of writing some of the details of the disagreement in his own book of stories.

Marco Polo had become a wonderful storyteller, and his adventurous tales of his travels entertained the Emperor. Like Herodotus before him, he repeated legends and hearsay that he heard from locals, even if they proved to be untrue or never really existed. Kublai Khan was deeply interested in the Christian religion and asked the Polos to explain more details of the religion. Marco was a practicing Christian until he left for China. Compared to his father and uncle, who had been away from the Church for a long time, he was better able to explain the philosophy of the religion to the Great Kahn.

The Emperor, a great administrator and intellect, immediately saw how clever, tactful, and diplomatic Marco was. Impressed with the young man's élan and daring, he began to employ Marco on public missions. Kublai Khan introduced the use of bright foreigners as administrators in his empire. His strategy was that such a move would more likely keep his people from colluding and developing schemes for bribery, fraud, and a possible revolution.

The Emperor often sent Marco, his new public servant, to distant parts of his empire. For him to be supplied with unlimited money, servants, excellent transportation, and traveling throughout the empire was thrilling! Marco made notes about the areas, cultures, and people, which amused and interested the Kahn.

Marco was particularly impressed with the effectiveness and hardiness of the Mongol soldiers, who were inured to war from their infancy and were expected to develop as fine soldiers. They strengthened themselves into furious warriors who could survive long distances with little food or shelter. Their modus operandi was to ride their horses with lightning speed as they attacked the enemy. Interestingly, when the Mongol warriors were on a series of battlefields for several years conquering foreign countries, their women managed the empire.

Becoming an astute diplomat, Marco was given important assignments that may have included assisting the governor of the city of Yangchow. Under the Khan's protection, Marco also visited Burma, then part of the Chinese dynasty, where he later wrote about the Silk Road. In addition, he traveled near to Japan, Sumatra, Java, and Sri Lanka.

While the Polo brothers stayed on, Marco continued to be fascinated by the different cultures and customs of the cities and provinces he visited within China's great empire. In a province called Manzi, South China, he described a special custom of the people in the community: "You must know that all the people of Manzi have a usage such as I will describe. The truth is that as soon as a child is born, the father or the mother has a record made of the day and the minute and the hour at which he was born, and under what constellation and planet, so that everyone knows his horoscope. Whenever anyone intends to make a journey into another district or a business deal, he consults an astrologer who tells him his horoscope, and the astrologer tells him whether it is good to undertake it or not. Often, they are deterred from the venture. For you must know that their astrologers are skilled in their art and in diabolic enchantment, so that many of their predictions prove true, and the people put great faith in them. When a marriage is planned, astrologers first investigate whether the bridegroom and bride are born under concordant planets. If so, it is put into effect, they are married; if not, it is called off."

Marco loved the construction and architectural details of the surrounding gardens of Kublai Khan's palaces. In one segment of his book, he wrote: "Between the inner and the outer walls of the palace, of which I have told you, are stretches of park-land with stately trees. The grass grows here in abundance because all the paths are paved and built up fully two cubits, about 3 feet above the level of the ground, so that no mud forms on them and no rainwater collects in puddles, but the moisture trickles over the lawns, enriching the soil and promoting a lush growth of herbage. In these parks, there is a great variety of game, such as, a male deer, a hornless male deer, a roebuck, stags, squirrels, and many other beautiful animals. All the area within the walls is full of these graceful creatures, except the paths that people walk on."

Today, that approach toward the environment is referred to as "sustainable development." Everywhere that Marco visited, there was either a fabulous building, cultural activity, or a new product that caught his imagination.

Marco loved Kublai Khan, writing, "This Great Khan is the mightiest man, whether in respects of subjects, or of territory, or treasure."

Marco also noted in his book his eyewitness account of a hunting trip. Like all Mongol warriors, Kublai Khan loved to hunt. As emperor, he had every possibility to hunt on a grand scale and utilized gyrfalcons, a special breed of hunting falcons that were exceedingly effective in locating game. The Great Khan also had a pet cheetah that had been trained to hunt, an eye-opening activity unfamiliar to Marco Polo, even though such hunting "leopards" were used by aristocrats during this period in India, Cyprus, and certain parts of Europe.

The Polo brothers prospered in the court of the Emperor, and they remained in China for fifteen years until the Great Khan became quite elderly, suffering from both gout and alcoholism. Feeling homesick as well as fearing that Kublai Khan's death would definitely endanger their lives by placing them in the hands of one of Kublai Khan's enemies, the Polo brothers sought permission from Kublai Khan to return to their native Venice.

Yet Kublai Khan had become very attached to the Venetian merchants and especially Marco, and would not consent to their departure.

The opportunity to leave finally came in 1292 when the Khan of Persia, the grandson of Kublai's brother, lost his favorite wife and desired that another be sent from the same Mongol tribe that his family had come from. The custom of obtaining a wife with a similar heritage as that of a Mongol leader had been a part of the culture for many generations. He sent an envoy to Kublai Khan to bring back a suitable bride. The right young lady of age 17 was located and brought to the court of Kublai Kahn.

A journey overland was considered too dangerous for a wedding entourage, so it was decided that the party would travel by sea. The Polo brothers, having come from the sea-faring nation of Venice, volunteered their services as navigators to pilot the ships to carry the bride, Princess Kokejin, and the returning envoy, to Persia.

Sorrowfully, the elder Kublai Khan agreed. Yet he equipped the party in the best manner at his disposal, which included a magnificent fleet of fourteen ships, a special crew, and military protectors. In all, the party reached six hundred people, not counting the seamen. There was a need for multiple ships just to carry two years' worth of provisions. With a great deal of melancholy, Kublai Khan said farewell to the Venetians. He also provided them with friendly messages to be delivered to the Christian kings of France, Spain, and England and to the Catholic Pope. And more, with expensive and exquisite gifts to add to their accumulated trade goods.

The Polo brothers, so fond of Kublai Khan, were also sad, yet glad to be on their way. Exchanging their acquired possessions for gold, jewels, and other precious objects that were easily carried and, with these concealed in their clothes, they set sail on the long, dangerous voyage.

Leaving Zaiton, China, they sailed through southern waters, touching on the islands of Sumatra, Java, Ceylon, and a few points along the coast of India. It took more than two years to reach Persia. Enduring a perilous journey on stormy seas in which they encountered various tragedies along the way, this led to the deaths of all but a few of the party.

Luckily, the survivors included the Polo brothers, Marco and the princess. In the meantime, the ruler of Persia had been killed, so they delivered the bride to his son. Sadly, Princess Kokejin lived only a few more years before she died at the age of 22.

With the wedding mission accomplished, the Polo brothers began the journey back to Venice. On their way home, they learned that their dear benefactor, Emperor Kublai Khan, had died at age 79.

They had no sooner left the protection of the Mongol territory when they entered the small kingdom of Trebizond on the Black Sea where they were robbed of some of the immense treasures they had accumulated. But they survived! Other difficult encounters were overcome, and, finally, they managed to reach home in 1295 after having been gone for twenty-four years. Amazingly, the brothers had been able to keep many of their precious jewels hidden in the clothes they wore. Yet they arrived in Venice looking like ragged Mongols. Having thought them dead, their relatives at first did not recognize them! However, they became delighted when the Polo brothers got home, settled, and invited them to a home-coming banquet. There, they ripped apart their raggedy clothes, and let all the hidden jewels clatter to the table!

Once the community learned of the remarkable adventures of the Polo brothers and Marco, they wanted to hear detailed accounts about the strange lands they had visited. Marco became a popular and sought after storyteller. Even the Venetian Government recognized his reputation and honored him with a commission as commander of a galley in a war against the rival Republic of Genoa.

Along came naval warfare between the Venetians and their trading rivals, the Genoese. Fighting with his troop, Marco was captured in 1298. He found himself rotting in prison in Genoa, an experience that could have ended tragically.

Instead, it took a lucky turn. In prison, Marco met a man named Rustichello da Pisa, who was a writer of romance novels, particularly about knights, heroic escapades, and beautiful women. To pass the time, Marco was luckily able to dictate his observations about his travels to Rustichello, who drafted a rough manuscript in French, the language preferred by romance writers. This combined effort led to a new book titled *The Travels of Marco Polo*.

Over the years, different translations have led to other titles as well, such as *Description of the World*. Yes, this is one of the greatest travel stories ever recorded. If this fateful meeting between the two prisoners hadn't taken place, the rest of us may not have learned about the Polos' fabulous journeys to the East. Rustichello most likely added some of his own words and stories and likely romanticized some of Marco's adventures in the version he wrote. Which reminds us of Herodotus! Why not, we smile!

We love sharing these dramatic, inspiring stories with you.

**Marco Polo recounting tales of his travels to
Rustichello da Pisa while in prison in 1298**
(Sharma, 2018)

Marco was able to gain his freedom when the Venetians and Genoese made peace in 1299. He was returned to Venice, and by then, he was in his mid-forties. He met and married Donata Badoer, a well-respected lady from a noble family, who bore him three daughters. At about the same time, his famous book, published in 1300, was already making him well-known throughout Europe.

Shortly thereafter, he took the French version of the manuscript *The Travels of Marco Polo,* added his personal edits and changes, and submitted it to a publisher who produced the book in French. It was first introduced to the reading public in limited quantities.

The book became an instant best-seller and was soon translated into many different languages, capturing the imagination of Europe. The books and translations were written by hand, usually by scribes from monasteries, as the Gutenberg printing press was yet to be invented. Later, once the Gutenberg printing press came into being, many copies of Marco Polo's book, in a multitude of different languages, were produced.

The monks making the translations likely added some of their own verbiage and diatribe.

Later, Marco wrote a revised version of the book in Italian, which, before it was lost, was translated into Latin. Then, the Latin version was translated back into Italian. The book began to suffer from so many translations. What fascinates us is learning there are about 150 versions of the book, and at best, no one really knows if there's an extant copy of the book in existence.

Marco had given a translated copy of his book to a French nobleman, which may be the most accurate copy available. This remains in the Paris Library.

By the beginning of the fourteenth century, Marco's book, chronicling the social, cultural, economic, and environmental conditions of the places he had visited; Central Asia, Mongolia, China, Tibet, Burma, Siam, Ceylon, Java, India, and other destinations largely unknown in Europe, became the *bible*, so to speak, for adventurers, explorers, mapmakers, intellects, and travelers outside Venice. Later, worldly travelers like Henry the Navigator, Ibn Battuta, Christopher Columbus, Ferdinand Magellan, and others were fascinated by Polo's book, and, after reading it, many were inspired to journey into the the their own unknown.

Marco Polo died January 9, 1324 at seventy years of age. He was buried in the Church of San Lorenzo in Venice. In his will, he freed his Tartar slave, Peter, never mentioned in the book, and he left most of his modest wealth to his wife and three daughters. He had never traveled to gain wealth, but, as he wrote and was loved for this, journeyed to gain knowledge about other people, cultures and to seek adventure.

He wrote, "I believe it was God's will that we should come back so that men might know the things that are in the world, since, as we have said in the first chapter of this book, no other man, Christian or Saracen, Mongol or Pagan, has explored so much of the world as Messer Marco, son of Messer Niccolò Polo, great and noble citizen of the city of Venice."

**Marco Polo shortly before his death**
(Biography, 2014)

Many Europeans were initially skeptical concerning the validity of what was written in Marco Polo's book. While they admitted to find it fascinating reading, they had nothing to compare it with. They wondered if maybe, it was more fantasy and fiction than factual and true. The story goes that when Marco was near death, a priest came to visit him. The priest had heard so many disparities and disputes about the validity of the book promoted by unbelievers. He decided to ask Marco if the book was really true.

Presumably, Marco replied: "I do not tell half of what I saw, because no one would have believed me."

Today, we know Venice as not only the birthplace of Marco Polo, but we know it as a beautiful and exciting Italian archipelago of 118 small islands. And we get into travel writing and learning, what we especially love. Venice has 400 bridges, 177 enchanting canals filled with attractive gondolas, fabulous art, magnificent architecture, interesting historic sites, wonderful museums, and a unique romantic atmosphere. It is one of our world's most popular international tourist destinations and the capital of both the community of Venezia and the region of Veneto, in northern Italy. Air service is centered at the Marco Polo Airport, and motorboat facilities are provided to transport passengers to the city. In addition, there are many hotels and restaurants in Venice and across the world named after Marco Polo. Venice was a special heart place in Marco Polo's era, and continues to exude a charm and sense of enchantment to this day.

Our worldly traveler has left us with many legacies. While Marco travelled 33,000 miles and visited 21 modern day countries, including areas where other merchants had traveled, he was the only known merchant traveler in that era to leave an extensive written record of where he had been. It was his book that made him famous and set him apart from other journeyers. If he had not written about his expedition to China, it's doubtful that people would have known much about the Polo brothers' adventurous travels.

Through his book, he introduced Europeans to Central Asia and China. While the Europeans were not as far advanced in science and engineering as the Chinese, the Polo family was presumably able to make even engineering contributions to the Great Khan.

Marco, the storyteller, sometime fantasized events and enlarged his role in helping his amazing mentor, Kublai Khan. One such instance occurred in Marco's description of the Polos' role when Kublai Khan's warriors had laid siege to a city for over six years with no results. Marco suggests that he, his father, and uncle helped design and build, presumably based on a European model, a large artillery catapult engine capable of hurling 300-pound stones at the enemy! While the Chinese had used catapults for centuries, during this siege time, they had not been successful. Marco would have us believe that the European model introduced by the Polo brothers during this siege helped win the battle. He went so far as to suggest that the Khan was not only grateful, but he used such catapults to his good advantage during this military situation. There's nothing written elsewhere to substantiate this story that appears in Marco's book; it may have been simply fiction dreamed up by Marco or by his co-author Rustichello da Pisa.

Marco's acute curiosity and courage, like that of other worldly travelers mentioned in this book, led to a dramatic new understanding of the world. As a result of these vivid descriptions of the eastern world, China and the history of the Mongols came to be better known to Europeans.

Lest it be forgotten, Marco traveled to China because of his father and uncle. The revelation that China was a country of great wealth and a land of engineering marvels, including the Grand Canal and the architecturally beautiful palaces of Kublai Khan, was unknown to Europeans, until they were able to read Marco Polo's book. Some readers of Marco's book wondered why he did not write about the Great Wall of China. When Marco came across a portion of the Great Wall in 1275, it had been abandoned, and was in disrepair. He did write about the advanced culture of China with its impressive art, bronze casting, and inspiring sculptures. It also became known that China had a larger population than Europe, as well as greater splendor, luxury, and scope of activities than was known at the time.

Imagine pulling in on your own boat to a well-established harbor? What do you see? To read one of his descriptions is enlightening, engaging and elegant.

\*   \*   \*

A major result from reading Marco Polo's book was that the attitude of Europe toward Asia was derived for centuries to come. Asia seemed to be a superior, wealthier, and more powerful part of the world, with Marco adroitly offering an unusual grasp of detail. Sometimes his descriptions defied the believable. One reason his book was so popular was because he made the world come alive to Europeans who thirsted for knowledge about China. They wanted to know just what kind of person could rule such a vast empire.

Marco, seemingly having the answers, included many pages of the book basically described the private life of Kublai Khan. He started with intimate details like: "Kublai Khan has four consorts who are all accounted as his lawful wives, and his eldest son by any of these four has a rightful claim to be emperor on the death of the present Khan. He also has many concubines…sends emissaries to this province to select for him out of the most beautiful maidens…some four or five hundred… After inspecting and surveying every girl feature-by-feature – her hair, her face, her eyebrows, her mouth, her lips, and every other feature – to see whether they are well-formed...barons' wives, who are instructed to observe them carefully at night in their chambers, to make sure that they are virgins and not blemished...Then those who are approved are divided into groups of six, who serve the Khan for three days and three nights...After three days and nights, in come the next six damsels...You should know further that by his four wives the Great Khan has twenty-two male children. There is no mention of female children, as they were not considered important to the Chinese culture at that time. By his mistresses, the Great Khan has a further twenty-five sons, all good men and brave soldiers. And each of them is a great baron."

Marco was fascinated by how much further advanced the Chinese were in comparison to Europe. Their mail and communication system on land was fast and efficient. Like the Persian's "pony express" in the time of Herodotus, riders in China were posted throughout the empire carrying communications from one city to the next. To make this happen efficiently, there were several thousand horses and hundreds of relay stations throughout China.

As we mentioned earlier, the Chinese printing machine was invented sometime before 1000 C. E., over four hundred years before Gutenberg's printing presses. The books that were printed covered topics in politics, economics, philosophy, religion, warfare, medicine, agriculture, painting, music, and other arts and sciences. Marco wrote and told of these new products from the East to the West, such as paper money, different spices, and pasta. He also explained the advancements that China had made with the uses of gunpowder.

China's use of paper money, as introduced by Kublai Khan, had a major impact on Europe. Europeans had no choice but to carry heavy coins around in order to make purchases. But Marco described Chinese paper currency in this way: "On this money, the Khan has such a quantity made that, with it, he could buy all the treasure in the world. With this currency, he orders all payments to be made throughout every province and kingdom and region of his empire. And no one dares refuse it on pain of losing his life. And I assure you that all the peoples and populations who are subject to his rule are perfectly willing to accept these papers in payment. The acceptance of these papers as payment ensures that wherever they go they pay in the same currency, whether for goods, or for pearls, or precious stones, or gold, or silver. With these pieces of paper, they can buy anything and pay for anything. And I can tell you that the papers that reckon as ten bezants do not weight as one..."

We suggest that Marco was possibly the first sustainable tourism advocate in the world. While he often spoke of the culture and the built environment during his trip, he also had an equally keen eye for the natural environment of the areas he visited. He talked of plants, birds, fruits, nuts, seeds, the geography, the ethnographical structure, the climate, and many other aspects of the environment and nature in China and elsewhere.

He was particularly fond of birds, and described five sorts of Chinese cranes: "One is entirely black, like a raven, and very large. The second is pure white. Its wings are beautiful, with all the plumage studded, with round eyes like those of a peacock but of the color of burnished gold. It has a scarlet and black head and a black and white neck and is larger than any of the others. The third species is like the cranes we in Europe know. The fourth is small, with long plumes by its ears, scarlet and black in color, and very beautiful. The fifth is a very large bird, quite grey, with a shapely head colored scarlet and black."

Like Herodotus before him, Marco was acutely observant. He was fascinated by the efficiency of the Mongol army and described their strategy. "When a lord of the Tartar, the Mongols, goes out to war with a following of 100,000 horsemen, he has them organized as follows. He has one captain in command of every ten, one of every hundred, one of every thousand, and one of every ten thousand, so that he never needs to consult with more than ten men. In the same way, each commander of ten thousand, or a thousand, or a hundred consults only with his ten immediate subordinates, and each man is answerable to his own chief."

Marco even made drawings and was able to portray clearly the highly effective Mongol military organization. These latter descriptions were invaluable as Europe prepared for the possible invasion by the Mongols.

One of his greatest gifts to Europe and the world was his astute understanding of the advantages of travel and explorations. While Marco did not invent the perception of travel, he was certainly one of the earliest travelers to understand its many ramifications. He noted throughout his travels how cruel and brutal much of the world was in the thirteenth century. Yet at the same time, he wrote about the excitement of visiting villages where the customs were charming and completely different from those of Europe.

His descriptions of the availability of gold, jewels, silk, and spices in the Far East provided incentives and inspirations for his readers to travel. As we wrote earlier, Prince Henry the Navigator, Christopher Columbus, Vasco da Gama, Magellan, and many others sought new routes to the east simply based on the writings of Marco Polo.

While Marco used the already popular word Cathay for China, he was the first European to use the word Cipango for Japan, which began to appear thereafter on maps of Asia. At that time, Japan was virtually unknown to Europeans. Marco had never heard of Japan until he came into contact with Kublai Khan and learned of the battles between his warriors and those of Japan. Columbus had read Marco Polo's book so many times that when he arrived in the Caribbean, he thought he had arrived either near Japan or in India! Hence, he named the natives "Indians." The book had a continuing influence on Columbus, on his interests of the riches of the Far East.

In some respects, Marco Polo is the greatest of the worldly travelers because he stimulated many later generations to journey and explore new areas. He revealed to the world new places, people, and discoveries never before described. He changed the world map. For two hundred years after his death, European explorers still studied his book and relied on it for the descriptions of China.

Most of the world in the thirteenth and fourteenth centuries was illiterate when Marco Polo wrote his book. This was not simply true of the common population, but also included much of royalty, government leaders and upper society. Recognizing that many of the nobles were illiterate, Marco started his book with the following note; "Emperors and kings, dukes and marquises, counts, knights, and townsfolk, and all who wish to know the various races of men and the peculiarities of the various regions of the world, take this book and *have it read to you*."

Though Marco Polo's bestselling book may not have been fully factual, it had a substantial impact by introducing new products and customs, and demonstrating by his writing that with imagination, commitment, and perseverance, people could move, reach, and surpass the bounds of the known world.

His book continues to be one of the world's greatest travel books. Present and future generations owe him special homage and gratitude for opening the world to travel and tourism, inspiring us to this day. What's your next project? Think of Marco Polo, and you can do it.

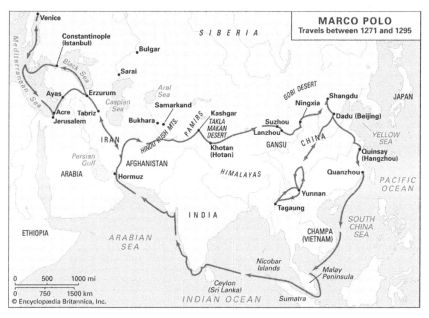

**Map depicting the places Marco Polo traveled to**
(Maraini, n.d.)

# CHAPTER FOUR

# IBN BATTUTA WANDERER FROM THE MIDDLE EAST

*"I do not tell half of what I saw because no one would have believed me."*
*-The Travels of Marco Polo, 1300 C.E.-*

*As a young man living in Morocco, Ibn Battuta had a special celebration related to his twenty-first birthday. Full of energy, he was anxious to travel and to expand his knowledge of the world, wishing for excitement and adventure. As he walked at home through the local bazaar in Tangier, he dreamed of faraway places. He had read Marco Polo's book over and over. He, like Marco, talked incessantly to merchants and sea captains in the local marketplace, continuously furthering his desire to journey to far-off destinations.*

*Ah, to explore the Middle East! How to get there and how long to stay? Little did he realize his various travels would consume thirty years of his life! He would go from Morocco throughout the Middle East, Asia, India, China, and parts of Africa, his travels amounting to over seventy-five thousand miles.*

*An incredible feat for our worldly traveler in the fourteenth century! Yes, Ibn Battuta traveled longer and farther than did Marco Polo. He eventually wrote a book that commemorated his journeys with the auspicious title; "A Gift to the Observers Concerning the Curiosities of the Cities and the Marvels Encountered in Travel."*

*Battuta's book is a classic profile of the life and culture of Islam during his era; still referred to "Rihla" which means journey. Like Marco Polo before him, Ibn Battuta's book "...does not tell half of what I saw..."*

*His desire was to proceed alone to destinations of interest with no set agenda. Other adventurers, merchants, and friends constantly advised strongly that traveling solo drastically increased all the dangers he would face. Everyone knew stories of independent travelers who had been attacked, robbed, and killed. What about warring tribes, political upheavals, and other risks in the areas he wished to go? Both land and sea travel in this age were treacherous with many hardships; you can't travel alone, you must join a caravan when moving overland!*

*None of this deterred him.*

*Battuta visited places where his predecessors, Herodotus, and Marco Polo, had also journeyed. Yet he went farther and was gone longer during his personal odyssey than either of these men. He often rode a horse, yet also depended on the highly reliable camel for desert travel, and his strong legs for walking.*

*Venturing forth as a pilgrim, a tourist, and through the years, Battuta became a scholar, jurist, ambassador, amateur naturalist, and anecdotal historian. Yet, like Herodotus and Marco Polo, he had his share of detractors who snickered at his adventures and stories, thinking his book was a fabrication of a traveler with a big ego and a runaway imagination. However, his recorded journeys by every means of travel available at the time, by camel, horse, boat, and considerable walking, make him one of our unique worldly travelers. As we study his legacy, we assert that he became one of the greatest Middle East travelers.*

**Ibn Battuta**
(Harcourt School, n.d.)

\*   \*   \*

The fourteenth century, in the era of the Middle Ages, was a period of turmoil and upheaval throughout the Middle East. War was regarded simply as an extension of commerce and politics. The formerly strong Byzantine Empire, with its highly cultured capital city of Constantinople was in decline, which had begun in the previous century. The Empire's military resources were exhausted, having fought the Christian Crusaders from the West in the Fourth Crusade as they responded to conflicts and threats from the East. What most severely impacted the Empire were the civil wars that took place in 1321 and 1341, which so weakened the Empire that the warlike Turks, referred to as the Ottomans, infiltrated the Empire from within and defeated the Byzantine Empire's armies on the battle fields.

The Byzantines were reduced to vassals and slaves of the Ottoman Empire.

At its height, the Ottoman Empire reached as far west as Hungry and east to Iraq. The first sultan of the Empire in 1299 was Osman the First and his Ottoman Dynasty lasted for six centuries. Osman I, an absolute monarch, controlled the political, military, judicial, social, and religious life in the kingdom. Under Islamic law, Osman I was, in effect, only responsible to God, at least as interpreted by Islamic law at the time. He ruled from 1299 until 1324 and was followed by his son, Orhan Gazi, as the Ottoman Sultanate until 1360. It was during this reign of Orhan Gazi in the fourteenth century that Ibn Battuta lived and traveled.

Young Battuta was well-aware of the power and leadership within the Ottoman Empire when he began his travels. While the Empire covered a large area, there were other Muslim rulers of lesser status throughout the Islamic world--- all seeking to expand their authority both militarily and culturally, which, of course, made it dangerous for his travels.

\* \* \*

He was born Sheikh Abu Abdullah Muhammad ibn Ibrahim al-Lawati, in Tangier, Morocco on February 25, 1304. He became known simply as Ibn Battuta. Tangier, an ancient Phoenician port city, on the coast of northern Morocco, at the southwestern entrance to the Strait of Gibraltar, was an important link from the Mediterranean Sea to the Atlantic Ocean. The city, rich in history, incorporated many diverse civilizations as early as the fifth century B.C.E.

During Battuta's youth, Tangier was important in international trade, providing supplies for military units, and housing warships. The town teemed with soldiers, traders, and adventurers. Growing up in a diverse community, seeing people from many different countries, and hearing their fascinating travel stories made many impressions on the intellect of our bright young man. He became well-educated in Islamic law and history, since his father and grandfather had been lawyers and judges, passing these interests on to him. Because of the academic scholarship tendencies and important positions held by the male family members, there was immediate respect in the community for the household in which he was raised. Raised with good manners, and learning gentlemanly conduct, he seized many educational opportunities available to him.

Battuta grew up as a strict Muslim. Like most young Muslims, he understood his holy duty of a Hajj, or pilgrimage to Mecca in Arabia. Those who completed the Hajj were told that all their sins before the journey are forgiven. Such a pilgrimage was expected at least once in the lifetime of a Muslim. Especially males who had good health and could afford the expenses of such travel. As he was able.

On June 14, 1325, Battuta, 21, left home in Tangier for a pilgrimage to Mecca. Later in life, he noted during some of his trips that he "… dreamed I was on the wing of a huge bird, which flew with me in the direction of Mecca, then made toward Yemen…and finally made a long flight toward the East, alighted in some dark and greenish country, and left me there."

Being well-educated and having read the travels of Marco Polo and others, he was motivated to move beyond the pilgrimage to Mecca. Amazingly, the 75,000 miles he traveled over thirty years, through most of the Middle East and beyond, which are 44 countries in today's count, was more than twice the distance traveled by Marco Polo.

Battuta wrote this about the beginning of his explorations: "My departure from Tangier, my birthplace, took place with the object of making the Pilgrimage to the Holy House at Mecca and to visit the tomb of the Prophet Mohammad in Medina. I set out alone, having neither a fellow traveler in whose companionship I might find cheer, nor a caravan whose party I might join. But swayed by an overmastering impulse within me and a desire long cherished in my bosom to visit these illustrious sanctuaries, I braced my resolution to quit all my dear ones, female and male, and forsook my home as birds forsake their nests. My parents being yet in the bonds of life, it weighed sorely upon me to part from them, and both they and I were afflicted with sorrow at this separation."

With his strength, and personal drive, Battuta's 3,000-mile journey to Mecca took two years as he ambled leisurely, making educational and sightseeing stops including visits to Syria, Egypt, and North Africa, simply traveling to learn about other places and cultures and the joy of adventure. His original intent was simply a pilgrimage to Mecca and to gain knowledge of the intricacies of religion and law. At home, it was expected of him to prepare to become a judge like his father and grandfather. He hoped these travels would lead him to meet Muslim scholars who could teach him to better understand his religion and expand his knowledge of law. He was quite lucky, as the scholars he met on his journeys graciously taught him in his quest for greater knowledge.

As Battuta traveled, he readily understood the advantages of joining merchant traders and religious pilgrims in caravans. Organized camel trains often included several thousand persons of different backgrounds and cultures. Over evening meals, he learned much about the demeanor of merchants, their strategies and plans for making a prosperous living by visiting other countries and trading goods. He even considered becoming a partial merchant trader as a means to support his travels.

We learn delightedly, again, that Battuta had an engaging personality, a winning way, and made friends easily. Throughout his journeys, he was often taken care of by the ruling families in the communities he visited or by the caravan commanders who seemed to appreciate his good humor, piety, knowledge, and informed conversations. It was noted that the Islamic religion, in many of the cities he visited, stressed giving alms to those in need, including wayfarers such as Battuta, himself, as a traveler. Becoming a gentleman scholar, he was often invited by the educated and wealthy persons in the communities he visited to partake of food in their company.

Yet staying healthy presented enormous challenges throughout any journey. The customs of sanitation and food preparation varied greatly;

it was common for travelers to get sick and for many to die. During this time, the Black Death was pandemic throughout Europe, in much of Asia and the Middle East. In some communities he visited, more than half the inhabitants suffered or were dying from disease or plague-related illnesses.

It's known that Marco Polo battled illness for a year, causing a delay in his travels. Battuta also endured bouts of sickness, but he managed to continue his journeys. In Damascus, during a trip to Mecca, he became so ill, he was advised to stay in the city to recover.

"If God decrees my death, then my death shall be on the road, with my face set towards the land of the Hijaz," he wrote. "As I continued my journey, the jurist who took care of me hired camels for me and gave me traveling provisions, and money, saying to me, 'It will come in useful for anything of importance that you may be in need of – may God reward him'."

Battuta's charm kept winning him respect, and friends who were willing to support his travel. Everyone knew of constant obstacles; highwaymen and robbers everywhere who preyed on individual adventurers. At one point, Battuta found himself to be one of their victims, learning the need to change routes and destinations. Also, as a member of a caravan, travelers felt strength in numbers would be enough to ward off an attack.

Crossing the desert during a sandstorm could cause any adventurer to get lost and perish. Seafarers weren't much safer. Pirates and storms could end the trip with the loss of possessions, death, and destruction. Each traveler constantly weighed the odds of safety and security with desire for the venture, the ability to obtain food, water, and shelter, and arriving at the longed for destination, he'd find appropriate accommodations and other amenities available.

During Battuta's first pilgrimage, though young, he was appointed *Gadi* of the caravan he traveled with. This title gave him legal authority within the group. In this role, he was able to earn an income for resolving disputes, marrying couples, and keeping the peace. Large caravans were like small moving cities, and to be appointed *Qadi* of a caravan at such a young age was an unexpected honor and privilege for him.

During this pilgrimage, an elder made arrangements for Battuta to marry his daughter when they arrived in Tripoli, Libya. During this time in history, marriages were arranged by parents, and women had little say in the matter. This marriage, for whatever reason, did not last, and the young lady was returned to her father. While still on the initial stage of his pilgrimage, Battuta married again after he arrived in Damascus. This marriage didn't work either, and he was able to divorce this wife before he left Damascus.

Battuta married many wives throughout his travels, but there is little information available about the women he wed, about his married life, or about the children he may have sired. During this era, the Muslim culture allowed that a man's business was private; no one should need to inquire about such matters. Wives were mostly *invisible,* having little influence over their own lives. The sparse personal information available about Battuta's wives is only what he included in his book, sparse in terms of personal relationships. Without explaining the circumstances, wives seemed to mysteriously appear during his travels, but discarded as he moved on to the next city. Also, questions regarding his relationships with slave concubines during the caravan trips are also left unanswered.

Battuta's group, traveling to Damascus, because of the lateness of their travel, missed an opportunity to join the grand caravans of pilgrims on their way to Mecca. This meant a wait of nine months to join the next seasonal journey to the Holy City. He never felt this was a problem; the delay gave him an opportunity to visit many additional areas, and to travel to Egypt.

When Battuta arrived in Alexandria, he felt at home, impressed with its ancient structures as well as its history and culture. He was amazed to learn that not only did Alexander the Great establish the city, he created the city's outstanding library.

Battuta then visited the grand city of Cairo, and it took him completely by surprise! A sophisticated, bustling community of over 500,000 people, Cairo was possibly the largest city in the world at this time; an intellectual capital, trading center, tourism destination, and crossroads of society in the Middle East. He was awed to see many shops, amazed by large crowds of people, and excited by the sights and sounds of this dazzling community.

After spending time touring Cairo and the surrounding areas, Battuta decided not to wait for the next grand caravan to Mecca. He redirected his route to pass by Syria, allowing him to visit Hebron in Palestine and to view the tombs of Abraham, Isaac, and Jacob, as well as the holy prophets to Muslims, Christians, and Jews alike. In his religious studies, he had read about the earliest recorded pilgrimage taken by Abraham, who left Ur, located in Iraq, 4,000 years ago on his way to Haran, Turkey. Abraham, an early worldly traveler, had also made visits to the present countries of Syria, Israel, Palestine, Jordan, and Egypt.

Mesmerized by the different societies, cultures, and people in the places he visited, Battuta loved spending time in these destinations which added to his education. He proceeded on to Jerusalem, another city known for its spiritual sites of great importance and interest to Muslims. Jerusalem represented all three of the world's major religions – Islam, Christianity, and Judaism. He visited the Noble Sanctuary, the Church of the Holy Sepulcher, and the Wailing Wall. Finally, his travel took him back to Damascus, allowing him to join a caravan to Mecca.

Upon arrival in Mecca, Battuta performed his necessary religious duties at the great mosque. He stayed on as a scholar, sojourner, and tourist, not only moved by the religious surroundings, but intrigued by the different people he met. "...The Meccans are elegant and clean in their dress," he wrote. "And as they wear white, their garments always appear spotless and snowy...The Meccan women are of rare and surpassing beauty, pious and chaste..."

Today, more than two million Muslims make their way to Mecca each year, the largest religious event in the world.

In his first pilgrimage to Mecca, Battuta resided in living quarters available for scholars and he lived well from monetary gifts and food. Since scholars were treated with great respect and given gifts or money to sustain their studies, he enjoyed his stay in comfortable conditions.

At one point, Battuta learned from wayfarers in Mecca that the government of the Sultanate of Delhi, India, provided qualified and educated individuals, regardless of their country, with high level positions. Hmmm, if he could journey to India and provide the Sultan with his credentials of education, experience, and worldly knowledge, perhaps he might be rewarded with a substantial position. This information gave Battuta the excuse he needed to travel in the general direction of India.

However, typically, when he embarked upon a journey, he found interesting side trips which delayed his eventual arrival to his planned destination. We conject often that time mattered differently in early history. Due to his engaging personality, education, and, by now, his knowledge about the many other places that resulted from his travels, Battuta began to attain a reputation as a sage. At each segment in his adventures, he received special aid from tribal rulers and local heads of state. He often saw people he had met during his pilgrimage to Mecca, and was invited to their homes. This recognition induced him to tell interesting tales, which the leaders and intellectuals in the local communities he visited were happy to hear.

So Battuta left Mecca and journeyed to Aden, in southern Yemen. He met and conversed with local officials. From there, in 1331, he traveled to the bustling Somalia city of Mogadishu, which had a prosperous port. The educated community leaders of the city took him to meet the Somali Sultan who bestowed upon him gifts. As well, Battuta was taken with the beauty of Yemen women and their sexual accessibility, outside of the prostitution that existed in the area.

From Somalia, he headed back to Mecca, with his sights still set on eventually reaching India. To take the most direct route to India, Battuta's small party of travelers left Syria and crossed the Orontes River into the Anatolia region of Turkey during wintertime. Once across the river, they moved toward the Black Sea in preparation to cross the mountains to travel east toward India. Their next obstacle was crossing the immense mountains in the dead of winter.

As his party journeyed toward the mountains, they encountered heavy snowstorms, and at a loss what to do next, they hired a guide to get them through the mountains. Sadly, the guide was unreliable, taking advantage of them by robbing them and fleeing the area. Battuta's party found themselves lost in the dead of night.

"...I had a good horse, however, a thoroughbred, so I planned a way of escape, saying to myself that if I reach safety, perhaps I may contrive some means to save my companions, and it happened so...God Most High guided me to the gate of a certain building..."

Grateful, he was able to get help from locals in the area, and to save his band of travelers.

Battuta and the group hired a new guide to get them through the mountains. While this person also stole from them along the way, they were able to get to their next destination, Kastamonu, Turkey, the capital city of the region. Even though his ultimate goal was to eventually reach India, Battuta spent a couple of years touring about Turkey. He moved through the Aegean lands that divided Turkey from Greece, along some of the same routes traveled by Herodotus several centuries before. As usual, a patron helped him in his trek toward India.

Wherever Battuta went, leaders of the communities seemed to know of him and wanted him to speak of his adventures. Due to his celebrity status gained from his travels, he kept receiving gifts, oftentimes without ever seriously working to gain them. This beneficence given to him included two slave boys which were provided by two different local leaders. He was also given large amounts of money, which allowed him to purchase needed supplies as well as two slave girls. Such acquisitions of slaves was not unusual for a Muslim man of substantial means during the fourteenth century.

This kept continuing! A most acceptable form in which important officials honored him, was to give him exquisitely designed honorary robes, money, excellent food and drink and comfortable accommodations.

On one occasion, Battuta received the special honor of accompanying the third ranking wife of the Khan of a large region on her travels to Constantinople. This invitation allowed him to travel in extravagant style as her guest and to share the splendor of her entourage, safety from marauders due to several thousand horsemen, servants, and slaves, whose only duties were to serve her. We can only imagine Battuta, smiling, arriving to the city astride a gallant horse, richly attired in his robes, happily leading the honorable lady to her destination.

**Ibn Battuta entering Constantinople**

Battuta's travels were made even more comfortable with his newly acquired retinue that included slave help, horses, and wagons. After seeing the sights in Constantinople, he was able to join a caravan headed toward India. Through his contacts with the Khan, he met many princes, princesses, and rulers in the regions he entered along his travel route. As usual, wherever he stopped, he received donations or gifts of one sort or another, which often included horses, money, and slaves. He also shared his wagon with three young women, and one gave birth to his child. Sadly, this daughter died shortly after the party arrived in India.

While his small party was traveling to New Delhi, Battuta's group was attacked by a group of Hindu bandits. A brief intensive battle ensued in which Battuta's group fought for their lives, they successfully repelled the attack, killing a dozen or so of the enemy. He was wounded. This region was always dangerous for travelers to travel throughout much of India for years into the future.

Arriving in New Delhi, Battuta was hoping and convinced he would be able to obtain a high-level position from the ruling Sultan of Delhi, Muhammad Tughluq. The rumor was that the Sultan particularly sought well-educated foreigners to serve him as top administrators and leaders in his kingdom. Battuta wrote in his book: "...The king of India...makes a practice of honoring strangers and showing affection to them and singling them out for governorships or high dignities of state. The majority of his courtiers, palace officials, ministers of state, judges, and relatives by marriage are foreigners, and he has issued a decree that foreigners are to be called in his country by the title of 'Aziz' is Honorable, so that this has become a proper name for them..."

After meeting and getting to know Battuta, the Sultan of Delhi gave him a major legal post as a *Qadi* of New Delhi, providing him with luxurious goods, servants, and liberal amounts of money. Battuta married again, to a high society well-connected woman. Shortly thereafter, he fathered another daughter.

Could this luxurious life go on? In the meantime, without him knowing, members of his new wife's family spied and plotted against the king and were caught, tortured, and killed.

Though Battuta apparently was not involved in any way and was not accused of any wrongdoing, he was concerned because a certain high-level person he had befriended, through his family connections, was clearly against the king. This friend was caught, tortured, and literally lost his head. Now Battuta was quite nervous as he saw people he knew, some friends, being accused of wrong-doing and eliminated by the king.

Under these circumstances, he asked to resign his post, with the excuse that he wanted to study religion, become a religious hermit, and live the life of a hermit.

But the Sultan was not happy with Battuta's request to resign and demanded his presence at court. Knowing Battuta liked to travel, and because of his impressive intellect, the Sultan offered a new position to be his Ambassador to the Mongol Court of China. After spending eight years in India under trying circumstances, Battuta was anxious to leave and readily accepted this opportunity. He would still have an extravagant lifestyle, a high title, and his entourage to China included horses, concubines and dancing girls, and a small army to protect him.

Battuta was entrusted by the Sultan to deliver special important messages and valuable presents to the Mongol leader. Included, among many presents were 200 slaves and other "gifts fit for a king".

However, the conditions of the travel were such that this trip had bad omens from the outset.

**Ibn Battuta's Delhi Escape**
(Dekkak, 2020)

Shortly after beginning this mission to China, yet still in India, Battuta's party was attacked by rebellious Hindus. This was a second frightening encounter for Battuta with such marauders. While the insurgents were defeated, Battuta had become separated from the main group of his party during the battle. This led to his being captured by a small unit of the retreating rebels. When it appeared that he was about to lose his life, suddenly his captors decided to let him go. While it's not clear why they released him; it may have been his charismatic personality that allowed him to talk his way out of this difficult circumstance. Or, they had no major reason to kill him.

Yet after he was released, Battuta became completely lost, unable to find his party. While they thought he was killed, not wanting to remain in this dangerous area, they simply wanted to continue their journey toward the boats that were waiting to take them to China. Battuta wandered for days, unable to find help or shelter or food. Near the point of starving to death, he was saved when kind strangers happened along. With their help, he survived the hostile environment and was able to locate his group of travelers.

The captains of the ships, on the lookout, who had been waiting for him, were relieved when they learned of the encounters of the ambassador's band with the rebels, that the troupe finally arrived mostly intact, and that Battuta had been able to catch up with them.

Because Battuta had so many gifts for the Great Khan, his entourage was now in a hurry to get to China. He contracted with the seafaring agents for four boats. These ships were of Chinese construction, better built and larger than any vessels Battuta had ever seen in any of the ports he had visited. Marco Polo, traveling before Battuta, had also noted, when he was in China, how superior the Chinese sea craft were to those of Europe. The only major drawback to such ships was their inability to navigate in shallow water.

**Chinese Junk Ships Commonly Used
in the Thirteenth Century**
(Saxena, 2017)

Once Ambassador Battuta's ships were loaded, the boats set sail in the Arabian Sea heading east. Typical of our worldly traveler, Battuta insisted on making numerous port stops along the way, as if his trip was one of pleasure instead of an official assignment. In one case, his stay in the port of Calicut lasted three months. Yet it wasn't as a result of his leisure pursuits, but because the captains needed to wait for better weather before they embarked.

In Calicut, after complicated negotiations with the port authority officials, Battuta's party was reorganized to fit aboard two large ships and one smaller one. He elected to sail on the smaller vessel so he could have a private cabin and be able to keep his personal possessions and certain selected individuals nearby.

Before the time to set out to sea, there was a severe change in weather. A storm brewed, making it unfit to sail. For the safety of Ambassador Battuta and because he elected to sail in such a small vessel, the captain suggested that his special passenger remain on shore. After dropping the ambassador off, the ship's captain took the other boats which were fully loaded with passengers and cargo out to sea for safety purposes to avoid them getting smashed on rocks and coral along the shoreline. This was a normal procedure for sailing in such weather.

Not long after safety precautions were taken, the torrential squall moved in their direction, with rain in torrents and gale winds. Horribly, two boats with the main party on board capsized during the storm. Both of the large vessels sank. Everyone drowned, including one of the slaves carrying Battuta's child, as well as the animals that were on board.

Thus, all the slaves, soldiers, horses, lavish gifts for the Great Khan, along with needed equipment and supplies, were tragically lost.

Ironically, the small vessel that survived was the one Battuta had chosen to be on. The vessel contained his concubines, some friends, and personal possessions. Yet the ambassador's boat was blown off course; it became necessary for it to continue the trip without Battuta, who remained on land.

Ha! Here was Ambassador Battuta without his credentials, important papers, or possessions, which were in the one surviving vessel now out at sea. This predicament left him totally at the mercy of the local population which knew nothing of him, nor cared. Who would care about his supposed rank or his pleas for help?

Here he was, totally lost, and so used to his privileged life, without any means to travel. He knew if he was able and capable of returning to the Sultan of India with nothing, having lost such an enormous amount of wealth, there was a great possibility his explanations would not be accepted; why Battuta might be jailed or executed!

Having witnessed the fate of others who failed the Sultan, he carefully, cautiously sought out a sponsor who might believe him and help him to continue his travel toward China. Yet, he was consistently confronted with problems by locals, who had no idea of his predicament.

Battuta found himself in the coastal town of Honavar, India; not a good place to be after he had lost such important possessions of the king. He took a chance and appealed to the Sultan of Honavar for help. But his initial appeals went unanswered. Yet, shortly after his requests for help, the Sultan became engaged in a conflict with a neighboring port city which left Battuta open to offer his services to the Sultan. Whatever was needed, he was sure he could accomplish! The Sultan, learning and realizing Battuta's seeming ability and competence, accepted, and, in the battle that ensued, Battuta fought and was on the winning side.

Again, he became restless, and with help from the Sultan, he was able to travel along the coastline looking to possibly locate his boat. Even though the boat had escaped the earlier storm, he hoped to find his personal entourage and possessions. After many inquiries in the coastal cities he visited, he learned that the boat had, indeed, taken refuge in an unfriendly port, and was seized by pirates. Of course, everything was taken.

Knowing that he would not be received favorably in China, Battuta decided to travel toward China anyway. He learned information about the Maldives, the islands off the coast of India, and decided to visit the islands before continuing his trek to China. He had heard interesting legends about these islands during his recent travels along the coast. The Maldives, as they exist today, rely heavily on fishing, limited trade, and tourism.

When Battuta arrived at the islands, they were known as simply an interesting way station for travelers on their course to India. These islands, then and now, are a picture-perfect paradise with swaying palm trees and beautiful beaches, although only a few feet above sea level. These small islands were ruled by a queen, and when she met Battuta and learned of his legal expertise, she wasn't about to allow him to leave. Desperately needing someone with the ability to oversee the legal activities of the islands, Battuta fit the bill perfectly and she put him in charge of all legal matters. She brought him into her inner circle of advisers and gave him comfortable accommodations.

Contented again, Battuta became enmeshed in the politics and problems of the area. Again, he was treated royally and showered with gifts including slave girls, a house, good food and servants. At this stage of his life, his book lets us in on more of his private life in the Maldives than in any other place he lived or traveled. He married a woman of noble status, and, like many marriages in that era, the union was as much to gain political favors as it was to obtain a suitable wife. This marriage elevated his social status, endearing him to the local elite.

Because Battuta knew the law and legal process better than anyone else in the islands, he proceeded to define and implement laws as he saw fit, even if the laws did not meet the social mores. His success rate in doing so was considered excellent, with one exception. The women of the Maldives wore no clothes above the waist, and when he tried to edict or proclaim that they must be fully dressed, they rebelled, resolutely disobeying him. They simply continued their normal custom of being topless, as this had been in existence for centuries. His limited victory in this regard was that if women came to see him or were involved in a legal matter that he adjudicated, they must be fully dressed and respectful of the law.

Shortly after Battuta got the legal system to his liking, he wed three more women, four wives being the limit under Islamic law, which seemed to fit his lifestyle. Again, he wed women that could further his political and social status. He also had slave girls and other servants to look after other of his needs. The limited evidence available suggests that he had a huge libido and likely an ego to match. As he took on more responsibilities and through his marriages, he gained enormous power and became feared throughout the islands.

Have we written with respect and surprise about his charmed life?

After a while, Battuta became bored with the Maldives, including its lack of a highly educated populace and limited facilities. Time to move on. Divorcing his wives, he wrote this in his book: "...It is easy to marry in these islands because of the smallness of the dowries and the pleasures of society which the women offer...When the ships put in, the crews marry; when they intend to leave, they divorce their wives. This is a kind of temporary marriage. The women of these islands never leave their country..."

Battuta sought out a captain on another island to transport him off the Maldives to continue his travels. While waiting for the captain to make the arrangements for his travels, Battuta married two more wives, only to divorce them when he left. The marriage system under Islamic law, allowing for multiple wives, only worked well if the husband had the financial means and ability to support such an extended family.

The wanderings of Ibn Battuta did not end in the Maldives. He became involved in another shipwreck, was robbed again, survived an additional illness, and yet he was able to tread a fine line of acceptance in different political situations. Somehow, he always rebounded in a positive light and moved on to his next destination. This worldly traveler seemed to have an innate halo effect or a lucky charm that got him out of extreme difficulties and pointed him in new positive directions.

He eventually reached China, newly amazed by their technology and progress. But he didn't stay long. With no ambassadorial title, nor gifts for the leader, he was uncomfortable in a society with so few Muslims.

"...China was beautiful, but it did not please me," he wrote. "On the contrary, I was greatly troubled thinking about the way paganism dominated this country. During my stay in China, whenever I saw any Muslims I always felt as though I met my own family and close kinsmen..."

He was able to leave China and returned to Mecca. When he finally got to Damascus, in route to Mecca, he called upon acquaintances from his earlier visits who gladly provided him with hospitality. Through conversations, he learned that his father had been dead for fifteen years and that his mother might still be living.

Traveling towards Tangier, he was again confronted with the ravages of the Black Plague, and thousands of people were dying in the cities he passed through, but somehow he never succumbed to the disease.

Battuta, anxious as he approached home, was aware of the many political changes and wars that had taken place in Morocco during his absence. By 1349, he arrived in Fez, the capital of Morocco, ruled by a Sultan named Abu 'Inan. He also learned from family members living in Fez that his mother had died from the plague.

Battuta arrived in Tangier, and after he visited the grave of his mother, he was happily reunited with family members. After briefly resting, with a true gypsy spirit, it was time to travel again. This time, he chose the Spanish city of Ceuta, along the Strait of Gibraltar bordered by Morocco. Much of Spain, at one point in its history, was conquered by the Moors and hence held a substantial Muslim population. This, of course, made it easy for Battuta to converse with the local population and make special visits in the area. From Ceuta, he visited the Spanish region of Andalusia, and found it fascinating. He visited the Spanish coastal port city of Malaga, and then to Ronda, Spain, in the mountains. From there, he traveled to the coastal community of Marbella, followed by a visit to the grand city of Granada.

In Granada, Battuta made an interesting acquaintance with a gentleman by the name of Abu 'Abdallah Muhammad ibn Juzayy. This meeting was fortuitous; Ibn Juzayy was a poet and author in his own right, and from a literary family. When they met again in Fez, they began to work together on a special project, to record Battuta's many journeys.

After his happy trip into Muslim Spain, Battuta returned to Fez in 1351. Later in 1351, he made his last journey, a caravan trip across the world's largest desert, the Sahara, to the Kingdom of Mali. Why Battuta wanted to go to Mali wasn't clear, but we realized this incessant traveler seemingly wanted to visit all the Muslim countries within his power to do so, and was still willing to accept the challenges and dangers he might encounter. He wandered throughout Mali and came away unimpressed with the leadership and the society. On two occasions in these travels he was quite ill, likely from food poisoning. By 1354, he was back in Fez.

The Sultan of Fez, Abu 'Inan, was impressed when he learned of all the fascinating and informative journeys of Ibn Battuta. He commissioned our worldly traveler to prepare a special narrative of his experiences in the various communities he had traveled. Another piece of luck; the poet and writer, Ibn Juzayy, whom Battuta had met, became employed by the Sultan to help write Battuta's travel stories. The two spent two years together working on the book titled *Rihla*.

When completed, the title was *A Gift to the Observers Concerning the Curiosities of the Cities and the Marvels Encountered in Travels*. This is generally referred to as *Rihla*.

**Ibn Battuta's book,** *Rihla*
(Casa del Libro, n.d.)

The book was formulated using Battuta's limited notes and his dictations to Ibn Juzayy based on his excellent memory. Battuta had few records at his disposal; throughout his earlier travels, he was robbed of all his possessions on many occasions. During his adventures, he was also forced to jump overboard a couple of times during shipwrecks, again losing all he owned. Ibn Juzayy had been hired as a literary collaborator with Ibn Battuta to wordsmith his various travels in words and to produce an exciting and interesting format. While Battuta was a learned legal writer, he was not skilled in writing in an interesting format for general public reading. Whether Ibn Juzayy was accurate in recounting the travels of Battuta, or added his own thoughts isn't known. But it worked well.

Historians and others who've studied his book suggest that during many instances Battuta's memory may have failed him with respect to names of places and time periods. We understand this. Also, Ibn Juzayy may have substituted information from other sources when certain descriptions given him by Battuta needed more accurate details. In addition, the book was designed to entertain the Sultan and his male guests, and, therefore, liberties were likely taken with some of the information to make it more exciting!

Battuta must have struggled, even with a good memory, to remember facts from a travel itinerary more than 30 years old. He had retraced his travel so many times that pinpointing certain destinations of his travels was a daunting task. For us, and you, who travel extensively, this is understood and appreciated. His book details visits to Saudi Arabia, Egypt, Palestine, Iraq, Syria, Iran, Oman, India, Russia, China, Ceylon, the Maldives, Burma, and Spain.

In addition, Battuta also wanted the book to present him as a reverent gentleman, scholar, and a recognized traveler of his era. Also noted is that he was judgmental in evaluating the social mores and customs in the different communities and countries he visited. If they did not measure up to his standards of society, he often was critical of the culture. For instance, in parts of northwestern Africa, he noted that women spoke freely with men even if they were not relatives, a custom he found mostly unacceptable. He was critical of the dress or undresses in societies or communities he was unfamiliar with as, the custom of slave women, female servants, and occasionally even the daughters of the Sultan appearing in public naked. He also felt strongly that the eating of "unclean" meats, such as dogs, that were not "ritually slaughtered" was very wrong. Yet beyond some of his personal standards and beliefs, he was fairly tolerant of most of the societies he visited, especially when their actions were more closely allied with what he expected.

"…I have indeed – praise be to God," he recounted in accomplishing his goal in life, "I have attained my desire in this world, which was to travel through the earth, and I have attained in this respect what no other person has attained to my knowledge…"

But like his predecessors, Herodotus and Marco Polo, Battuta is accused of exaggerating his stories. Like them, it may have been possible that he did not visit all the places mentioned in the book. Some historians have challenged the validity of some of his stories. It is left to us, the readers, to decide what might be true and how much was fiction.

It may not be possible to find a better book than that of Ibn Battuta's in providing the best account of governments, politics, people, cuisine, and social structure of the Islamic countries he visited during his era of travel.

Posterity has learned a great deal about the upper strata of society of the period because Battuta paid special attention to the kings, princes, and rulers of the day. The book has little to report about the general populations of the countries he visited and his travels were sponsored by wealthy patrons of the places he visited.

When Battuta crossed the frozen steppes of Russia, he wrote: "...I used to put on three fur coats and two pairs of trousers, and on my feet, I had a pair of woolen boots with a pair of boots quilted with linen cloth on top of them, and on top of these again, a pair of horsehide boots lined with bearskin..."

Battuta unintentionally became an important historian, a recognized social scientist, a legal expert, and indirectly an untrained geographer. As a student of law, he was aware of the importance of utilizing records, and he mentally attempted to record the important places, events, and rulers in the countries he visited. As a news commentator of the day, a pre-international newsman, he learned of new events in his travels and passed on what he had learned to the local authorities or others with whom he came in contact.

After the book was published, Battuta appeared to have vanished. Unlike Marco Polo's book that became an instant best-seller, the *Rihla* was initially unknown. Since it was written for the enjoyment of the Sultan and his friends, it possibly received little publicity. Unlike Herodotus and Marco Polo, his book was almost unknown for centuries.

Though the book didn't make Battuta famous, there were rumors that he had received a modest judgeship in a Moroccan community near home. He would now have been in his fifties, possibly married again, and having fathered more children. How many children he sired throughout his life with wives, concubines, and slave girls is simply unknown.

Battuta is believed to have died in Morocco around 1368, possibly from the plague.

In the 1800s, the book was rediscovered and published in different languages. Over the past hundred years, his text and his stature as an important historic figure and worldly traveler has gained in popularity. There are many in the 20th and 21st centuries who assert that Battuta was history's most important traveler prior to the age of steamboat travel, which revolutionized the ability to travel long distances in relative comfort.

In the twenty-first century, new investigations of Ibn Battuta's journeys suggest that he may very well have been the greatest worldly traveler ever.

Look at the chart. He certainly was the busiest!

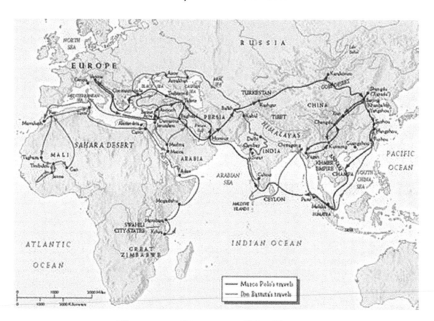

**The mapped journey of Ibn Battuta**

# CHAPTER FIVE

# ZHENG HE
# WORLD'S GREATEST SEAFARER

"I have indeed – praise be to God – attained my
desire in this world, which was to travel through
the earth, and I have attained in this respect what
no other person has attained to my knowledge."
-Ibn Battuta, *Rihla* [*Journey*], 1358 C.E.-

*As the clouds parted, sun sparkled on the water of the
Yangtze River at Nanjing, China, a major event was
unfolding. This river, the longest in Asia and emptying
into the East China Sea, was the site of the most
magnificent fleet of ships ever assembled. The flagship of
this grand armada, named the "Treasure Ship", was an
impressive 417 feet long, to be the longest wooden boat
ever constructed.*

*Sailing 87 years later, Columbus would have been elated
to have such a vessel several times larger than his 77-
foot flagship, the Santa Maria. Certainly, in Columbus'
time, the Venetians, Portuguese, and Spaniards had ships
larger than the Santa Maria, but they likely had nothing
to match the Chinese boats of an entire century earlier.*

*By 1405, the Chinese had sea craft far superior to any vessel
then in Europe or elsewhere in the world. By the beginning*

*of the fifteenth century, the Chinese imperial navy was organizationally and functionally the best in the world.*

*While the merchant marine sailors loaded their ships with necessary provisions for a long voyage, a tall and distinguished looking Mongolian arrived to inspect this fantastic array of vessels as they were all about to embark. His large frame, dark hair, penetrating eyes, good looks and bronze complexion suggested a man of strong character. The sea breeze gently touched the face of this giant seafaring Fleet Admiral, who was rumored to have been six feet, six inches tall, quite tall, especially during the 15th century.*

*He smiled, silently admiring his own work in developing this extravagant group of seagoing craft. When he walked along the main deck of the Treasure Ship and glanced across the queue of 300 ships of every size with the more than 37,000 officers and men aboard, he smiled again. All his men were capable of performing any task needed during any extended journey. These vessels contained horses, cargo, food, water, military supplies, and valuable trade goods to meet the special circumstances they might encounter during their sojourns. The ships had enough food and water to remain at sea for more than four months. There was even a group on board who spoke the different languages of the countries they were soon to visit.*

*To be the leader of this splendid armada required the personal confidence of China's supreme ruler, Emperor Yongle. Such a leader had to be an able commander, an exceptional organizer, and a goodwill ambassador, capable of negotiating treaties and agreements in the name of the emperor.*

*On the dock, the tall, handsome man smiled again. He was optimistic about the coming voyage as he walked to the prow of the magnificent Treasure Ship. Through his dreams, he had already communicated with the necromancers, which meant communicating with the spirits of the dead in order to predict the future. The prognosis for the trip was good; the spirits would be with him.*

*These ships were laden with valuable trade goods and impressive gifts for rulers in countries along the way. As special ambassador, he would be able to explain to the kings of the countries to be visited that China was the world's most powerful and wealthy country.*

*This is our next future famous worldly traveler, mariner, explorer, and diplomat, by the name of Zheng He. China and the world would never know of a more amazing set of expeditions than these, sailing the China seas and beyond…*

*Let's learn about the seven voyages of Zheng He.*

**Zheng He in all his splendor**

**A likeness of the Treasure Ship**

\* \* \*

Zheng He's voyages to Southeast Asia, South Asia, East Africa, and Arabia began early in the 1400's. Other notable seafaring explorations were led in the East by the Chinese, and in the West by the Portuguese, Venetians, and Spaniards.

The fourteenth century brought progressive technological development between the Middle Ages and the Early Renaissance, leading into what was known in Europe as the "early modern period" and culminating in the Industrial Revolution. The country of China, little understood by the Europeans at the time, truly led the world in technology, military strategies, organizational and administrative attributes, and ship building. Various power struggles taking place in Europe dominated the politics and military concerns, so that happenings in East Asia and the Pacific were almost completely unknown.

In Europe, in the late fourteenth century and early in the fifteenth century, constant wars were fought, mostly on land, but to a lesser extent on the oceans. Progress being made in China, the other side of the world, was of little interest to the Europeans. The so-called Hundred Year's War (1337-1459) between England and France dominated the concerns in Europe. As we said, these wars had no interest to political leaders in China.

In Europe, two of the principal seafaring nations, Spain, and Portugal, were always at war with each other, much like England and France. These continuous conflicts emptied the royal coffers that might have been available to expand ship technology and development. By 1411, there was peace between Spain and Portugal, allowing both nations to turn toward more international trade and commerce, which led to the need for better ships and new trade routes.

European leaders, especially those of Portugal, supported famous Portuguese sailors such as Vasco de Gama and Bartolomeu Dias. Spain's support of Christopher Columbus, and England's support of John Cabot, all European adventurers were leading to new discoveries.

Portugal, in the Renaissance period, grew more than other countries in Europe; her mathematicians and scientists made major breakthroughs that included cartography and naval technology, as well as enlightened royal leadership that supported explorations in new areas. Yet, with these positive improvements being made in Europe with respect to ship building and seafaring, it was China that made the most progress in the early fifteenth century.

That was our historical background in Europe.

Back to China and our fascinating worldly traveler, Zheng He.

During the fifteenth century, the Chinese led the world in oceangoing ship construction and technology, developing large, compartmentalized ships and effective sails. Some Chinese vessels had six masts and four decks that could carry as many as a thousand men aboard. Enlightened leaders in the Ming dynasty fostered the construction, development, and use of new technology in shipbuilding and improved equipment and techniques in navigation.

Both Marco Polo in the thirteenth century and Ibn Battuta in the fourteenth century, sailed on uncomfortable, ill-conceived vessels. Now, new larger, better, and more magnificent Chinese vessels had 50 or more cabins, whereas European ships had only six or eight cabins. During his visit to China in 1347, Ibn Battuta had noted the superiority of the Chinese vessels, swooning and writing; "...We stopped in the port of Calicut, in which there were at the time thirteen Chinese vessels...China Sea traveling is done in Chinese ships only...The large ships...has four decks and contains rooms, cabins, and saloons for merchants; a cabin has chambers and a lavatory, and can be locked by its occupants..."

*   *   *

Throughout Zheng He's lifetime from 1371-1435, much of the world was in turmoil, especially, as was noted, during the European wars. Also, as we previously mentioned, the Chinese knew little of what was taking place in Europe, and the Europeans knew almost nothing of the great Chinese empire during this period. The Chinese were concerned about whether they might be invaded by the Mongols, following the Mongol invasion of Syria in 1400. The Mongol leader, Tameraine, with great interest, had not only invaded Syria, but also defeated the Georgians, Russians, most of Iraq, and the Ottoman sultan. In 1405, just as Tameraine was preparing to invade Ming China, he died. Following his death, the Mongol Empire began to crumble.

Prior to Zheng He's birth in 1371, the Chinese had already successfully rebelled against the Mongol rulers of China, but they were still not totally in control. Just before the final rebellious conflicts initiated by the Chinese, the Mongols, in a last-ditch effort to save their empire, forbade the Chinese to have arms or to gather and communicate in large groups.

According to Chinese legend, the Mongols apparently had forgotten the Chinese custom of exchanging "moon-cakes" at the beginning of a full moon. An innovative Chinese revolutionary, Chu Yuan Chang, began hiding messages about coming events in the "moon-cakes" which became known as fortune cookies, which were passed on to others. Such communications were used to convey the date of a possible Chinese uprising.

The rebellious Chinese army was led by Chu Yuan Chang, the son of a poor farm laborer. When he was seventeen, his family had died from an epidemic, and he entered the Buddhist monastery. By age twenty-five, having had time to contemplate and dwell upon the injustices of the Mongol empire, he took up arms, organized an army of rebels, and went on the offensive to attack the Mongol army. After thirteen years of struggle, Chu Yuan Chang and his rebels defeated the Mongolians, and, by 1368, the rebels occupied Beijing and most of China.

And so Chu Yuan Chang was able to name himself the first emperor of the new Ming dynasty. Now known as Emperor Hongwu, he went about uniting the various provinces, setting up new administrative procedures, and modernizing and advancing the Chinese government.

Emperor Hongwu had enlightening ideas and was a constant crusader over many years for a strong united China, but he also became dictatorial and ruthless. If he thought his efforts were being thwarted in any way, he had no compunction in killing thousands of people. If a government minister was not sycophantic enough in his dealings with Emperor Hongwu, he might find his life ending. As time wore on, the emperor became suspicious of the administrators surrounding him, and he began to put greater trust in his eunuchs. For him, the eunuchs were loyal servants willing to implement his decisions regardless of the end result. During his rule, the eunuchs were given a good education and trained in almost all aspects of work and military prowess that was needed to advance and administer the empire.

Beijing's fabled Forbidden City was in fact mostly forbidden to all males, except the eunuch employees of the emperor. The emperor felt that he had full rein and trust in his associations with his wives and concubines in the presence of the eunuchs, the only males allowed to stay all night in the Forbidden City. During most of the Ming dynasty many eunuchs became rich and powerful through their connection with the emperor. This began an animosity between the eunuchs and non-eunuch civil administrators that led to a disenfranchise of much of the power of the eunuchs. The most famous and most powerful of the eunuchs was Zheng He.

Our Zheng He.

Zheng He was born in 1371 as a Muslim Mongol. At this time, two societies were colliding; the Chinese of the Ming dynasty, who were powerful with a large army that quickly increased the size of the Chinese empire. Yet, the other society, the Mongols, had successfully conquered much of China under the famed military leadership and organizational genius of Genghis Khan.

The earlier history is that Genghis Khan conquered more than twice as much land as any other person at that time in history. His third son, Ögedei Khan, following him, became the second *Great Khan,* continuing the expansion of the empire his father had built. Ögedei Khan was now a world figure when the Mongol Empire reached its farthest extent west and south during the Mongol invasions of Europe and East Asia.

Like his father, Ögedei Khan was feared in Europe because of his own military prowess and desire to conquer new lands. He was succeeded by Genghis Khan's grandson, emperor Kublai Khan, who ruled during the time Marco Polo traveled to China, and was a great administrator who advanced the empire substantially with innovative technology.

The point here? Despite such enlightened rulers, huge cultural and heritage differences abounded, colliding the two societies, between the Mongols and Chinese.

Back to the birth of Zheng He, born in China's southwestern Yunnan Province, who was born into a poor Muslim family. Yet his father, grandfather, and great-grandfather were all able to make the important religious pilgrimages to Mecca. Even though the Chinese Ming dynasty was gradually taking over all of China, and the Yunnan Province was still ruled by the Mongol Yuan dynasty.

Ironically, his great-great-grandfather had been appointed governor of Yunnan Province by Emperor Kublai Khan.

At the age of ten, Zheng He was captured along with other children, when the newly powerful Chinese army invaded many regions. His father and others connected to the family were killed resisting the Chinese army. For three years, it wasn't clear as to whether Zheng He would be killed, or in what capacity he would be allowed to live.

At age thirteen, along with similarly aged male prisoners, Zheng He was castrated. The procedure of castration at this time, and even later, was not unusual in China. A eunuch was considered highly desirable among royal families of the day. Such men were trusted to intermingle as servants in the ruler's household and, in some cases, to become administrators in the government. A few, like our young worldly traveler, were given increasingly high-level assignments, which eventually led to his becoming famous and powerful.

As a eunuch, Zheng He became a household servant of the Chinese Emperor's fourth son, Zhu Di, Prince of Yan. He made himself indispensable in the household, rewarded with more responsible duties. While born a Muslim, he adopted the household religion of Buddhism. As his talents continued to be recognized, he was trained in the highly effective Chinese "art of war" and he also became skilled in diplomacy and eventually served as an officer under Prince Zhu Di's military command.

Emperor Hongwu did not trust many of his officers and decided to give greater military control of the provinces to his sons. He gave Prince Zhu Di the frontier province on the northern border that included Beijing.

After a thirty-year rule, Emperor Hongwu died in 1398. He was succeeded by his son, Jianwen, who became the second emperor of the Ming dynasty. Prince Zhu Di intensely disliked Jianwen in all respects and rebelled against his appointment as Emperor of China. Interesting that Emperor Jianwen succumbed to a tragic death after ruling for four years.

Succession in the Ming dynasty was based firmly on primogeniture, which is the right of the eldest son to inherit the estate. This left out

Prince Zhu Di as a possible new emperor. But he was a revolutionary and strong leader, and his intent was to become the emperor of China. In 1402, Prince Zhu Di led a revolt, assisted militarily by his loyal servant, Ma He.

Prince Zhu Di's army defeated the opposition, which provided him with the opportunity to become the new emperor of the third Ming dynasty. He chose the title and name of Emperor Yongle, which stood for Perpetual Happiness. He was also referred to as "Son of Heaven" which was a recognition he wished to represent his people before the heavenly spirit.

In due course, Emperor Yongle brought his trusted aide, Zheng He, who had grown up with him, coached by him and now spent much time with him on horseback and in camps during his military campaign. He was designated in the Imperial Palace as director of palace servants, as a staff assistant, and military advisor.

Further, in recognition of his service to the Emperor, Zheng He became the Grand Eunuch of all the emperor's servants and staff, given immense powers and new responsibilities. Zheng He's developed military prowess and devoted loyalty to the emperor led to his special friendship with Emperor Yongle that lasted a lifetime.

As Emperor Yongle's power over the progressive China grew, the concept on his mind was that China represented the best of everything and e ruled the greatest empire in the world.

In 1403, Emperor Yongle ordered the construction of an imperial fleet of ships, organizing a massive naval expedition. He wished to spread the message of his grandeur, of China's great wealth, and superior military power and advanced technology in comparison to all the countries in the surrounding seas. China need not conquer other countries, did not need additional territory, wealth, or new technology, because the country had everything of importance.

The Emperor also had an alternate motive and mission for the voyages. He thought that the former Emperor Jianwen, who had disappeared, might still be alive hiding in a country outside of China. Thus, wherever the ships docked, a search was made to determine if Emperor Jianwen might be found.

Again, who could the Emperor trust with complete confidence for organizing and implementing this grand seafaring expedition? That person must have leadership skills, understand military strategies and tactics, and be completely loyal to him. .

Zheng He, educated, had grown into a great intellect and trusted individual. And he had grown to six feet, six inches tall, with a mighty build. This proved to have a powerful influence on the men he led.

Emperor Yongle designated Zheng He to be his personal ambassador to the countries that would be visited. He presented Zheng He with blank scrolls stamped with his seal so that the new Admiral Zheng could issue imperial orders during the voyages and negotiate treaties or agreements with the countries visited.

Feeling this honor, Zheng He went about the daunting task of organizing the greatest sea armada ever known at that time. In his forthright manner, and all that he had learned, he had the best boats built, hired the best military personnel, and obtained the most accurate seagoing maps available. The fleet included three hundred ships with over thirty-seven thousand crewmen, sailors, soldiers, and officials. On board were explorers, navigators, doctors, specialized craftsmen, translators, and scribes. The members of the fleet were from different countries and represented a multitude of different religious beliefs. The ships were designed and organized such that they could sail for up to four months, again, without having to be resupplied with food and water for the crew and passengers. The intent of the expeditions, largely of peace and goodwill, with the purpose of communicating to the world that China was the most powerful empire in existence.

**Zheng He's Treasure Fleet**
(Kim, 2012)

Zheng He also had the responsibility for ensuring that the subservient countries owned up to the monetary and other tributes demanded by the Emperor. It was presumed in advance that such an assignment might require the need for military action in certain circumstances, thus, the regular military crews on board the ships were well equipped to fight, if necessary, to fulfill the emperor's wishes.

The first expedition, from 1405-1407, had 317 ships and 27,870 men and left the important port of Nanjing, China on July 11, 1405. The boats were loaded with trade goods as silks, porcelain, and spices along with special gifts of gold, silver, porcelain, and silks for kings and dignitaries in countries they would visit.

On this first expedition as well as on subsequent voyages, Zheng He demonstrated his strong leadership characteristics such as: a) a desire to effectively accomplish the goals for the mission as outlined by the emperor, b) ability to inspire his men to resolve potential conflicts before such became a major problem, c) a demonstration of a high level of emotional leadership, spiritual wisdom, and maturity, and d) gaining the respect and trust of the crew and soldiers due to fair and equal treatment.

**Zheng He commands his Treasure Fleet**
Zheng He (Cheng Ho – Chinese Explorer, 2012)

During the time of the first voyage, the South China Seas were infested with marauders of all types and a major conflict ensued; a large pirate army that roamed the seas preying on ships of trade made a grave mistake in thinking they could attack Zheng He with his well-armed and seasoned army and navy personnel. The pirates never had a chance against the large well-trained military instructed by one of history's best military commanders.

In this era of battle readiness, Zheng He's soldiers were equipped with advanced weapons, some of which used gunpowder, unheard of in other societies at this time, for rifles, cannons, and grenades. The rest of the world was still fighting battles using bows and arrows. They killed the pirates, and later the principal lieutenants of this plundering group were captured and executed.

In the first expedition, Zheng He's fleets visited Brunei, Java, Thailand, Southeast Asia, India, the Horn of Africa, and Arabia. Whichever country visited was duly impressed with a strong show of force and diplomatic leadership that espoused peace and tranquility at every stop.

After a highly successful venture and visits with the leaders of the countries on their itinerary, the ships returned to China in 1407. Zheng He noted on their return to the home port that the entrance into the harbor was not always easy to see. To help guide his ships on returning voyages, he had a thirty-three-foot structure erected, a prelude to a lighthouse which gave off smoke in the day and fire at night, marking a good channel for the ships to follow.

Preparations for the second expedition began in 1407, shortly after the ships had returned from the first mission. Again, the ships were carefully inspected, repaired, and resupplied with food, water, trade goods, and special gifts for foreign dignitaries. During the previous expedition, many ambassadors from the countries visited requested the opportunity to visit China and pay their respect and homage to the Emperor. Since Zheng He's mission was one of *goodwill*, he welcomed ambassadors and high officials from the countries visited to board his flagship for the return voyage to China.

Once in China, these passengers met the Emperor and were allowed to travel extensively throughout China. The ambassadors were vetted in their travels in a style "fit for a king" and were shown how advanced and powerful the Ming dynasty was in every respect. They were feted with celebrations and festivals. Young ladies were available to socialize with or provide sex to these special guests as protocol determined. After more than two years in China, the ambassadors joined the second expedition in 1408 and were returned to their respective homelands. The second voyage, with the main purpose of returning the ambassadors to their home countries and learning about and exploring new destinations, went smoothly. Zheng He's ships performed this mission admirably. After visits to additional countries, the ships returned to port within a year.

In the third expedition, 1409-1411, Zheng He was confronted with a rebellion by the king of Ceylon. Really? Confusion existed as to which of three groups of Ceylonese were loyal to the emperor of China. Zheng He made a careful evaluation of the situation, launching a sizable contingent of soldiers from the ships to conquer the entire Ceylonese population. His military savvy, large military force, and his well-orchestrated operations ended in a spectacular assault to defeat the unruly king of Ceylon. He was able to weed out those who were not loyal to the emperor and had them taken prisoner or killed. As mention of this operation quickly moved through the leadership of the surrounding countries, the rest of the mission was accomplished without further protest.

On his fourth expedition, from 1413-1415, Zheng He had to again resort to a military force to extinguish a rebel group in Sumatra. Zheng He's troops easily dwarfed and squashed the forces of the rebel leader Sekandar, in northern Sumatra. These confrontations on certain expeditions were the exception to the rule in Zheng He's peaceful diplomatic missions, but his willingness to use force and military power demonstrated the strength of his military forces and the growing power and influence of the Chinese empire.

One of the most impressive voyages in terms of distances traveled, was that of the fifth expedition in 1417. With some 30,000 men on board, Zheng He sailed to the major trading ports of Arabia, including reaching the mouth of the Red Sea and beyond. No one in that part of the world had ever seen such a magnificent armada. The excitement in the region was remarkable.

Before the voyage was over, 19 countries had sent ambassadors to board Zheng He's ships. Zheng He sailed along the east coast of Africa, stopping at Mogadishu, Mombasa, Zanzibar, and other ports along the way.

On his sixth voyage, Zheng He returned to East Africa to further explore the area. This took place in 1421-1422. Like many of his former expeditions, this would likely fit today's definition of international diplomacy. In most of these voyages, including this one, the expeditions were partially organized to return ambassadors and diplomats back to their homelands after their visit to China. Such an operation improved relations with the countries visited through the advancement of peace and goodwill, added opportunities to explore new areas not well known to the Ming dynasty, and continued to spread the word of China's great power and wealth.

In most of the countries Zheng He visited with his vessels, the citizens stood in wonderment at this magnificent fleet, its commander, crews, and military personnel. They wanted only to honor and receive them in the best way they could. Recognizing the impact of these voyages on the countries he visited, the Emperor of China bestowed monetary rewards, precious gifts, medals, promotions, and other honors on the crew and military personnel participating in the voyages. Everyone felt this good will.

During these various expeditions, Zheng He usually took goods such as Chinese silk, porcelain, jewels, and other items for trade with the various countries visited. The Arab and African merchants bartered with such products as spices, ivory, medicines, pearls, and other goods sought by the Chinese.

From 1405 until 1422, six of the seven expeditions took place. During that time, the ships visited thirty-seven countries. Zheng He had certainly made the potent leadership of Emperor Yongle well-known, while promoting China as the most powerful and influential country in the Far East and beyond.

Sadly, in 1424, Zheng He's patron, Emperor Yongle, died. This was a devastating blow to Zheng He, who had devoted his entire life to the Emperor. Taking over power in 1425 was Emperor Yongle's studious elder son, Zhu Gaozhi. It was shocking to Zheng He to learn that Zhu Gaozhi worked to reverse his father's policies and was adamantly against navel expeditions, military campaigns, and international diplomacy, implementing an anti-maritime and isolationist policy, resulting in a complete close-down of all expeditions.

However, the reign of Emperor Zhu Gaozhi was short, lasting nine months. He was followed by an enthusiastic maritime emperor, Yongle's grandson, Xuande. Emperor Xuande, like his grandfather, had great respect and confidence in Zheng He and asked him to organize "The Seventh" which would be the grandest of all the expeditions.

As Zheng He left on this voyage, he stopped at Change, in Fujian province, on the East China Sea, to erect a unique tablet to the goddess Tianfei, which means "Celestial Consort" as the protector of sailors and fishermen. The tablet had this inscription: "The power of the goddess, having indeed been manifested in previous times, has been abundantly revealed in the present generation. In the midst of the rushing waters, it happened that, when there was a hurricane, suddenly a divine lantern was seen shining at the masthead, and as soon as that miraculous light appeared the danger was appeased, so that even in the peril of capsizing one felt reassured and that there was no cause for fear."

Because of the political intrigues in China between 1424 and 1430, it was felt that the other countries beholden to the Chinese empire needed to be reminded of their strong leadership and power. Thus, the seventh voyage, which included Admiral Zheng He, and many other of the emperor's influential officials and important diplomats of ambassadorial rank. This voyage went as far west as Hormuz, an island south of Iran in the Strait of Hormuz, before returning.

During a violent storm during the seventh voyage, most of the party on board the ships became frightened; many members of the expedition began to pray for their safety. What isn't clear is whether Zheng He, under the duress of the situation, might have unconsciously prayed, based on his Muslim upbringing or instead sought solace in the Buddhism religion which he had adopted.

We suspect he probably became an advocate of syncretism, adjusting to a multitude of faiths, because his crew represented so many different religions. It's been suggested that more than likely he would have joined his crew and prayed to the goddess Tianfei. Prior to the first voyage, Emperor Yongle had hosted a huge festival for the officers and crew, providing them with sumptuous food and wine and giving them gifts and wishing them success, followed by prayers and sacrifices to the goddess Tianfei, asking her for a safe voyage and her protection of the passengers.

After the highly successful first voyage, Emperor Yongle, at the behest of Zheng He, had erected a temple to the goddess Tianfei in the harbor of Nanjing. Before each voyage, Zheng He worshipped at the temple and asked the goddess for protection. Today, in China alone, there are many such temples to the goddess Tianfei.

The prayers worked.

In 1432, Zheng He erected a second special tablet in Changle, stating: "We have traversed more than one hundred thousand li [40,000 miles] of immense water spaces and have beheld in the ocean huge waves like mountains rising in the sky, and we have set eyes on barbarian regions far away hidden in a blue transparency of light vapors, while our sails, loftily unfurled like clouds day and night, continued their course as a star, traversing those savage waves as if we were treading a public thoroughfare…"

This legacy of Zheng He helps us to better understand this great worldly traveler. There is no seafarer, before or after Zheng He, who successfully traveled to many incredible destinations by sea with the diplomatic assignment of establishing peace and goodwill.

After his successful seventh voyage in 1433, China purposefully moved toward a total policy of isolationism. But the reasons for Emperor Xuande moving toward an isolationist policy were not clear. One may have been that the emperor realized the expeditions had emptied the country's treasury without making China more prosperous. The gifts given to the leaders of other countries during the voyages cost considerably more than the tributes received. Additionally, many Chinese officials felt that it was no longer necessary to pronounce the greatness of China to other countries. The voyages had accomplished all that was originally intended.

No matter what the reasons, Emperor Xuande lost interest in the sea expeditions and turned inwardly to address domestic issues. Immediately, the emperor proclaimed that all sea-related activities were canceled and the emperor ordered Zheng He's entire fleet burned. Researching this, we can only imagine that while the loyal Zheng He was horrified, he was wise not to question the reasons for burning the fleet. But he must have been so saddened and deeply frustrated to see such a spectacular array of beautiful ships destroyed.

New isolationist policies were shocking; a 180-degree turn-around; Chinese citizens were forbidden to even leave the country, let alone go sailing for any purpose. No boats of any size or shape were allowed to be built. The communications and contacts made with other countries during the seven voyages dissipated as if they had never existed.

Now it became Europe that took over the lead in ship building technology and navigation techniques. And as the countries began to explore the oceans and established colonies, their leaders began to battle for dominance in world affairs without knowing much, or even caring about the great era of China.

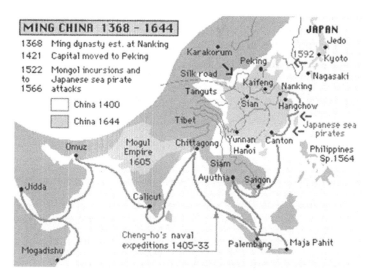

**Map of the route of the Seventh Expedition
of Zheng He, also known as Cheng-ho**

In 1434-1435, after the seventh voyage, Zheng He was named the military commander of Nanjing. It was befitting that he was stationed at the headquarters where his ships of the great era of his voyages had been anchored and would have formerly left the great harbor of Nanjing. Now, in this new, devastating position, he no longer had any major responsibilities and was still stunned by the lack of interest by the new leadership about any of China's future ventures on the oceans.

Zheng He died in 1435, recognized as the most powerful court eunuch in China's history, the greatest seafaring mariner and admiral, an outstanding military commander, a unique explorer, a very special kind of diplomat, and a fascinating worldly traveler.

Appropriately, he was buried at sea.

Shortly thereafter, the new government purged the power of the eunuchs. As a result, many of the records that had included important information about the accomplishments of eunuch administrators, including those of Zheng He, were altered to give a negative view of eunuch power. The new non-eunuch officials deliberately left out the accounts and accomplishments of the celebrated expeditions of Zheng He.

Because the new government advocated isolationist policies, they debunked the international diplomacy advances made in prior regimes, basically now ignoring their neighbors. They discredited many of Zheng He's exploits, attempting to diminish his reputation.

Over several hundred years, new research and information has become available about Zheng He. As a result, he's been recognized for his outstanding accomplishments. By the twentieth century, an increasing curiosity about his great seafaring achievements burgeoned, as well as a resurgence of interest in China's great accomplishments in shipbuilding. Historians and others began to recognize how innovative Zheng He was in employing the latest seagoing inventions by the Chinese in his voyages. In addition, the accumulation of geographic and cultural information on the countries he visited added immeasurably to understanding the knowledge base of China and Southeast Asia in the fifteenth century.

Unlike Zheng He's predecessors, Herodotus, Marco Polo, and Ibn Battuta, we have no known book written by this admired worldly traveler. We marvel at how this amazing household eunuch left such an impressive list of legacies, making it safe to travel the South China Sea and Indian Ocean by ridding the area of pirates.

In addition, his boats were the largest wooden vessels ever to sail the seas. His ships, voyages, and command decisions were never entirely matched in the history of the world. He added substantially to the use of scientific instruments, navigational techniques, and a better understanding of East and Pacific cultures.

In 28 years of travel, Zheng He sailed to and visited 37 countries and studied the culture and political structures of each. There's an unsubstantiated theory that Zheng He may have traveled as far as the Americas, but it is highly unlikely according to most knowledgeable experts.

Zheng He's legacy as a worldly traveler explains some of the social and cultural values of fifteenth century China. His voyages were not designed as military expeditions, but as peaceful extensions of the great power of the Emperor of China and were never meant to be conquests. While the Chinese national religion was Buddhism, there was no attempt during the voyages to change the religion of the areas or countries visited.

Although Zheng He was buried at sea, a traditional tomb monument was built on land in Nanjing to honor him. China also built an impressive *Zheng He Treasure Ship Park* in Nanjing, the historical seafaring city in east China's Jiangsu Province. This large and impressive park is architecturally built as a replica of the era in which Zheng He traveled. There is a hall of treasures in a temple in the park that exhibits the gifts and tributes from the countries Zheng He visited during his voyages.

**Statue of Admiral Zheng He at Zheng He Treasure Ship
Park in Nanjing as he looks out over the shipyards**
(TripAdvisor, 2011)

It was not until the twenty-first century that Zheng He's exploits became known to much of the world. The book, *Biography of Our Homeland's Great Navigator Zheng He*, written by the Chinese author Liang Qichao in 1904, first published, did not enjoy a large circulation. This was followed in 1911 with the discovery in Galle, Sri Lanka, of a trilingual stele, a stone monument left by Zheng He. The inscription on the stele mainly praises Buddha.

There are a few written documents from other countries that Zheng He visited that have survived. Later, two important books were published that received attention. The first is *When China Ruled the Sea: The Treasure Fleet of the Dragon Throne, 1405-1433* by Louise L. Levanthes (1994) and *Zheng He: China and the Oceans in the Early Ming Dynasty, 1405-1433* by Edward L. Dreyer.

In 2005, the Chinese government organized special voyages of "peace and goodwill" to many parts of the world as missions to celebrate the six hundredth anniversary of Zheng He's expeditions. July 11th is also celebrated in China as Maritime Day in honor of Zheng He's first voyage.

Furthermore, during the opening ceremony of the Olympics in 2008 in China, a special tribute and display honored the legacy of Zheng He. Such recognition is well deserved, as this fascinating worldly traveler changed the part of the world in which he visited, and his contributions to shipbuilding, sailing, and seafaring technology have never been equaled. His ascendancy to power was absolutely remarkable for an individual with no special connections to the ruling families, except as a loyal eunuch who seized opportunities to become a very powerful leader and to serve his emperor in an exemplary way.

While Zheng He never wrote a book about his travels, and many of the records of his impressive feats were destroyed, he did, however, in 1431, leave the world to contemplate the notion that "The countries beyond the horizon and from the ends of the earth have all become subjects and to the most western of the western or the most northern of the northern countries, however far away they may be."

And we add, "The distance and the routes may be calculated…"

We think about all of this.

# CHAPTER SIX

# CHRISTOPHER COLUMBUS LOST ADMIRAL OF OCEANS AND SEAS

"We have traversed more than one hundred
thousand li [40,000 miles] of immense water
spaces and have beheld in the ocean huge waves
like mountains rising to the sky, and we have set
eyes on barbarian regions far away, hidden in a
blue transparency of light vapors, while our sails
loftily unfurled like clouds day and night."
-Zheng He, 1433 C.E.-

*Young Christopher Columbus clutched a book in his
hand tightly, as if someone were trying to pry it loose or
even to steal it. The volume, titled "The Travels of Marco
Polo", was so fascinating that he read it over and over
again. The stories, especially of China, Japan, India, and
certain other countries, captured his willing imagination.
He dreamed about these stories, as told by the author, and
became restless about the adventures of his own traveling.*

*When he met with his brothers and friends and tried
to explain to them what he read frequently and how it
pertained to their lives, they pretended to be interested.
But they did so only because his passion was so intense
and his enthusiasm so obvious.*

*The book he held described the dangers and difficulties of overland travel. He noted, with particular interest, the passages describing sea travel and the rich countries that Marco Polo had visited in the East, writing about distant destinations containing gold, spices, silks, and other exotic goods located in the Greater Indies, as the East Indies, China, India, and Japan. He heard from other sources about perilous seagoing trips to the East and the riches brought back if the traveler was able and capable to endure the hardships of the journey. His young mind was ablaze with thoughts that perhaps he might find a shorter route to the riches of the East Indies by sea by traveling west instead of east!*

*If Marco Polo had not been in a Genoese prison, he would never have met fellow prisoner and writer Rustichello. Without this fateful encounter, Marco Polo's written work about his travels would not have been published, nor made available to other travelers and explorers. Inspired by Marco Polo's work, it changed his life and altered our understanding of the world.*

**Christopher Columbus bids farewell to the King and Queen of Spain as he prepares to leave on his first voyage.**
(Roth, 2012)

\*    \*    \*

E vents of great magnitude were transpiring in Europe as
Christopher Columbus was born in the middle of the fifteenth
century C.E. His life mirrored the beginning of the Modern Age
in Europe, a time of sea discoveries and power struggles in Europe.
Eighty years earlier, China had been the greatest world sea power, but
was no longer interested in sailing and nor explorations. As a result, the
great ships were no longer in use, or had been destroyed.

Columbus' birthplace, Genoa, Italy, and its main rival city-state for
ocean trade routes, Venice, were beginning their decline as great sea
power city-states. Being replaced by Portugal, Spain, the Netherlands,
and, to a lesser degree, England and France.

Portugal took the early lead due to the insightfulness of Prince Henry
the Navigator, the son of King John I, who foresaw that sea explorations
would lead to destinations with possible rich resources available to the
nation that got there first. His efforts and support of new explorations led
him to be a key player in the Age of Discoveries in the fifteenth century.

By 1429, the French national heroine Joan of Arc had gone to battle to
unite France. Her efforts set in motion an opportunity for King Louis XI
to rule over an expanded kingdom by the time Columbus was born. By
1440, German goldsmith and printer Johannes Gutenberg had perfected
the printing press in Europe. In 1469, the marriage of Ferdinand II of
Aragon and Isabella of Castile led to the unification of Spain. The union
of these two leaders advanced Spain to become a major seafaring nation.
By 1481, during the reign of Ferdinand II and Isabella, the infamous
Inquisition was initiated in Spain. This religious cleansing continued for
many years. When Columbus landed in the Bahamas in 1492, the Jews
of Spain who would not convert to Catholicism were being expelled.

In 1485, Henry VII defeated Richard III to become King of England.
Subsequently, John Cabot, the Italian explorer in the service of England,
discovered Newfoundland. France was also exploring new territories.
While Columbus made Spain an early conqueror of the New World, other
European nations were beginning to encroach on the claims of Spain.

By 1501, Michelangelo began work on his famous statue, *David*, which he completed in 1504, the year Queen Isabella of Spain died. In 1503, Michel Nostradamus, the French astrologer, medical doctor, famous prognosticator, and author of *Les Propheties,* was born. Also, in 1503, Italian scientist, mathematician, engineer, writer, and artist, Leonardo da Vinci began painting *Mona Lisa,* which he finished in 1506, the year Columbus died.

The time between the fifteenth century and the early sixteenth century was highly competitive for countries seeking to dominate ocean routes. In addition to the Genoese and Venetians, now the Portuguese, Spaniards, and Dutch, already seafaring nations were intent on opening new trade routes. Even the French and English began to have an interest in sea power.

More than any nation at the time, the Portuguese dominated the oceans; as a result, they explored much of the continent of Africa. Traveling around the tip of Africa, the great Portuguese seafarers reached the East Indies. The problem, from an international trade perspective, was that the voyages took so long. The Portuguese sailor Bartholomew Dias, a great fifteenth century sea explorer, had already sailed to the Indies in 1487-1488. His voyage took him around the southern tip of Africa, a trip which lasted sixteen months.

In 1497, building on knowledge gained from this voyage, the famous explorer and seasoned navigator, Vasco de Gama, left Portugal and made a journey to India. He returned after almost two years.

* * *

"He who has gold," Christopher Columbus said, "makes and accomplishes whatever he wishes in the world and finally uses it to send souls into paradise." His search for gold began to make him impervious to his surroundings and led him to inflict maltreatment on many native populations he encountered. It is a fact that he was a great navigator, but we learn, as he matured, that he was also vain, irascible, and unfaithful to his wife, yet curious, brave, courageous, and loyal to the Queen of

Spain. The pursuit of gold and riches was his driving force for his four ocean-going voyages. He was full of pride and ambition, and fully convinced that going west across the ocean would bring him to the wealth of the East Indies.

Columbus grew up in Genoa, an ancient seaport community on the northwestern Italian coast. This seaport had been receiving seafarers for hundreds of years. Throughout its history, the city was destroyed many times only to be rebuilt more magnificently than it was before each destruction.

During the fourteenth and fifteenth centuries, Genoa was a constant rival of Venice, aspiring to be the most important commercial port in the area. The two city-states, Venice, on Italy's west coast and Genoa, on its east coast, had similar governmental structures because the Genoese noted how progressive Venice was and copied most of the Venetian form of government. These two seafaring nations fought many times for dominance of the sea trade.

However, by the middle of the fifteenth century, Genoa became a part of Spain. Later, in 1805, it was a French territory as a result of the Napoleonic wars. Finally, after many other battles, Genoa became a major port city of Italy, as it is today. Its historic buildings and great art centers make it a highly desirable tourism destination.

There is not much known about his early childhood. He had a younger brother, Diego, and an older brother, Bartholomew, both of whom played important roles in his life and travels. He had a third brother, but there is little information about him. Throughout his life, he wrote many documents, but had little to say about his childhood and family life.

In 1470, his family moved to Savona, a region located west-southwest of Genoa on the Ligurian Sea. It is likely Columbus began his seafaring experiences here. There's a story that in 1476, when Columbus was twenty-five years old, he sailed on a Flemish vessel as part of a Genoese convoy, and his ship was attacked by a French armada. While the ship that Columbus was on sank, fortunately, he wasn't far from land, and using one of the long boat oars as a life raft of sorts, he half swam and half floated to shore.

After his first near death experience, he joined his brother, Bartholomew, in the progressive seaport of Lisbon, Portugal. There, Columbus helped his brother develop the growing business of making and selling mariner's charts. The Portuguese had taken the lead in sea explorations, and their ship captains brought back their notes, hand-drawn maps, and other information that were used to produce new mariner's charts.

Constantly reading *The Travels of Marco Polo,* Columbus reviewed maps and charts and began to develop theories about of sailing west, instead of east, to reach the East Indies. He made ample notes in the book so he would know just how to act in the China court when he arrived.

In 1479, Columbus married Felipa Moniz Perestrello, the daughter of Bartolomeu Perestrello, the former governor of the Island of Porto Santo, Portugal. He, also was a Portuguese navigator who had been given the Island of Porto Santo in recognition of his service to the Portuguese crown. Sadly, Bartolomeu had already died by the time his daughter Felipa married Columbus.

To his delight, as part of his wife's dowry, Columbus received Bartolomenu's navigation charts on winds, currents, directions, and other notes. This information excited him and helped him to prepare for his voyages to the New World. Felipa and Columbus had a son in 1480 they named Diego. Columbus' documents, including his will, tell us nothing about his married life. Apparently, he was so wrapped up with his work and in his quest to find a direct sea route to the Orient, all else in his life seemed secondary.

The more Columbus talked with sailors, mapmakers, and others in Lisbon, the more convinced he became that the riches of the East Indies were easily reached by sailing west from Europe. All he had to do was convince the skeptics, financiers, and royalty that he was right. But not many believed him. Some of his intellectual detractors, advisers to the monarchies, felt he had many strikes against him. For one, Columbus was not capable of speaking or writing any of the more acceptable languages of the area; Latin, Italian, or Portuguese. Growing up in Genoa, most likely with little formal education, he initially spoke Genoese, which wasn't really a language but a dialect which few people spoke. By the time he became literate, Spanish clearly became his language for all intents and purposes.

Yet by 1484, Columbus felt he had enough information to approach King John of Portugal about his theory for reaching the East Indies. King John was also interested in seafaring expeditions, seeking to gain new territories and wealth for Portugal. After considerable knocking on doors and begging for assistance to get an audience with the king, in the presence of the king and his special advisors, he quoted information from Marco Polo's book and made a strong attempt at convincing the king to sponsor an expedition. While the king was impressed with Columbus' enthusiasm, it was not enough to support such a sea adventure. Greatly disappointed, Columbus next tried to convince the leaders of both Genoa and Venice for help. He was turned down in both cases.

In 1485, Columbus' wife died. Shortly after, he left Lisbon with his five-year old son, Diego, and they headed towards Spain. Two years later, he met Beatriz Enriquez de Arana of Spain who became his mistress. They had a son named Fernando. Based in Spain for the next seven years, Columbus met and spoke to anyone in Europe who would listen to his proposal. While he found a few interested individuals, no one was willing to provide the needed finance for such an expedition. One who did support Columbus throughout his life was his brother, Bartholomew, who believed in his brother's project.

In 1486, Columbus made an impassioned appeal to King Ferdinand and Queen Isabella, joint rulers of Spain. Some of the Queen's advisers listened to his infectious optimism, but they were skeptical of his reasoning. Again, nothing was forthcoming.

Again, Columbus approached King John in Portugal, trying to use the intense rivalry for the dominance of the seas between Spain and Portugal as a way to gain the King's attention. Yet again, no decision.

In the meantime, the Spanish King and Queen learned of his trips to Portugal, and they were concerned that King John might agree to his venture. Aha! In an effort to keep Columbus in Spain, they continued to demonstrate some interest in his project.

Finally, in 1489, the King and Queen agreed to give him an annual allowance and a regal letter that ordered cities he traveled to in Spain to provide him with food and lodging at no cost. These benefits were helpful, but they still did not advance his cause for support for a voyage.

Early in 1492, as he was about to board a boat bound for France, he was summoned by Queen Isabella. On advice from her husband, the Queen decided to personally listen to his theory. Just what changed her mind and caused her to become interested remains unclear; although, it likely had something to do with her aspirations for her own kingdom. The reasoning here supports the contention that she was afraid that the King of Portugal, or another nation, might sponsor Columbus and gain an advantage over her kingdom, in sea travel.

While Queen Isabella wasn't totally convinced that Columbus could be successful, she saw in him a possibility for replenishing the monarch's treasury since she desperately needed a war chest to support her quest for additional power in Europe.

If Columbus could sail to the Indies, he might provide the gold she needed. The Queen arranged for a private and public investment in Columbus' project, committing only a small amount from the royal treasury. She conferred on Columbus the title of "Admiral of the Seas". In addition, her financial advisers developed a contract that was mutually beneficial to Columbus and the monarchy. If he were successful in discovering new lands for the crown, he would be appointed viceroy and governor of the new lands, as well as share in financial gains.

**Christopher Columbus receiving from Queen
Isabel of Spain his nomination as Viceroy of the
territories he will discover on his voyages.**
(Wellcome Collection, 2018)

Credit must be given to Columbus for his considerable and unstoppable research that led him to eventually become a master mariner. His notes are everywhere in books, on charts and in the Captain's logs. He read anything available to help on this next expedition and carried Marco Polo's book everywhere; again, the book's pages extensively marked with notes in the margins, especially the sections dealing with China and Japan.

At age 41, full of confidence, Columbus was eager to assume command of the expedition. And he looked the part; over six feet tall, much taller than the average European at the time. He, like Zheng He, towered above most of his men. Yet finding a crew that believed in an admiral who had little actual experience as a commander was a challenge. While he had spent most of his efforts in selling his idea with great enthusiasm and patience, he had not allotted himself time for actual training or gaining experience as a sea captain.

Yet he felt his considerable research about sailing, his understanding of the east and west winds, and his self-assurance were all he needed to begin his journey. While this knowledge did not necessarily convince Spanish sailors to join a captain from a foreign country with little seaworthy credentials, the royal secretary of Spain announced a special grant giving certain convicts their freedom if they agreed to join the expedition. Only four took advantage of this offer. However, others helped him to recruit sailors, and he was finally able to assemble an experienced crew. A few officials joined the expedition, but there were no priests, soldiers, or settlers aboard.

During the fifteenth century, many Europeans believed in predictions that the world would end in 1492. Columbus wrote, "I make the journey in my imagination…to see the world before it ends…1492…"

Yet, such eschatological beliefs of such a cataclysmic outlook for 1492, and its aftermath, did not stop him from making his final preparations to sail west to reach China and the Far East.

On August 3, 1492, Admiral Christopher Columbus set sail from Palos de la Frontera, Spain, near the mouth of the Rio Tinto. With him were 104 men and three small ships, the Niña, the Pinta, and the Santa Maria. He sailed southward to the Canary Islands, in Spanish territory, to take on fresh water and supplies. Since Columbus noted that the Canary Islands were on the same latitude as Cipangu, Japan, his initial destination in the East Indies, he sailed west from there.

La Pinta     La Niña     Santa Maria

**Depictions of the ships on which Columbus' crews sailed for
the first voyage – the Niña, the Pinta, and the Santa Maria**
(Marin, 2015)

On the voyage, strong winds pressed the vessels rapidly and dangerously, making some of the crew nervous as they wondered what air currents might eventually bring them back home. By now, Columbus had studied and developed expert knowledge of the trade winds, knowing how to use the winds to sail west, and how to change sail to capture the winds to head east, when needed later on. He taught his men, truly "men of the sail", how to constantly adjust sails to capture the wind--- as directed by the Admiral.

Yet, the expedition was a mysterious voyage to an unknown place causing some of the crew great anxiety and a lack of confidence in their leader. Possibly the most difficult aspect of the trip for Columbus was keeping up the morale of his men. They constantly worried they might sail off the edge of the horizon of the earth, as the concept of a round earth was not so easily understood by an uneducated crew. Or that they were led on a journey to a destination from which they would never be able to return. From the outset of the voyage, Columbus led, reasoned and prevaricated about the ship's location when communicating with the crew.

He had promised that after 750 leagues at sea, they would reach land in the Indies. Realizing that he wasn't sure of his estimates, he deliberately falsified the logbook by indicating they hadn't traveled as far as they thought they had that day. Since most of the crew did not understand speed calculations or many other measures, his deviousness worked. And they believed him. Besides, most of the crew thought that surely an Admiral would not deliberately mislead the seamen he depended on.

However, ten weeks of sailing failed to bring them to land; the crew began to lose confidence in their Admiral. Most had never really bought into the concept of going west to reach the East Indies. Some were ready to consider mutiny. They noted that if the sea were calm, they could not continue moving forward, but they could turn around and go back in the other direction instead. If it didn't rain, they feared the lack of fresh water for the journey, a major concern. The promises that they thought they would be sharing in the riches of the East began to be less of an incentive as they moved farther into the unknown without sighting land.

The first sighting of land arrived just in time to ward off an impending mutiny. Columbus offered a handsome reward to the first seaman to sight land, and it was with much relief that, on October 12, 1492, it happened. At about 2:00 a.m., Rodrigo de Triana, a seaman on the Pinta Shouted "Tierra! Tierra!" The Captain ordered the cannon fired to signal the other boats so all would know that at last they were about to reach land.

**Christopher Columbus plants the Spanish
flag in the presence of the Taino Indians**
(Moody, 2018)

Columbus and members of his crew spent ninety-six days exploring many islands in the area, which he thought were a part of the East Indies. However, he had really landed on one of the present-day Bahamian islands. They also visited the islands later referred to as Cuba and Hispaniola. Today, Hispaniola is divided into the countries of Haiti and the Dominican Republic. Columbus was simply an adventurous tourist, not knowing what lay around the next corner.

To the question, if Columbus discovered America, where was it? While Columbus first landed on an island in the Bahamas, which can be counted as "part of the Americas," but was it North America? While He discovered many Caribbean islands, his closest contact to being a "discover of the U.S." was visiting and naming St. Croix. It only became part of the U.S. in 1917 when the U.S. bought the island from Denmark.

As they traveled throughout these islands, he was constantly surprised by the amazing cultures of the new natives he met. He came upon indigenous populations thoroughly enjoying their leisure time; dancing, singing, playing ballgames, engaging in sex, eating, hunting and other endeavors. One of the ballgames, he noted, included a bouncing ball made of a sticky substance coming from a tropical tree. It wasn't until 1896 that B.F. Goodrich began making tires from this "sticky substance", *rubber*, which became known as "black gold". Columbus found the indigenous population to be friendly, pleasant, and helpful in loading fresh water on to the boats, and seemingly unselfish. When he first met the natives of the islands, he called them Indians since he was sure he was in the East Indies.

Columbus was also amazed at the expertise of the Indians in knowing how to grow crops and otherwise provide ample food to eat. He noted how well-built their lodges were and he appreciated their innovative use of local materials for construction. The houses had thatched roofs, which were constructed using available nearby palms that were held together with closely woven branches and vines over cane poles. These homes were able to withstand the winds and rains. He especially noticed how clean and well-kept the homes were.

What made him uncomfortable was the nakedness of the Indians. In his generation in Spain, such a lack of clothing was unacceptable. However, notwithstanding their nakedness, he was impressed with the handsome features of the natives. Apparently without asking the Indians if they might be interested in traveling back with him to Spain, which they would not have understood anyway, we read that he kidnapped a few and took them on board his ship to present to the King and Queen on his return voyage.

In his explorations of the islands, he looked for gold and other treasures. In the short term, it was clear his party had not yet found anything truly valuable. This presented a unique set of problems. He had promised the Queen that his journeys would yield riches for all who supported his venture. Many of his crew had signed on as seamen, willing to take on the dangers of such a voyage, only because they were told they would become rich. How to deal with not finding the wealth of the East Indies created many problems, no less than the dissension among crewmembers.

Without the Admiral's permission, the Captain of the Pinta revolted and sailed away on their own from the main party looking for gold. While they did find a small amount of gold and obtained gold trinkets from the Indians, it was not enough to be convincing to anyone who had been promised the fortunes of the East Indies.

On Christmas morning in 1492, the Santa Maria went aground. As a result, Columbus had to leave 39 men behind to develop a settlement called *La Navidad* in present day Haiti. He then set sail for his return trip to Spain on the Niña. The Pinta, under troubled circumstances for disobeying the commander, did rejoin Columbus, and both ships headed back to Spain. But when the boats were hit by a terrible storm, Columbus was able to land the Niña in Lisbon.

Meanwhile, Captain Pinzon landed the Pinta on the northwest coast of Spain. King John II of Portugal apprehended Columbus, but later in March 1493, he released him, and Columbus sailed into Palos, Spain. Captain Pinzon arrived later, but before he could report on his voyage, he died.

When Columbus arrived back in Spain on March 15, 1493, he addressed a letter of his discoveries to the Honorable Luis de Santangel, official representative of King Ferdinand and Queen Isabella. The Honorable Luis de Santangel was the one who had persuaded the Queen to support the voyage in the first place. His letter, written in Spanish, was quickly translated into the universal church language of Latin. Later, it was published in other languages. The letter was immediately a document of the day, even though its distribution throughout Europe took some time.

In this famous letter, Columbus never mentioned his potential mutinous crew. He also left out the insubordination of one of his Captains and the loss of the Santa Maria. He skipped over other problem areas, but he did admit he had not met the great Khan of China, nor located the riches of the East he had promised. He truly believed that in a future voyage to other islands in the area, he'd find China and Japan.

He had encountered Taino Indians smoking tobacco in the islands he visited. Many years later, this became the rage of Europe, making many boat captains and tobacco farmers very rich. But such a find did not materialize in the marketplace during Columbus' era. He rechecked his book of Marco Polo's travels, convinced he had traveled near to China on this first voyage.

Columbus was eager to appear before King Ferdinand and Queen Isabella at the royal palace in Barcelona to recount his voyage. He was invited to sit with them and eat at the same table. He paraded before them the handsome natives and exotic, colorful parrots, while he reported on his voyage. While he did not have all the gold and spices he had promised, he did have enough gold to convince them that, truly, he must have been close to the East Indies. They were impressed by the success of his voyage, and rewarded him handsomely monetarily, which gave him considerable publicity.

In effect, Columbus' fame and fortune led to his being Europe's new celebrity. And as a religious man, he was convinced that God had placed him on this earth as a prophet. This belief that he was God's personal messenger kept him persistently confident, an integral part of his life throughout his travels. In addition to the importance of religion, being wealthy was an important driving force of his life as well.

To keep Portugal from trying to claim the territories that Columbus visited on his first voyage in the name of Spain, he wrote a letter to the Pope, Alexander VI, to make him aware of his discoveries. In 1493, the Pope issued an official edit granting Spain the areas Columbus had discovered. The Pope drew a demarcation line; all undiscovered land west of this line belonged to Spain, and any land east belonged to Portugal.

This document left Portugal unable to explore what later became North and South America. The Pope realized his mistake, *and* in 1494, he re-drew the demarcation line. The new division allowed Portugal to have an area that would later become Brazil. Spain then received most of the rest of the Americas. Later, of course, many changes took place; the New World would be impacted by many European nations.

Over the next twelve years, Columbus made three more voyages of discoveries to the Indies. He was always sure the wealth of the Indies was just beyond the horizon. After all, one of the many books he had read spoke of some 5,000 islands in the Indies. Early on, he made up stories to convince his supporters and much of Europe that he had found a short-cut to China.

Praised lavishly after his first voyage had been deemed successful, at the height of his power, he quickly assembled larger expedition for his second voyage. This journey, which he took only six months to assemble after he returned, included seventeen ships and over twelve-hundred men.

In some respects, Columbus' voyages were not unlike today's Caribbean cruises. He sailed from island to island, stopping to go ashore to see what he might find. He enjoyed the sights and the sounds of the islands and the smooth sailing of the Caribbean Sea. We say he was our first Caribbean cruise captain, and his crew were the first tourists. Initially intermingling with the natives, he had liked them and had positive things to say about how great they were as hosts, their living conditions and providing kind hospitalities as he traveled.

An event took place in the Western Caribbean on his second voyage which included a fleet of 17 ships. On November 14, 1493, the fleet came upon the island that the native islanders, the Taino Indians, called "Ay-Ay". The Carib Indians, invaders, and conquerors of the Taino Indians, referred to the island as "Cibuquiera" or the Stony Land.

146

Columbus named it Santa Cruz. Of course, we know it is called St. Croix, in the U.S. Virgin Islands. Columbus sent armed men ashore to explore the Carib village and to search for fresh water on the west side of what is now called Salt River Bay. The men seized some of the Taino Indians, who were working as slaves to the Caribs, from the village. On their return from the village to Columbus' flagship, which was anchored outside the bay, the Spaniards rammed a Carib canoe containing four Carib men and two Carib women. A fierce skirmish ensued. The Carib Indians were excellent with the bow and arrow. One Carib, while treading water, shot an arrow with great accuracy and killed a crew member. But the Spaniards also shot and killed one of the Indians. This conflict is the first documented example of Native American resistance to European encroachment. Christopher Columbus named this cape "Cabo de la Flecha", or Cape of the Arrow, in honor of the seaman who died from arrow wounds in the battle. This reference to St. Croix is the only known area where Columbus' crew touched land that is now a part of the United States of America.

Also on the second voyage, there was an attempt at colonization of the islands and in converting the natives to Catholicism. Yet; finding gold was still his main priority. A town named after Queen Isabella was constructed on the island of Hispaniola as the headquarters of the new world. At first, Admiral Columbus assumed the title of Governor, and then, from 1495-1500, he was officially named governor and viceroy of the island by the Queen of Spain. But Columbus was a terrible administrator, with likely many reasons. He was raised with no education or training that might suggest any administrative preparation. His total and only interests had been in sea explorations. During this second voyage, he was besieged with illness, resulting in a condition that kept him ill for his remaining years; therefore, he may not have been mentally or physically up to the task of being a governor. And being stuck on an island as governor did not fit his character.

His passionate interest remained with sea travel, and his psyche was focused on the goal of finding the riches of the East. Still fully convinced that his voyages had successfully landed in the Indies, he believed he would definitely meet the rich and powerful rulers of China. Whatever the situation, he failed miserably as a government official. Since most of the crew and others he left behind on the island were not reputable individuals to begin with, their actions and behaviors created much difficulty and trouble for him. They had signed on for an adventure and to become rich and had no desire to work or make a commitment to improving conditions on the island.

By now, they deplored Columbus and his two brothers, Diego, and Bartholomew, who served as assistants to the Admiral. The brothers earned contempt and loathing from the crew as a result of their actions.

As Columbus' sickness rendered him bedridden for a long time, he appointed his brother Diego in charge of Hispaniola. No surprise that chaos broke loose. The men, those who had not mutinied, ran helter-skelter with no special purposes in mind. They killed natives without reason, and also, because they had not found the gold they had demanded. Some of their punishments for the natives were cruel, raping native women at will, and creating hatred and animosity among what had been friendly natives. When the natives rebelled and tried courageously to fight back, it was total disaster on both sides. .

**Columbus' harmful actions against
the natives turns fatal**
(Topbuzz.com, n.d.)

When he was able to feel better, Columbus' answer to this chaotic situation was to put his older brother, Bartholomew, in charge. So that Columbus could continue and go off exploring in Cuba and the other islands; always seeking the East Indies and the riches he knew were there.

This time, when Columbus returned from his explorations of the islands, he found Hispaniola in even worse shape. The supposedly Christian men had perpetrated even worse evils on the natives during his absence. Instead of having sympathy for the poor natives who were being abused, he ordered his soldiers to set about killing and torturing them because they had begun to fight back. Because his men would not work, either at agriculture or mining, he instituted slavery of the natives at a time when it was not legal in Spain. In every situation, Columbus rationalized his actions to use native slave labor on the islands.

When he returned to Spain in 1496, after his second voyage, without having found the riches he had convinced his sponsors existed, Columbus was not well received. His credibility and honesty were in question, with recriminations that he stooped to devious means and was deceptive in his dealings. There were no celebrations as had been the case after his first voyage. While he had been recognized for his discoveries, now Spain was engaged in conflicts with other countries and needed gold to support her armies. The monarchs had little time or interest in Columbus' petitions for a third voyage.

But finally, in mid-1497, they relinquished. They allowed six small boats to return to the islands with provisions for the colonists. On the third voyage, he discovered the mainland of South America when his vessel arrived off the coast of Venezuela. At first, he thought he had again arrived on islands of the East Indies. When he realized this coast was not an island, he was really confused, thinking it must be a part of mainland Asia in the China Sea.

Even though natives in the area told him that many pearls existed off the coast of Venezuela near the island of Margarita, he did not even try to search for them. The coast of the island was abundant in pearls, which would come to represent almost a third of all New World tribute to the Spanish Crown. Why Columbus did not stay longer to gather the pearls is still a mystery.

He continued on to Hispaniola and spent time organizing his governors' house and his thousands of acres of property. By then, most of the inhabitants' conditions had deteriorated. Word had gotten back to Spain about his lack of properly administering the island.

The result was that the crown sent a new administrator, Francisco de Bobadilla, to take over control as governor. However, before the new governor arrived, Columbus did discover a productive gold mine. Though this yielded some profits for him and gold for the royal treasury, it wasn't in the amount everyone had hoped for. But it did help to make the venture mostly worthwhile.

Governor Bobadilla found Columbus truculent and temperamental. He thought Columbus was unwilling to tolerate others and most conditions in Hispaniola. So he brought formal charges against Columbus and his older brother Bartholomew for complete mismanagement of the island, putting them in irons. He was able to send all three brothers back to Spain to stand trial. This horrifying setback demoralized and demeaned Columbus, again, ill.

Our worldly traveler was no longer a hero, or had he even been?

His medical problems and often bizarre demeanor caused him difficulties for the rest of his life. After their arrival in Spain, and when the monarchs were made fully aware of Columbus' arrest, all the brothers were released.

Yet, once again, Columbus was able to get back into the good graces of the Sovereigns, and gained their support for a fourth voyage. He led a group of four vessels and left Spain on May 9, 1502 on his last voyage to the new world. Altogether, they carried 143 men and boys, including, for the first time, Columbus' thirteen-year-old illegitimate son, Fernando. His faithful brother, Bartholomew, also accompanied him.

On this voyage, Columbus had only one thing on his mind; to find gold and the riches of the East Indies that he had read about in Marco Polo's book. He was quite aware that the Portuguese had sponsored a trip by Admiral Vasco da Gama, who sailed to India by going around Africa. Anticipating that they might meet somewhere in India or China, he carried special letters to present to the Portuguese Admiral. However, on this voyage, he finally came to the conclusion that he was not in the East Indies. Thus, if he was not in the East Indies, he must be in the "West Indies"….

While not of significance to Columbus, during this voyage, his party encountered a large canoe carrying 25 men, women, and children. This group included a Maya trading party. While the magnificent Maya civilization was in decline, Columbus' brother, Bartholomew, noted in his report that the Mayans were able to dominate the salt and goods traffic in and out of the Maya region. Even though the captain of the canoe pointed in the westerly direction in describing an area of Maya treasures, Columbus chose to go eastward.

The Maya treasures were westward, but Columbus, still suffering from numerous illnesses and having taken suggestions in the past from local natives that did not result in finding the riches he so desperately sought, clearly ignored the captain. It was a big mistake, indeed. The Mayans did have gold.

This voyage was handicapped by bad weather and the fault that Columbus continued to be ill. On December 5, 1502, the expedition was hit with a severe storm. He wrote in his journal: "For nine days I was as one lost, without hope of life. Eyes never beheld the sea so angry, so high, so covered with foam. The wind not only prevented our progress, but offered no opportunity to run behind any headland for shelter; hence, we were forced to keep out in this bloody ocean…All this time the water never ceased to fall from the sky; I do not say it rained, for it was like another deluge. The men were so worn out that they longed for death to end their dreadful suffering."

Luckily, in a way, all four boats were heaved ashore and became shipwrecked with few supplies on the shores of Jamaica. They spent a tempestuous year on the island of Jamaica, with chaotic conditions, mutinies, starvation, and sickness. Yet what was left of the crew was rescued in June of 1504 by a ship from Hispaniola. After a month's rest, and the rebuilding on one ship, Columbus set sail for Spain with 22 others, but little to show from his travels.

He arrived in Spain broken-hearted, ill, and disoriented and without bringing any of the wealth he had promised. Mostly ignored by representatives in Spain and for the remaining year-and-a-half of his life, Columbus was held in disrespect by the local population.

Worse, was that shortly after his arrival, his initial supporter, his dear Queen Isabella, died. Although King Ferdinand initially ignored Columbus, he hired his son, Diego, now grown, as part of his personal guard. Finally, after a year, the king granted Columbus a brief audience. Ferdinand patiently listened to all the petitions made by an ill and now somewhat mentally disturbed Columbus. He basically ignored what Columbus had to say.

For the next year, Columbus lived in Valladolid, Spain, bedridden with compounded illnesses and little support. On May 19, 1506, he summoned as much energy as he could to make out his last will and testament, leaving the major share of his inheritance to his son, Diego, a separate amount to support his mistress, Beatriz, and small amounts to his other son, Fernando, and to his brother, Bartholomew.

The next day, hardly noticed by the country of Spain or the local community, Columbus died. And it would be many years later before Spain and the world would realize the importance of the many discoveries made by Admiral Christopher Columbus.

Interestingly, Spain paid little tribute to the Admiral for the next three to four hundred years. It was in the nineteenth century that the Americas became intensely interested in Columbus' discoveries and were able to review Spanish documents about his voyages.

While Christopher Columbus' legacy in the domains of discovery and sailing were heralded, he often viewed as a tragic soul. That he was a great worldly traveler is substantial, yet in many respects, he remains controversial. There' is no question that his voyages and explorations changed the world during his lifetime and into the twenty-first century.

Here's more. Columbus was not the first European to explore the Americas; that honor possibly rests with the Norseman Leif Ericson. However, while the Norseman was 500 years ahead of Columbus, his brief settlement was only temporary and mostly unrecorded. Other than the Native Americans, most others in Europe and the Americas consider Columbus as the great discoverer of the American continents.

Columbus' expeditions certainly foreshadowed great wealth for European countries as they exploited and colonized the New World. Because in finding riches for his benefactors, (the King and Queen of Spain had been a part of his mission,) he was deemed belatedly successful. . Though he never found the silks, spices, and large quantities of gold that he had promised.

While his travels also transformed the Americas by introducing them to European languages, culture, and ideas, his negative impact on his behavior with the native populations raised serious issues. In the beginning, Columbus' initial contact with the natives of the Caribbean islands was positive. In fact, he had stated in his official letter to the majesty's court about the natives: "They are so ingenuous and free with all they have, that no one would believe it who has not seen it; of anything they possess, if it be asked of them, they never say no; on the contrary, they invite you to share it, and show as much love as if their hearts went with it, and they are content with whatever trifle be given them, whether it be a thing of value or of petty worth."

Despite his admiration of the natives' generosity and living conditions, Columbus' subjugation and subjugations, led to Indian slavery, decimation, and cruelty to many of the natives. When he first arrived, the natives provided him with hospitality, friendship and shared whatever they had with the admiral and his men. Some of his detractors in history repeat that he repaid them with death, disease, and destruction, setting the stage for future generations of Europeans to do the same.

Many seafarers in his day traveled by using the heavens: stars, moon, and sun to help them locate where they were going. They figured out latitude much better than the more difficult longitude. Not knowing much about longitude had largely kept European explorers from locating the new world. Using the latest technology, maps, compasses, research, and charts helped Columbus, to decide he could find the riches of the east by going west. While his theory was correct, he severely underestimated the diameter of the Earth, which conveniently left out the American continents. His use of the compass was important in sailing to the new world. While the Chinese invented and used the compass in the twelfth century, by the fourteenth century, it had found its way to Europe. And it was in the fifteenth century that it became widely used by European ship captains. The compass allowed Europe to become a dominating leader in sea navigation and exploration.

While Columbus did not know there were two enormous continents between, his theory of going west to get to the East Indies was certainly right, adding a great deal to the knowledge of sailing in the fifteenth and sixteenth centuries. He did have the courage to test his knowledge of geography, having been a mapmaker earlier in his career, and to boldly strike out into the unknown regardless of the circumstances.

What Columbus might have lacked in terms of experience and of captaining ships, and kindness, he made up for in research, reading, navigation, and talking with seafarers. Because he had worked early in his career as a mapmaker, he wisely recognized and named Juan de la Cosa to be his cartographer. He could not have picked a better person. Juan de la Cosa owned one of the ships, the *Santa Maria*, and was probably the best mapmaker of that time period. As a result of his being on the first and second voyages, there are excellent maps of where Columbus had been and what he saw. His maps completely changed the known geography of the world.

Unlike his predecessor and idol, Marco Polo, Columbus was not as interested in the cultures he encountered. In the islands, he seemed to be indifferent to the many positive characteristics of the natives. And he paid seemingly little attention to the flora and fauna of the islands. These beautiful islands with fantastic trees, flowers, and grasses seemed of little concern to him. Comparatively, he had little to say about this beauty of the islands, which easily surpassed the barren lands he encountered in Europe.

Columbus' legacy is an enigma. There's no question that he is one of the greatest worldly travelers. His discoveries changed the world for better or worse, depending on one's viewpoint. He had the courage to travel routes no one had travelled previously. And he had no idea if he would ever be able to return to Spain. Over the years, we've come to realize that he traveled little for the interests of pursuing travel for travels' sake, but remained narrowly focused and geared toward increasing the wealth of his patrons and himself. Rank, privilege, and stature were important to him. He was certainly partially driven by simple greed.

Some historians see Columbus as a sanctimonious, avaricious individual caught up in his own world of power, and unable to grasp reality as it was presented to him during his travels. Despite all the negative aspects of his travel, he will be remembered for his contributions to the maritime industry and for expanding a world well beyond anyone's belief.

His riches sprang after he was gone. Today, thousands of communities, buildings, schools, and other edifices are named after Columbus. Some notable ones include the Republic of Colombia, Washington, District of Columbia, Columbia River, Columbus, Ohio, Columbia, South Carolina and many more.

These honors, posthumously bestowed on Christopher Columbus, are lasting memorials of the degree to which this worldly traveler forever impacted the Americas.

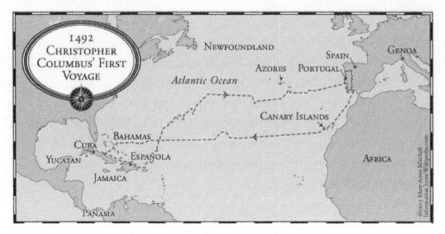

**The first voyage of Christopher of Columbus**
(Garr, 2018)

# CHAPTER SEVEN

# JEANNE BARET DISGUISED WORLDLY TRAVELER AND BOTANIST

"Life has more imagination than
we carry in our dreams."
-Christopher Columbus-

*Hmm…as a woman, might I be able to live my dream of traveling in a man's world? With imagination tis can be possible! What if I dressed up like a man? Oh that's ridiculous! And acted like a man? Oh God, really? Yes, travel as a man? Lord, help me!*

*I received an amazing offer today! My benefactor and friend, the distinguished naturalist Dr. Philibert Commerson, has been invited to join the renowned French admiral and explorer Louis Antoine de Bougainville on a round-the-world expedition! Dr. Commerson needs my help, since I have worked a long time with him in his botanical garden. I love being here and I keep learning a great deal about the various plants. This knowledge, combined with what I already knew from practical experience as a herbwoman, has made me realize what an important ally I am to Dr. Commerson.*

*He wishes me to accompany him as his assistant on the round-the-world expedition. But there are "rules" about "a woman" traveling on French naval ships. We both know the rules: No women are allowed aboard a French naval vessel. What's the penalty for breaking the rule? Prison? Lashings? Humiliation? What am I to do?*

*The doctor and I have put our heads together and came up with a ridiculous plan; disguise me as his male assistant. I must be nuts to consider it, but I really need to have this travel adventure of a lifetime, this opportunity to circumnavigate the world and learn to be a naturalist. Also, as I respect and care for Dr. Commerson, who is sickly and needs my help, I must do this. If I really put my mind to it, I think I can pass as a young man, ready to sail the seas. It's dangerous, but then all aren't all such ventures present unknown trials and tribulations?*

*I put our plan to the test: I dressed up like a young sailor, which wasn't so hard. The only major problem was hiding my breasts in a sailor's outfit. I practiced lowering my voice, which seemed to work reasonably well. I watched the sailors down by the dock as they worked, strutted, and drank rum at the local tavern and studied them closely. I attempted, successfully, to mimic their antics. Well, it's appeared to be working. No one has seemed to recognize me as a female. I think I can do this. I am now committed, smiling, looking in the mirror as I practice acting like a young man, yes, ready to set sail on this adventure.*

*My dear Dr. Commerson and I are ready to put this façade to the test as we board the ship. While I am, of course, nervous, I wonder... because Dr. Commerson is so highly recommended for the expedition, why no one has questioned him about his assistant named Jean.*

*So I slink by without initially raising any eyebrows from the boat's occupants.*

*So far.*

**Guesses of sketches of Jeanne Baret dressed in male sailors clothing. She is pictured on the left. Pictured on the right she is dressed in traditional female attire.**
(Meet Jeanne Baret: The First Woman to Circumnavigate the Globe, 2020)

\*   \*   \*

Most early travel for adventure and discovery throughout the world, especially by boat, took place by men. There were rare exceptions, like for example, the travels of Queen Hatshepsut of Egypt. However, it was generally considered too strenuous and dangerous for women to travel long distances by boats.

We reconsider this for Jeanne Baret, again remembering that sailing ships in the eighteenth century proved to be dangerous; ships were often poorly constructed, liable to catch on fire, sink during a storm, or be seized by pirates. The food was atrocious, living conditions on board were cramped, and diseases were rampant. Those adventurous and courageous worldly travelers and explorers during the early centuries were almost exclusively men.

Women were generally not allowed to travel on government-run naval vessels, which were the ships most often used for global travel expeditions. Women on board military vessels were considered "bad luck" and superstitiously might lead to a disaster at sea. In addition, ship captains were concerned that women on board a ship clearly proved distracting to the male sailors in getting their work done as well as possibly leading to violence. Most of the men on board the ships were hard-drinking tough seaman living in cramped conditions; their behavior, card and dice games and storytelling, was not fit, they laughed often, for the "weaker" sex.

However, there were exceptions: women who dressed up like young male sailors sometime snuck aboard. And, of course, the tales of female pirates is part of the early naval history. However there were examples like the British navy, more lenient than most other government navies, in that a certain number of naval officers' wives were sometimes allowed on certain of the British expeditions.

Women also encountered restrictions on many of the private ships, and often were required to travel with a husband or male chaperon. However, even under these difficult circumstances, occasionally a woman would find a way to travel throughout the world. Such women as Jeanne Baret, Isabella Bird, Nellie Bly, Gertrude Bell, Harriet Chalmer Adams, and Lady Hay Drummond; these women were truly the pioneer women worldly travelers. This story is about Jeanne Baret, the first worldly traveler of this group to find a unique way to travel around the world. But even Ms. Baret needed a "male chaperon" to help her illegally travel on an official French naval vessel.

*   *   *

Some basic background. The world was experiencing many changes during the lifetime of Jeanne Baret (1740-1807), including dramatic shifts in the directions of policies, programs, and political transformations within and outside her home country of France. France was constantly in peril of not being able to protect its position as a world power, always checking to see what other European powers were doing throughout the world.

By 1740, Frederick II, by name Frederick the Great, became the king and ruler of the German Kingdom of Prussia. A daring and highly successful military leader and statesman, he was a renaissance man interested in the arts and sciences. He preferred speaking French to German or English, recognizing French as the international language for statesmen and intellects. During his reign from 1740-1786, he introduced state policies which made Prussia a formidable power in Europe, giving Prussia the capability of challenging the major eighteenth century European powers that included France, Great Britain, Sweden, Austria, and Russia.

In 1740, the devastating Irish Famine also took place. By the time it ended in 1741, the Kingdom of Ireland had seen some 13-20 percent of the 2.4 million citizens die from the Famine, with many years before the Kingdom was able to recover.

The eighteenth century also saw a major change in the Middle East when the First Saudi State was established in 1744. Co-founded by Mohammed ibn Abdal-Wahhab and Prince Muhammed bin Saud, they perpetuated a unique socio-religious reform movement to unify the many states of the Arabian Peninsula. In today's geography, the First Saudi State would have included parts or all of Jordan, Iraq, Oman, Qatar, Saudi Arabia, United Emirates, and Yemen.

From 1754-1763, the Seven Years' War occurred with the Kingdom of France and her allies on one side battling against Great Britain and her partners on the other. The feud spilled over into their respective North American colonies. In North America, this conflict was referred to as the French and Indian War, with both the Kingdom of France and Great Britain utilizing their colonists and Native American confederates to help in the war efforts. Great Britain was the victor, and in the Treaty of Paris in 1763, the Kingdom of France ceded her territories on mainland north to Great Britain.

During the eighteenth century, many European countries founded colonies throughout the world. The Kingdom of France and Great Britain both established and supported colonies in North America. With help from the Kingdom of France, American colonists broke away from Great Britain and fought the British from 1775-1783. This became the American Revolutionary War. As a result of the help from France, the American colonists defeated Great Britain, and with the Treaty of Paris in 1783, (not to be confused with the Treaty of Paris in 1783,) the United States of America was born.

During the 1780s, the greater population of France was suffering from increasing poverty and social injustice, which led to the breeding of a revolutionary spirit, especially among the poor. This turmoil led to the French Revolution of 1789-1799, which abolished the Ancient Regime and created a constitutional monarchy.

By 1799, Napoleon Bonaparte was named First Consul of France, which allowed him to consolidate his power from 1799-1804. He began to set a course of world conquests t eventually led to his downfall. Yet as Napoleon began his quest to increase France's power and return France to a colonial owner in North America, he acquired the Louisiana territory from Spain in 1800. Shortly thereafter, needing money for his European conquests, he sold what became known as the "Louisiana Purchase" to the United States of America for $15 million dollars. This purchase doubled the size of the United States of America, allowing the country to expand its western borders and to increase its economic opportunities.

France, realizing the great sea explorations by her European competitors, became incensed with jealousy witnessing the Pacific voyages that had been taking place from 1768-1771 by British Captain James Cook and later, from 1791-1795, the British expedition to circumnavigate the globe by Captain George Vancouver. The British and Dutch were sailing in the Pacific Ocean, acquiring new possessions as they did so. France had colonies in the Pacific, but did not have wealthy locations like the Dutch East Indies. It was time for France to launch worldly voyages, and as part of this progressive policy, to accidentally anoint Ms. Jeanne Baret as the first female to circumnavigate the globe.

\*   \*   \*

In the eighteenth century, few women traveled, and they certainly did not travel to explore new territories, or to conquer or colonize new lands, or to discover new flora and fauna. Since this was the case, how did a certain young lady named Jeanne Baret become a self-educated botanist/naturalist, explorer, and worldly traveler? It is fascinating to learn this mysterious young woman who traveled illegally on a French navy ship accomplished her quest to circumnavigate the globe.

In five of the first six chapters of this book, the authors introduced several men who became worldly travelers and who changed the world as a result of their travels. There were certainly ample reasons to add additional men to this list of worldly travelers and explorers.

However, there was no apparent opportunity to add a female to the list of early worldly travelers until Jeanne Baret made sail on her global adventure.

With Jeanne Baret's background, and the lack of opportunities for women to travel globally, she would not have appeared a likely candidate to travel the world. Her education was limited, and her poor family lacked the funds to pay for her travels. Her lifestyle and the circumstances for a French lady to travel internationally did not bode well for the likelihood that she would accomplish global explorations. There was considerable discrimination against women traveling in the same way as men in the eighteenth century.

We must wait for dramatic changes in travel by women until one of the most significant fighters for women's rights appeared in the twentieth century in the embodiment of the celebrated aviatrix and worldly traveler: Amelia Earhart.

Jeanne Baret was born in humble beginnings on July 27, 1740 in the small town of Autun, France. Her parents, Jean and Jeanne Baret were poor; her father was a local laborer. An entry from a priest in the local parish record of Autun reads as follows: "On the twenty-seventh of July 1740 was born and on the twenty-eighth was baptized Jeanne, the legitimate issue of the marriage of Jean Baret, day laborer from Lomé, and Jeanne Pochard. Her godfather is Jean Coureau, a day laborer from Poil, and her godmother Lazare Tibaudin, who are not signing."

During the 1700s France was growing and by 1740 had a population of over 20 million or about three times the population of England. France had reasonably good fertile soil for farming but lacked efficient farming techniques or good rivers for shipping grain to other parts of the country. Few farmers had enough land or produced large enough crops to make a profit and thus were poor and usually in debt to landlords who had little interest in their welfare. While the French elite and intellectuals were into the Age of Enlightenment, the poor folks in rural areas were largely illiterate. The Bourbon family ruled France and by the time Jeanne was born King Louis XV was the sole monarch and ruler. France was on the losing side in the Seven Years' War and lost the colony of Canada and its presence in India to the British. This loss was a wakeup call for the king and finally he began to seek ways and means to bolster the image of France and to seek new territories to improve the economy of the country. Growing up in a poor rural area of France, Jeanne knew little of what was happening in the French government or society. Her life evolved within a few miles from where she lived.

While highly intelligent, Jeanne had almost no formal education, yet early on, she learned about certain herb plants that could be used by humans for food or medicinal purposes. In effect, she was what during that era was called an "herbwoman", a woman who learns about the medicinal and food properties of plants through oral tradition handed down from generation to generation. Some women knew considerably more about the qualities of plants than the highly educated male botanists of this time. Little did she realize that her love of plants would become an integral part of her travels and explorations and lead to her designation as both a worldly traveler and a botanist.

While the history books note that Jeanne was the first woman to circumnavigate the globe, there is nothing in her early life that seemed to lead her in this direction. The story of her life and accomplishments skip over her childhood and move into her twenties when she became a housekeeper, lover, and caregiver to Dr. Philibert Commerson, a well-educated and well-known naturalist.

Jeanne Baret's global travels began with Dr. Commerson.

**Dr. Philibert Commerson**
(Krulwich, 2012)

Philibert Commerson was born November 18, 1727 at Chatillon-les-Dombes in France to Wealthy parents who could afford to pay for his excellent education. He was educated at the great University of Montpellier, established in 1220, one of the oldest universities in the world and the oldest medical school still in operation. During his medical studies, the headmaster, who was interested in natural history, imbued him with desire for knowledge for becoming a naturalist. To his father's dismay, Philibert became excited and interested in natural history, zoology, and botany. To please his father, he also studied medicine and in addition to his knowledge of plants and animals, he was known as Dr. Philibert Commerson, a practicing physician.

His education and travel led him to befriend several important people. He conducted a special scientific project for the world-famous Swedish scientist and botanist, Carl Linnaeus. As a result of his work he met Carl Linnaeus's patron, Queen Louisa Ulrika of Sweden who was the founder of the Royal Swedish Academy of Letters, History, and Antiquities. In addition, he also met Francois-Marie Arouet, known by his nom de plume Voltaire, the famous French writer, historian, and philosopher. These contacts later helped him in his career to become a well-known naturalist. When he returned to Chatillon-les-Dombes, he partly occupied himself with medical studies to please his father and continued his readings of natural history. But even though he had a physician's title, he remained fascinated with botany projects.

In 1758, while he was teaching a young lady by the name of Antoinette-Vivante Beau the basics of botany, he fell in love with her. She was bright, attractive, and commanded a sizable fortune. On October 17, 1760, 31-year-old Philibert married 38-year-old Antoinette and they settled in the small town of Loire, which was less than twenty miles from Autun, where Jeanne Baret was born. In early 1762 Antoinette became pregnant but died shortly after giving birth to a son. As a widower, he inherited considerable resources from his late wife.

The question of when Dr. Commerson met Jeanne Baret is somewhat of a mystery. Jeanne likely gathered herbs near her parents' home in Autun and her skill in identifying plants may have become known to Dr. Commerson. Often learned men in botany sought out herbwomen to help them identify plants. Or possibly at some point between 1760 and 1764 Dr. Commerson may have been botanizing near Autun while Jeanne was gathering herbs and a meeting may have taken place. The complete answer to just how they met is unknown. However, sometime during this period Dr. Commerson hired Jeanne both as a household servant and assistant; as a person who could manage the household and also share her practical knowledge about plants and herbs with him. Furthermore, sometime before 1764 Dr. Commerson and Jeanne became lovers, as we know that Jeanne Baret was pregnant in 1764 and that all indications were that Dr. Commerson was the father.

What we do know for sure about the Commerson household is that in 1764, Dr. Commerson left his young son by his late wife in the care of a family member and that he and the pregnant Jeanne left Loire to travel to and live in Paris. For Jeanne, the travel to Paris opened a whole new world that was generally impossible for someone from her background. Because of Dr. Commerson's ill health, Jeanne became both a housekeeper, lover, caregiver, nurse, and conservationist about medicinal qualities of certain plants.

In early 1765 Jeanne gave birth to a son which she named Jean-Pierre. But Dr. Commerson had already left his first son with family and was not interested in caring for a second child. The result was that Jean-Pierre was given up to a special Parisian hospital where care was provided by a foster mother.

During the mid-eighteenth-century Paris was a center of education, commerce, and enlightenment. A major political conversation in Paris was that France was falling behind other European countries with respect to explorations and commerce throughout the world. In short, France needed to immediately begin to explore new territories throughout the world to increase her prestige, increase her colonial lands and to expand her trade opportunities.

Thus, in 1765, French King Louis XV, in an effort to improve the country's economy and to boost the image of France as a leading European nation, ordered his favorite son and military commander, Admiral Louis Antoine de Bougainville to make France's first global expedition to discover new territories, to improve trade, and to potentially investigate new products for France. Such an expedition would need a highly qualified naturalist to identify new plants that might have commercial and medicinal qualities benefiting to France.

In 1766, on the recommendation of Dr. Pierre Poissonnier, a French physician, professor, and member of the Paris Academy of Sciences, and based on Dr. Philibert Commerson's reputation, was invited by the well-known French admiral, navigator and explorer, Louis-Antoine de

Bougainville, to be Dr. Commerson's assistant as the royal naturalist on an around-the-world exploration voyage. Admiral Bougainville was popular and close to Louis XV. The Admiral had two ships, the *Boudeuse* and the *Etoile*, with a total crew of 300 assigned to this venture. During this worldly expedition, the Admiral would become the first Frenchman to sail around the world.

While Jeanne did not set out in life to become a worldly traveler, circumstances, mostly beyond her control, resulted in her becoming the first woman to circumnavigate the globe. With her intimate connection to Dr. Commerson. If he were to accept an invitation to become the royal naturalist on a worldly expedition, he would need help. He was not a well man, and not capable of handling the rigors of a long venture aboard a ship, nor hiking throughout new lands in search of undiscovered plants that might lead to health or commercial benefits for France. Dr. Commerson's solution would be to take Jeanne, who he trusted with his life, and who understood intimate details of plants, as an assistant co-naturalist on board the ship for this around-the-world adventure.

The only problem with this solution was that Jeanne was a woman. Women, based on a royal ordinance of 1689, were not allowed on French navy ships. Dr. Commerson and Jeanne decided that with careful costuming and imitations on her part, they might be able to pass her off as his *male* assistant. With considerable trepidations they decided to try it. Initially, the plan worked. Jeanne was able to board the ship without raising questions as to her sex. The question became: would this ruse work for the long, entire expedition? Dr. Commerson worked with Jeanne to carefully dress her as his male assistant. The most difficult part of dressing her as a male was to hide her breasts with bandages. In comparison to manipulating uncomfortable and tight bandages across her chest the rest of the male dress was relatively easy as males on board ship usually dressed in baggy clothes. A young female face, with male-type haircut and baggy clothes could be construed to imitate a young male – it had happened before.

In 1766, Admiral Bougainville's two ships, the *Boudeuse* and *Etoile*, were ready to set sail to circumnavigate the globe. Dr. Commerson and his assistant boarded the *Etoile* without difficulty. The ship's captain and 116 sailors on board accepted her as a male, using the rubric name of Jean Baret, as the male assistant to Dr. Commerson.

The ship's captain, Francois Chenard de la Giraudais, gave up his large cabin to Dr. Commerson and his "assistant" as they needed space to keep plants on board the ship. This gave Dr. Commerson and Jeanne the privacy they needed as well as a place to keep their supplies and later their plant specimens. Although she was nervous, she looked forward to the three-year voyage. The ship *Boudeuse* left first, and then the *Etoile* left the port of Rochefort in Nantes, France on February 1, 1767. Both ships later joined each other in Rio de Janeiro, Brazil. Jeanne knew she'd have difficulties adjusting to the protocols on board a navy ship, but by making certain adjustments she was able to make the initial voyage and beyond.

The *Etoile* first pulled into port in Montevideo, Uruguay. During this stop, Dr. Commerson, who suffered from seasickness and a recurring leg ulcer, felt ill, allowing Jeanne to leave the ship to identify and collect a variety of different plants. She brought back several specimens so that they could be logged into Dr. Commerson's record book. Their system of Jeanne doing the hard work of collecting plant specimens and bringing them on board so that she and Dr. Commerson could identify them was working.

From Montevideo they proceeded on to Rio de Janeiro where the *Etoile* caught up with the *Boudeuse*. Admiral Bougainville decided, while in this port, to carefully inspect both ships for needed repairs and to take on supplies for the long voyages that were next on the horizon. During Bougainville's inspection, based on his ship logs and journals noted after the voyage, he apparently concluded that it might be possible that Jean was a young lady. Whatever his reasons were, he decided not to reveal his findings nor to put her ashore at that time.

This long stopover gave Dr. Commerson and Jeanne an opportunity to botanize in the area where again, due to Dr. Commerson's health, the work of climbing through the brush and up the hillsides searching for plants fell to Jeanne.. Later, at one point in their botanizing, Dr. Commerson would refer to Jeanne as his "beast of burden" since she carried all the equipment and plants. Meanwhile, she was happy learning about plant life while seeing new lands and novel sights. The story goes that while in Brazil, as Jeanne climbed up a small incline, she discovered a woody vine with heart-shaped leaves and beautiful flowers. While there is no clear proof, but based on Dr. Commerson's reputation, or maybe it was her idea, he named this beautiful, newly discovered, woody vine plant after Admiral Bougainville: hence, the plant flower is now known as bougainvillea.

Bougainvillea
Forest & Kim Starr [CC BY 3.0 (http://creativecommons.org/licenses/by/3.0)], via Wikimedia Commons

**The plant discovered by Jeanne Baret, known as bougainvillea**
(Swapping Skirts for Trousers: The Price for a Trip Around the World, 2015)

The next stops were Argentina and Patagonia, both Spanish colonies, where Dr. Commerson and Jeanne collected additional plant specimens. Then, the *Etoile* and the *Boudeuse* began their arduous journey through the difficult Straits of Magellan, always a challenge for sailors due to the uncertain climate conditions and stress on the ship. This long stretch of ocean through the strait linking the Atlantic to the Pacific was known as Tierra *del Fuego*, in English as the Land of Fire, surrounded by many small islands. They noted the native inhabitants, whose ancestors had lived on the islands for over 12,000 years, to be quite healthy in adjusting to this cold climate. They saw considerable wildlife in the area, especially in the sea, including many species of dolphins and whales.

The two ships anchored along the shore of the main island for quite some time waiting for better weather conditions to allow them to sail through these treacherous waters. During several land stops, Dr. Commerson and Jeanne searched this southern part of Chile for medicinal plants. Glynis Ridley, in her book *The Discovery of Jeanne Baret: A Story of Science, the High Seas, and the First Woman to Circumnavigate the Globe* noted the following about Jeanne Baret: "She climbed rock faces and scrambled up and down scree slopes, bagging specimens of ferns, and lichen, anemone and grasses." Once through the Strait of Magellan, they sailed into the Pacific Ocean and on to Tahiti.

By 1767, the *Etoile* reached the island of Tahiti where they confronted a group of beautiful partially clothed native women. Interestingly, Admiral Bougainville named this new island *New Cythera* after the Greek Island of Cythera (now Kythera), the birthplace of Aphrodite, goddess of love and beauty. This encounter with the native women taxed the leadership of Admiral Bougainville in trying to keep his sailors in line to perform their necessary chores instead of their pursuing the beautiful native women. A few years later in 1789, Captain William Bligh, captain of the ship *Bounty*, had similar problems with his crew on Tahiti as his crewmen fell in love with the Tahitian women. This situation led to a "mutiny on the *Bounty*" which became a famous story and movie.

It was in Tahiti that Jeanne's gender was revealed. Apparently a group of Tahitian men immediately, either through scent or by some other means, recognized that the valet/botanist Jean Baret was a woman.

The ruse of Jeanne's identity changed the landscape of what to do next. Although there had been rumors about Jeanne's sex, it was in Tahiti that the mystery of her gender was over. The fact that a woman was on board his ship did not disturb Admiral Bougainville, but it presented problems with the crew, who now saw her in a different light. This meant that she had to always be on guard to avoid being a "sexual" object to the crew.

The next stop was a small island called New Ireland, a province of the large island of Papua New Guinea. There is speculation and strong hints in journals by some of the officers on board the ship, that while Jeanne was onshore in New Ireland collecting plants, unprotected, some members of the crew raped her. This caused her considerable trauma and this time the roles of Dr. Commerson and Jeanne were reversed. Dr. Commerson began treating her medical and emotional condition. From that point on, whenever the ship docked, she and Dr. Commerson took precautions to avoid any association with the crew.

After leaving New Ireland, their next destination was sailing to the Dutch East Indies. The Dutch East Indies yielded extensive types of spices in high demand by the upper classes in Europe. The Dutch guarded these Spice Islands with great care, as such spices, especially nutmeg, were like owning gold. The Dutch governor allowed them to obtain provisions and water but disallowed any botanizing or opportunities for obtaining spices.

Finally, in 1768, after two years of sailing, the ships anchored at Port Louis next to the city of Pamplemousses on the French territorial island of Mauritius. It was time to restock the ships with supplies before finally heading back home to France. After the many travails aboard the *Etoile*, Jeanne and Dr. Commerson decided to stay on the island as guests of Pierre Poivre, the highest-ranking French civil administrator of the island and a botanist in his own right.

Apparently one of the main reasons for staying in Mauritius was that Jeanne was pregnant from the rape incident on New Ireland. Both Dr. Commerson and Jeanne did not want to risk the possibility of giving birth on a vessel at sea.

An expected bonus for the pair of botanists was the large ninety plus acres of the Pamplemousses Botanic Gardens that had been constructed by Pierre Poivre. He was excited to have Dr. Commerson as a scientific colleague who knew so much about plants. Poivre had been thinking for some time about a special plant exploration project on the island of Madagascar. With Dr. Commerson here, it might be possible to begin the project. The only major drawback for Dr. Commerson, and hence Jeanne, was that once Dr. Commerson left Admiral Bougainville's expedition, he would no longer be on the French Government's payroll. And being a long way from his home in Paris, unable to access his financial resources in France.

Pierre Poivre gave Dr. Commerson and Jeanne excellent accommodations in his large colonial mansion. After two years at sea, they both relished the quiet and tranquil surroundings on the island of Mauritius. In one of their forays away from the city, they befriended a coffee plantation owner in the small settlement of Flacq who was fascinated by their knowledge about coffee plants. It was in the small community of Flacq, near the coffee plantation, where Jeanne's baby was born. Not knowing who the father was, and Dr. Commerson's lack of interest in raising a child, led to Jeanne giving the baby to the plantation owner who had no children and who had the means and interest in raising the boy.

While on Mauritius, they were informed by Poivre that the island of Madagascar, about 500 miles away, had an abundance of exotic plants. For years Poivre had wanted to visit and botanize in Madagascar, but his governmental responsibilities on Mauritius didn't allow the time he needed to do so. With Dr. Commerson and Jeanne, highly qualified and available, he was able, in 1770, to give them the official papers to investigate the plants on Madagascar.

They were amazed at the incredible number of plants and animals that had not yet ever been identified and named. For the four months that they were in Madagascar, they wrote that they felt like they were in "plant and animal heaven" and because of the unique location of Madagascar, the mostly isolated island was a virtual paradise for the growth of plants. Madagascar became known as the home to the profusion of plants and animals found nowhere else on the planet. According to scientists, more than 80 percent of Madagascar's over 14,000 plant species are found nowhere else in the world. Dr. Commerson and Jeanne were overwhelmed what they had found on the island. When they returned in 1771 to Mauritius, they continued their work of cataloguing the hundreds of plant specimens they had gathered from Madagascar.

In the meantime, Admiral Bougainville returned to France, and in 1771, he wrote a travel book about his circumnavigation of the world titled: *Voyage autour du monde par la fregate du roi La Boudeuse et la flute L'Etoile* or simply *"A Voyage Round the World.* He noted in the book that Jeanne Baret was on board the *Etoile* as valet and assistant to Dr. Commerson. His book revealed that it was his surgeon, Dr. Francois Vives, who was the first to discover that Jeanne was a woman. Dr. Vives was housed on the *Etoile* and had something to say in his written journals on board the ship which collaborated this comment. What we don't have is the opinion of the Captain of the *Etoile*, Francois Chenard de La Giraudais. He would have been required to keep a detailed log of the voyage of the *Etoile*. However, at some time after the voyage the log was either lost or destroyed. As a result the official comings and goings of the voyage was also lost.

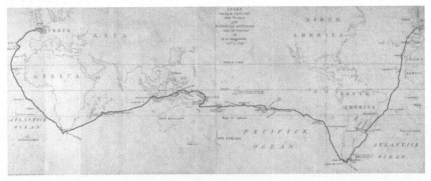

Bougainville's voyage.
From: Jeanne Baret: the first woman to circumnavigate the globe. Londa Schiebinger

**Map of Jeanne Baret's travels as shown in a
map in Admiral Bougainville's book**
(Swapping Skirts for Trousers: The Price
for a Trip Around the World, 2015)

Dr. Commerson's work on Mauritius was frequently interrupted due to his declining health. By 1773 he was bedridden with Jeanne constantly at his bedside to look after him. And finally, on March 13, 1773, at the age of 45, he died. Jeanne was devastated. The man that she had depended on for many years as a companion, workmate, lover, and provider was gone. This tragedy left her with minimal finances and certainly not enough for her to pay for a passage back to France. Now she was alone on Mauritius without a place to stay or means to pay for food and shelter.

While Dr. Commerson had provided for financial benefits for Jeanne in his will in Paris, there was no way for Jeanne to obtain any of those funds until she got back to France. What could she do in the meantime? After suffering from hardship and loneliness, she was able to get a job as a barmaid at a local tavern. But she knew that she would not be able to earn enough money for a trip back to France.

The tavern was near Port Louis which was frequented by many military personnel on their way back to France. At one point at the tavern, she was able to meet a French soldier named Jean Dubernat. They became friends and lovers and shortly thereafter, they were married in May 1774. Luckily, Jean Dubernat had enough rank and resources to obtain passage back to France for both of them. For Jeanne, once she left Mauritius and returned to France, she had, in effect, completed her circumnavigation of the world. She and her husband moved to Jean Dubernat's hometown of Saint-Aulaye. Jeanne did receive a considerable inheritance from Dr. Commerson's will. This allowed her and her husband to buy a house. They lived a comfortable rural life together. Jeanne died in Saint-Aulaye on August 5, 1807 at the age of 67.

Having circumnavigated the world, Jeanne's legacy as a worldly traveler was not initially recognized. Likewise, her work as a naturalist and her collection of exotic plants that provided important information for the scientific community only became known at a later time. Jeanne did not keep a diary of her travels, but there were ships logs and writings by Admiral Bougainville and Dr. Commerson and a few others to confirm her worldly travels and her work as a botanist. Dr. Commerson, in his notes, credits and honors Jeanne as the first female to circle the globe, noting that Jeanne should be recognized for her collections and recordings of plants.

Jeanne Baret was somewhat of an enigma to much of the world, as it is difficult to find the facts of her life, her accomplishments as a botanist, and her status aboard the *Eioile*. Initially, there was little recognition of her circumnavigation of the globe and her considerable contributions. While on Madagascar searching for new plants, Dr. Commerson and Jeanne came across a plant that Dr. Commerson named *Baretia* in recognition of her considerable scientific contributions to botany. However, the genus of this plant was later reclassified as *Turraea*.

While it took a while, a decade after these voyages, the French navy recognized Jeanne Baret's achievements. Even though she was a woman, the government authorized a yearly pension for her. The French government recognized her accomplishments in 1785 with these words: "Jeanne Baret, by means of a disguise, circumnavigated the globe. She devoted herself in particular to assisting Dr. Commerson, a doctor and botanist, and shared with great courage the labours and dangers of this savant." One more tribute in recognizing Jeanne Baret as a *worldly traveler*.

In Admiral Bougainville's travelogue, he noted this about Jeanne: "…she well knew when we embarked that we were going around the world and such a voyage had raised her curiosity. She will be the first woman that ever made it, and I must do her the justice to affirm that she has always behaved on board with the most scrupulous modesty. She is neither ugly nor pretty and is not yet twenty-five." From an Admiral who knew that Jeanne disobeyed French navy policy, this is high praise and provides world recognition that Jeanne was the first female to circumnavigate the globe.

An additional honor for Jeanne that came about in 2012, a few hundred years after her unexpected, awe-inspiring voyage, was the fact that botanist Eric Tepe named a new plant, *Solanum baretiae*, in recognition of Jeanne's accomplishments of collecting plants under very difficult circumstances. She was curious, courageous, and determined to see the world and leave behind a legacy as the first female to circumnavigate the world.

*Solanum baretiae*
By Tepe E, Ridley G, Bohs L (2012) [CC BY 3.0
(http://creativecommons.org/licenses/by/3.0)], via
Wikimedia Commons

**Plant discovered by Jeanne Baret,
later called Solanum baretiae**
(Swapping Skirts for Trousers: The Price
for a Trip Around the World, 2015)

# CHAPTER EIGHT

# AN ADVENTUROUS SCIENTIFIC EXPLORATION EXPERIENCE WITH CHARLES DARWIN

"Nature is full of infinite causes which
were never set forth in experience."
-Leonardo da Vinci-

*It was one of those cold, damp, rainy days prevalent in early spring in England as a boyish Charles Darwin awakened from a restless sleep. He had been dreaming of running through a forest of magnificent tall trees surrounded by pretty multi-colored flowers. In the dream, he chased beautifully colored butterflies. Then, all at once, he saw himself on the ground seeking out and picking up beetles. It was his curiosity about nature that ultimately enticed him to travel. Yah, beetles.*

*Charles was sickly as a child. Afflicted by various illnesses, he was often forced to stay in bed. To pass the time, he entertained himself by reading about different places in the world that perhaps he might one day visit. One of his favorite hobbies was collecting franked international postage stamps. He loved to observe the different colors and markings on each stamp as well as its country of origin. Then he would retrieve his set of maps and locate the particular nation from where the stamp came, thinking that, yes, one day he might visit such a destination.*

\*   \*   \*

C harles Robert Darwin was born February 12, 1809 at The Mount, a large Georgian home in Shrewsbury, Shropshire, England. He lived in an exciting time when great changes were taking place throughout the world. New philosophy emerging in this era came about in 1848 when Karl Marx and Friedrich Engels published the Communist Manifesto. The nineteenth century saw many of the great empires crumbling or on the verge of doing so. These great empires included those of Portugal, Spain, China, Ottoman, Holy Roman, and Persia. Different theories and new ideas were bandied about in terms of determining the best form of government. There were monarchies, dictatorships, democracies, and everything in between during this century. On the other hand, the Kingdom of Great Britain and the Kingdom of Ireland merged to form the United Kingdom. Furthermore, during this century, Britain began to reach its peak as an empire, controlling almost a quarter of the world's population and developing into an overseer of a huge land mass. Charles Darwin noted, during his worldly travels, that he was able to find British citizens wherever he went, which was often very comforting and helpful to his work.

The nineteenth century awakened the world to the evils of slavery. The Slavery Abolition Act of 1833 abolished slavery in the United Kingdom. The thirteenth amendment of the United States Constitution abolished slavery in the United States in 1865 after a bitter Civil War. Finally, the last major country in the Western world to abolish slavery, Brazil, did so in 1888. A form of slavery, known as serfdom in Russia, was abolished in 1861.This social progress seemed to invigorate the world, and the century saw unprecedented movements toward inventions and industrialization. Improved transportation, more favorable world economies, and the desire of people to travel began to grow.

As exploration and adventurous travel blossomed in the nineteenth century, there were many great explorers/travelers during Charles Darwin's lifetime. Mentioned later in this chapter is Charles Darwin's favorite explorer, Friedrich Alexander von Humboldt, the impressive German explorer, geographer, and naturalist who traveled extensively in South America. Another who captured world attention, especially in Great Britain, was the Scottish physician/explorer David Livingstone. His explorations of Southern and Central Africa, his quest to find the source of where the Nile River began. His discovery of Victory Falls captured the imagination of people around the world. Much of the world followed his expeditions in Africa. Given his fame and his large following, it was a shock to many when no one heard from him for six years. So in 1869, Henry Morten Stanley organized and headed an expedition to search for David Livingstone. After considerable travel, in 1871, Stanley was able to locate a very sickly and exhausted human being and greeted him with the now famous words: "Dr. Livingstone I presume?" To which Livingstone replied: "Yes, I feel thankful that I am here to welcome you."

We'd be hard pressed not to mention the impressive nineteenth century French statesman and military leader Napoleon Bonaparte and many of his successful campaigns in the early part of the nineteenth century. Between 1804 and 1815, Napoleon was the best-known individual in all of Europe. In 1804, after a successful military victory, he named himself Emperor of France. By 1807, he controlled the greater part of Europe. Things changed in 1815 when the British defeated Napoleon at the Battle of Waterloo in Belgium. Under the military leadership of Arthur Wellesley, the 1st Duke of Wellington, the British military sent Napoleon into exile on the British island of Saint Helena. Napoleon's defeat and exile brought much relief to Europe, allowing them to breathe more easily and move ahead.

Other changes in the nineteenth century stirred the imaginations and curiosities of adventurers and explorers throughout the world. This century saw the United States of America experience its greatest Manifest Destiny. With the "Louisiana Purchase" for $15 million from France in 1803, the United States almost doubled its land mass and began expanding westward. After buying Alaska in 1867 for $7.2 million from Russia and conquering land from Mexico, Britain, and Native Indians, the United States was fast-moving toward becoming a powerful nation. The Napoleonic Wars were finally over, which hastened the United Kingdom to flex its muscles and become the world's major colonial power under the banner of the Victorian era. At the same time, Portugal and Spain were losing their influence and holdings in South America. The dynamics of change during the century opened new opportunities for exploring and traveling. It was not just the adventurers who took advantage of these new opportunities.

Charles became one of our most famous naturalists. His discoveries and theories of the species of life are well-known by the scientific community and by many in the general public. What is lesser known about this scholarly individual is that much of his knowledge about nature and natural selection resulted from his five-year voyage on the ship *HMS* (abbreviation for His/her Majesty's Ship) *Beagle*. Naming a ship after an animal was common in the British Royal Navy. In fact, this particular *HMS Beagle* was the third of nine vessels to be called the Beagle. And this ship became known around the world as a result of Charles Darwin's travelogue and scientific journal writings resulting in his famous book called *The Voyage of the* Beagle. It was the travels, explorations, and scientific discoveries made during the voyage aboard the *HMS Beagle* that led Charles Darwin to study and write about the evolution of the species.

**H.M.S. Beagle**
(HMS Beagle 1:60 Scale, OcCre. n.d.)

\* \* \*

182

He was born on February 12, 1809 at The Mount, a large Georgian home in Shrewsbury, Shropshire, England. He was the fifth of six children in the wealthy family of Robert and Susannah Darwin. Robert Darwin was strong-willed and controlling, traits which likely contributed to making him a highly successful physician and businessman. Susannah Darwin was a well-educated lady and from the English society family, the Wedgwood's, who were well-known for their wealth and artistic pottery.

Charles' grandfather on his father's side of the family was Erasmus Darwin, a medical doctor, naturalist, evolutionist, and author. Sadly, Erasmus Darwin died prior to Charles' birth. However, he left many published and unpublished papers behind, which became important reading materials for Charles. His grandfather on his mother's side of the family was Josiah Wedgwood, an intelligent, wealthy broadminded thinker and nonconformist, who had also had a great impact on Charles' life. Thus, Charles grew up in a family of learned, open-minded, and ambitious adults.

The English society of this era was generally conservative. The Church of England, referred to as the Anglican Church, heavily impacted the daily life of most British households. In the eighteenth century, the well-known philosopher David Hume, as well as various other famous philosophers, put forward many enlightened ideas. Hume's writings on naturalism, including his well-known publication of *A Treatise of Human Nature*, became important concepts for Darwin's own studies of naturalism. Hume's views on religion, especially with respect to organized religion, later on, kept him from obtaining the chair of philosophy at the University of Glasgow.

With respect to religion, Charles' parents and grandparents on both sides of the family were Unitarians. They were freethinkers, and within family discussions, they crossed the line in questioning the Anglian Church's views. However, the family was careful in public not to voice many objections to the Church as such a move might counter against their successful businesses and social standing in the community. It was not good politics to argue with a Church representing the views of an overwhelming majority of the population. Charles, while baptized as an Anglican, initially attended Unitarian church services and later, after his travels, became an agnostic.

When Charles was sixteen, he worked one summer with his father helping to administer medical treatment to the poor in Shropshire, England. His job was to record the patient's medical histories and, in so doing, attempt to make a diagnosis of the person's illness. Based on this initial work experience, his father immediately saw in his son potential for Charles to become a successful doctor. With this career in mind for Charles, his father sent him off to study medicine at the University of Edinburgh in Edinburgh.

Within a short time, Darwin found his medical studies boring regarding a career in medicine. He took a couple of courses in natural history, excited and fascinated by many subject matters. Certainly, he had some of the right genes for studying natural sciences. His grandfather, Erasmus Darwin, had conducted extensive research on the metamorphosis of flowers which he published in a poetic work called *The Botanic Garden*. Some of Erasmus' other research related to natural science and his views on evolution had raised eyebrows throughout the country and beyond. His viewpoints greatly influenced Charles' future studies and outlook on life.

Charles' father was highly displeased that his son was neglecting his medical studies to meddle in the business of studying natural sciences. So he pulled him out of the University of Edinburgh and sent him to study divinity at Christ's College in Cambridge, England. Here, Charles dutifully studied and received a Bachelor of Arts degree that was consistent with preparing him to become a minister in the Anglican Church. However, a career as a minister in the Anglican Church did not appeal to him. During his theological studies, he was most inspired by professors and friends who discussed books and information on botany. He became interested in becoming a naturalist. The more he read and studied, the more excited he became about yearning for a career in this field.

One particular professor at Christ's College, Reverend John Stevens Henslow, became Charles' dear friend and had a lasting influence on his life and career. Professor Henslow was a Professor of Botany who saw scientific work as consistent with religious natural theology. This combination appealed to Charles, and under the tutelage of Henslow, he began intense reading in such areas as natural science, natural history, and natural philosophy. He read the first volume of the book called *Principles of Geology* (1830), written by the great Scottish geologist Sir Charles Lyell. Lyell became recognized for demonstrating the power of known natural causes in explaining Earth's history. Later, Charles was able to become his good friend, and much later, they consulted when Charles was writing his own book, titled *On the Origin of the Species*. In this book, Charles noted that: "He who can read Sir Charles Lyell's grand work on the *Principles of Geology*, which the future historian will recognize as having produced a revolution in natural science yet does not admit how incomprehensibly vast have been the past periods of time, may at once close this volume."

Charles accepted the work and writings of Georges Cuvier, the French naturalist and zoologist who was involved in the fields of comparative anatomy and paleontology.

Professor Henslow took him on field trips in the area and taught him about many different aspects of natural history, including botany, entomology, chemistry, mineralogy, and geology. He also made arrangements for Charles to accompany the renowned professor of geology, Adam Sedgwick, on a geological trip to North Wales. Little did either professor realize just how soon their protégé would be putting his studies to practice...?

At the request of Captain Robert FitzRoy, in 1831, the British Admiralty was searching for a "gentleman naturalist" who would accompany FitzRoy during the voyage of the *HMS Beagle*. He was looking for company: fortunately, Charles, became that gentleman. Though the 22 year-old student lacked many academic credentials and experience as a naturalist, Charles was chosen for the position by *HMS Beagle*'s Captain Robert FitzRoy.

Charles' father strenuously objected to this venture for his son, as he saw no long-term opportunities for a career in such an endeavor. Wanting his father's approval, Charles initially rejected the offer from Captain FitzRoy. However, other family members convinced his father that it was a unique opportunity for the young man. Reluctantly, his father agreed to his son's wishes. Once his father accepted the idea of the journey, he insisted on helping with expenses for the voyage. Had Charles not been chosen, or had he not accepted the position, it is likely he would have had a career as a clergyman in a local community or rural area somewhere in England. However, chosen, and he became e world's most recognized scientific worldly traveler.

The main mission of the voyage of the *Beagle* was to be a two-year expedition to map the east and west coasts of South America. An additional objective was to complete a series of chronometric readings and other measurements while circumnavigating the globe. Chronometric readings were an essential method used by navigators to determine longitude. Of equal importance was the charting of shorelines and navigable waters, a technique known as Hydrography, a relatively new initiative by the British Royal Navy in the 1830s and important to the safety of English ships. Also of interest to the British government was to learn more about the natural history of the places to be visited as well as the culture and heritage of the inhabitants.

Professor John Henslow kept in touch with Charles throughout his five-year voyage on the *Beagle*. They corresponded on a regular basis, to the degree that the antiquated postal service allowed. Professor Henslow looked after many of the specimens sent to London by Charles during his voyage. The professor saw to it that Charles' samples were appropriately and quickly analyzed. He also published information from Charles' letters in scientific journals. So, by the time Charles returned from the five-year voyage, he was already recognized as a budding scientist thanks to Professor Henslow. Later in life, in an 1861 letter written to one of Charles' friend, the famous British botanist and explorer Joseph Hooker, Charles wrote: "I fully believe a better man than my Professor John Henslow never walked this earth." In Charles' autobiography, he acknowledged that Professor Henslow was the most important person in his whole career.

**Charles Darwin (pictured on the right) and**
**Professor Henslow (pictured on the left)**
(Charles Darwin – the Man Behind the Evolution, 2015)

The voyage on the *Beagle* forever changed Darwin's life. The two-year planned trip became five years of physical hardships and mental challenges. They traveled to Brazil, Uruguay, Argentina, Chile, Ecuador, El Salvador, the Falkland Islands, Peru, Australia, and Tahiti. And the *HMS Beagle* was ideally suited for a world surveying venture. It was a *Cherokee*-class ten-gun brig-sloop, 90 feet long and 24 feet wide. The British Royal Navy had more than 100 ships in this class. According to Charles, there were 74 individuals on board the *HMS Beagle* for this voyage. It was so crowded that he had to sleep in a hammock slung above the drafting table in the poop deck, the back cabin.

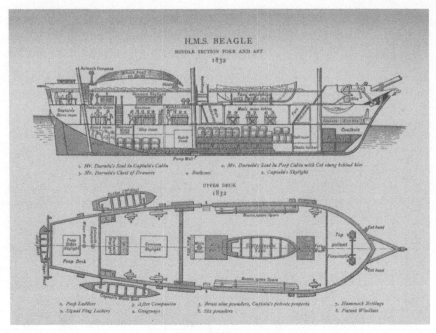

**H.M.S. Beagle**
(King, 2014)

Charles and the rest of the *Beagle's* crew were extremely fortunate to have an experienced leader in Captain Robert FitzRoy, who was from a wealthy family that was well-connected with the British Admiralty. The Captain's seamanship had been thoroughly tested, and he received high marks for leadership from the British Admiralty. Charles learned to appreciate his great intellect and knowledge of many different subject areas. Captain FitzRoy had already circumnavigated the world on an earlier trip; he knew the *Beagle* inside and out. In fact, he had completely refitted the *Beagle*, making her not only fully seaworthy but a ship with all the trappings that needed on this voyage, including an impressive library. In many respects, Captain FitzRoy became another mentor to Charles, regarding areas new to this young naturalist.

Captain FitzRoy wrote in his journal at the beginning of the voyage; "Never, I believe, did a vessel leave England better provided or fitted for the service she was destined to perform, and for the health and comfort of her crew, than the *Beagle*. If we did want anything which could have been carried, it was our own fault; for all that was asked for from the Dockyard, Victualling Department, Navy Board, or Admiralty was granted."

On this voyage, the *Beagle* followed a continuous 360-degree route around the world. While he was a member of the crew, Charles was, in reality, simply a passenger with limited knowledge of the sea. He had the basic responsibility of noting natural attributes of plant and animal life and making other observations, including of the culture and heritage of the inhabitants when opportunities arose to go ashore. While Charles was not an experienced naturalist, he kept studying intensely topics as geology, mineralogy, entomology and energy.

The circumnavigation of the world by the *Beagle* was to begin on December 26, 1831. However, much of the crew was missing, and others were suffering from drunkenness from celebrating Christmas the day before. As a result, the voyage of 74 men, according to Charles' count, began on December 27, 1831, as they departed from Falmouth, England. As the *Beagle*, heaved on the upward swell of waves, with the susurration of the wind producing sounds of the sails snapping in the strong breeze. And this jolly wind and rocking waves taking place throughout the entire trip caused Charles to become seasick. Many times during the voyage, he questioned his judgment in joining such an expedition! Yet, he began to realize, once underway with stops planned in the Spanish Canary Islands and the Island Republic of Cape Verde off the western coast of Africa, what such a voyage could mean! Everything was new and he was fascinated by the geological structure of the Cape Verde Islands, entering this in his diary.

During the initial phases of the voyage, Charles felt useless since he had no sailing experience. He could only contribute research knowledge with respect to his position as a naturalist. Once into the journey, he studied and read about natural history and related fields every day, grateful that Captain FitzRoy was a learned individual, with the *Beagle* having a state-of-the-art library of about 400 volumes. He became interested in the work of the famous German physical geographer, naturalist, explorer, and worldly traveler Baron Alexander von Humboldt.

Humboldt's book, *Personal Narrative of Travels to the Equinoxial Regions of America during the Years 1799-1804*, described his own five years of traveling and exploring the plants, animals, and cultures of numerous countries. The book, in six volumes, was released each year from 1799 until 1804. Humboldt's travels had taken him to Brazil, Venezuela, Columbia, Cuba, Ecuador, Peru, and Mexico. These books became Charles' principal handbooks. Later in life, Charles referenced Humboldt's findings many times in his own publication, *The Voyage of the Beagle*. In effect, Humboldt's writings had an overpowering impact on Charles in much the same way that Marco Polo's book had influenced Christopher Columbus. As far as Charles was concerned, Humboldt was his role model; "...the greatest scientific traveler who ever lived...I have always admired him; now I worship him."

Another major influence on Charles' education aboard the *Beagle* was that of Professor Charles Lyell, who had given him a copy of his new book, titled *Principles of Geology*. This book and Charles' close relationship with Professor Lyell, his mentor, had a major impact on our young traveler and his approach to nature.

After a few months into the voyage, the *Beagle* made a brief stop in Pernambuco, Brazil, and then, on February 29, 1832, it anchored off Bahia, Brazil. When the boat dropped anchor, Charles was ready to begin his work in earnest. He jumped off the rowboat as it approached the shoreline, he was so eager to investigate plant and insect life in the forests near Bahia.

Charles enjoyed every moment in the dense jungle canopy and the majestic rain forests adjacent to Bahia. The luxuriant foliage was well populated with numerous species of beetles, (ah, beetles,) spiders, and other insects which he collected. When he saw the first rainforest of his life, he was amazed. He wrote in his journal about every detail of his investigations and explorations. He noted: "...To a person fond of natural history, such a day as this brings with it pleasure more acute than he ever may again experience..." Yes, a prodigious note-taker, his diary of the voyage eventually reached 800 pages. As a prolific letter writer, fortunately, his expressive letters sent back to England survived and added more information on his many adventures.

Charles and some of the crew got a special treat on March 4, 1832 when the Bahia Carnival and other festive activities commenced. Brazilians, then and now, know how to have an exciting time dancing, drinking, and merrymaking during the carnival season. Charles, at six foot two and being an extremely light complexioned individual, definitely stood out in the crowd. As a result, he received a great share of attention during the celebrations. This was all a part of the wonderful tourism event and festival. However, right after the celebrations, he went right back to work. After collecting many specimens of plants and animals in the region, he gladly reboarded the *Beagle* and began arranging and classifying his finds.

On the Brazilian portion of the trip, the next stop of the *Beagle* was in Rio de Janeiro, a hotbed of revolutionary and political uprisings during the 1830s. While Charles loved much of what he saw of the people of Brazil, he was dismayed from his observations of the treatment of the slave population. While Brazil struggled for independence from Portugal, her neighboring Spanish-speaking countries had successfully extricated themselves from Spanish rule; Brazil was anxious to accomplish the same results with respect to its mother country, Portugal. For Charles, anxious to get into the interior jungle areas, the political events meant many bureaucratic delays. However, he finally got permission and traveled inland, overcome by the beauty of the interior of Brazil and its exotic plant and animal life; truly a naturalist's heaven. Charles always brought his collections on board the *Beagle*, and the ship headed south. Luckily, he was given a big cabin by the Captain.

Leaving Brazil, it was time to head towards Montevideo and Maldonado, Uruguay, where he next disembarked. Uruguay also had political problems and an internal civil revolt on its hands. Once things settled enough, Charles left the *Beagle* and went ashore. As in Brazil, he was amazed at the variety of plant, insect, and animal life. He also met local gauchos, and in numerous conversations with them, became enamored with their exploits, their horsemanship, and their freedom to live as they pleased. Also catching his attention, and duly noted in a letter to his dear sister Caroline, was the beauty, poise, and exoticness of the Uruguayan women.

The *Beagle*, anchored on a river dividing Uruguay from Argentina, allowed an opportunity for Charles to also explore Argentina. It was from Buenos Aires that he sent the first 100 pages of his travel diary and many specimens from his collection to Professor Henslow at Christ's College. Eventually, these notes and other documents would be included in his book, *The Voyage of the Beagle*.

In Buenos Aires, he partook in several social events including a presidential ball. As in Uruguay, he was smitten by the beauty of the Argentinean women, and wrote about them in another private letter to Caroline. However, he spent most of his time in the outback areas of Argentina and became fascinated conducting research in Patagonia.

As in Brazil, even with respect to his observations of slavery, Charles continued his rigorous travel throughout the area to observe the remarkably different kinds of flora and fauna and to collect numerous bones of extinct mammals. Often, during his explorations, he became quite ill and needed bed rest, but he recovered and moved forward with his work. Again, finding new specimens of plant and animal life that added to his collection. We imagine his stateroom.

In 1833, the *Beagle* rounded Cape Horn, at the southern end of the Tierra del Fuego archipelago of Chile. This is the farthest point of the South American continent. One of the passages through this archipelago which the *Beagle* took was by way of the Strait of Magellan. The waters around Cape Horn are particularly hazardous for sailing, owing to strong winds, cold weather, giant waves, strong currents, and icebergs. Sailors obviously hated the area, knowing the dangers and of the many shipwrecks that had taken place. Charles wrote in his diary: "It is a grand spectacle to see all nature thus raging, but Heaven knows everyone in the *Beagle* has seen enough in this one summer to last them their natural lives." His observations and experiences were similar to those of his predecessor Jeanne Baret; however, her work and travels, and that of Dr. Commerson, were not known to him.

Many crew members, though exhausted and sick, fulfilled their mission in mapping the coastline. Here Charles briefly went on land to observe the native Fuegians, an experience which he later described: "...nothing... more completely astonished me than the first sight of a Savage; it was a naked Fuegian, his long hair blowing about, his face besmeared with paint. There is in their countenances, an expression, which I believe, to those who have seen it, must be inconceivably wild. Standing on a rock he uttered tones and made gesticulations than which, cries of domestic animals are far more intelligible..." Charles was amazed that, despite the cold weather, the people went about their business naked, keeping themselves warm with fires.

Not long after a second passage past Cape Horn in 1834 to map the coast, Charles and the crew of the *Beagle* witnessed a major volcanic eruption. The *Beagle* and its occupants were frightened by the impact the earthquake had on both land and sea. Later, in a voyage off the coast of Tahiti, Charles remembered this encounter with the earthquake in Chile and became fascinated by the Tahitian volcanic island of Moorea. He was greatly moved by such natural phenomena. He later wrote in *The Voyage of the Beagle*: "We feel surprise when travelers tell us of the vast dimensions of the Pyramids and other great ruins, but how utterly insignificant are the greatest of these when compared to these mountains of stone accumulated by the agency of various exceptionally small and tender animals! This is a wonder which does not at first strike the eye of the body, but, after reflection, the eye of reason."

Following his voyage down the long seacoast of Chile, Charles wrote; "July 23, 1834, the *Beagle* anchored in the Bay of Valparaiso, in the seaport community of Concepcion, Chile." The crew was happy to go ashore after their difficult encounter around Cape Horn.

As it turned out, there were many British living in Concepcion, Chile, which surprised and comforted Charles, and he even came across an old schoolmate. There were also bundles of mail from England for him, including a considerable number of documents from Professor Henslow. The specimens and diary notes he had sent back earlier had arrived back to England in good order and had created extensive interest and excitement in the scientific community. But Charles, like many members of the crew, was still quite ill from the effects of rounding Cape Horn, and sought a chance to rest. He decided to stay with his classmate friend to recover. As he began to feel better and after happy times socializing with the locals, he was anxious to get back to work.

His next destination was to the capital, Santiago, Chile, to obtain permission to travel throughout the country. Here he had the opportunity to socialize and to observe the people and customs of the area. He was particularly enamored with the Chilean women and noted in his journal "...where there were several pretty senoritas..." In general, he seemed fascinated with the looks, dress, and customs of South American women. His focus, always on his work.

Though Charles was not in the best of health, his spirits were good, and he was anxious to explore the Andes. He quickly organized supplies and obtained guides for this next set of adventures. He noted the air in the Andes was crisp, cool and soothing. The valleys were beautiful and picturesque, and he found the magnificent mountains to be alluring as the trip began. He wrote in his diary: "I did not cease from wondering at finding each succeeding day as fine as the foregoing. What a difference does climate make in the enjoyment of life...How opposite are the sensations when viewing black mountains, half enveloped in clouds, and seeing another range through light blue haze of a fine day...August 14th [1834] ...and ...I set out on a riding excursion for the purpose of geologizing the basal parts of the Andes..."

While his expedition neither took extra food nor made provisions for shelter, the Chilean farmers and ranchers were more than happy to provide him with whatever he needed. This trek and his explorations and specimen collecting, lasted a long time. By March 7, 1835, he was high in the Andes heading toward Portillo Pass near the Chile-Argentine border. At this point, he now succumbed to altitude sickness in the mountains, which included a fast heart rate and heavy breathing. However, the beauty of the area and his work were enough to keep him going.

In June 1835, after more than 200 miles overland by horse and walking, he came down from the mountains into the seaport of Copiapo, Chile. The *Beagle*, according to previous plans, waited at anchor in the bay. The ship was a welcome sight after this exhausting land excursion. The long trek had been well worth it. His journal now contained over one hundred pages about what he had seen, his accomplishments, and about the culture of Chile. In his notes about the Chilean Patagonia, he was amazed at its splendor, an amazing showcase of glaciers, beautiful lakes, scenic rivers, snow-capped mountains, lively marine life, pristine wilderness, and unique flora and fauna. After a brief stop in Iquique, Chile on July 16, 1835, he joined the crew and they continued the voyage toward Peru.

Initially, Charles was disappointed with his six weeks' stay in Peru. While he was fascinated to learn about Inca history, he was less than impressed with the communities and natives of the area. He found the people crude, the weather during his stay to be miserable, and the political uproar among the landowners depressing. The negative political situation kept him from going too far into the interior, and it was only when he arrived in the capital, Lima, that he had some pleasant days.

Possibly the large number of British merchants in Lima and the good conversations with the British consul general helped him gain some respect for the Peruvian culture. Maybe, more importantly, it was the Peruvian women that caused him to be interested. His writings in his diary reveal that: "Their [Peruvian ladies] close elastic gowns fit the figure closely and oblige the ladies to walk with small steps, which they do very elegantly and display very white silk stockings and very pretty feet..."

Charles' last visit in South America occurred on September 17, 1835, when the *Beagle* put into the cove of Chatham Island, an island within the Galapagos archipelago, over 600 miles from the mainland of Ecuador. Ecuador had claimed the islands a few years earlier after the country had received its independence from Spain. Though not initially, the visit to the Galapagos quite possibly influenced Charles the most. Several years later, after he had an opportunity to study his notes from the specimens he found in the Galapagos, he understood the importance of all he had observed. The evolutionary sequences of birdlife that he observed here became the basis for his book on evolution, *On The Origin of Species*.

When he first left the *Beagle* in the Galapagos, he was disappointed. He had hoped to find an island jungle paradise overflowing with flora and fauna. What he initially discovered, for the most part, was volcanic rock which supported little, if any kind of life except for giant tortoises weighing several hundred pounds. However, as he moved to another island of the Galapagos, he found about 300 people living there in exile. They had been sent to the island by the Ecuadoran government for politically related offences. It happened that the leader of this small enclave was an Englishman who was happy to see a British ship, since most of the visits to the islands were whaling vessels. He became a helpful guide for Darwin's work.

Each island here was unique with different, but limited, plant life, birds, and reptiles, but containing especially numerous land iguanas. From his notes, he wrote in his book in 1839 that "The natural history of this archipelago is remarkable: It seems to be a little world within itself; the greater number of its inhabitants, both vegetable and animal, being found nowhere else." It was Charles' study of bird life, especially the finches, which eventually led him to his theory of evolution. After exploring these islands for five weeks, it was now time to head back to England.

Returning to England, the *Beagle* crossed the South Pacific with stops in Tahiti, New Zealand, Australia and Tasmania. The wildlife in Australia also fascinated Charles. He noted: "Anyone who has faith in his own reasoning is sure to cry out: Surely there have two creators at work here – one for Australia and one for the rest of the world."

The ship then rounded the Cape of Good Hope, passing on to Bahia, Brazil for the second time, and finally returned to Falmouth, England on October 2, 1836. The planned two-year voyage had taken four years and two hundred seventy- eight days, a remarkably extensive voyage around the world. The crew was indeed happy to be back on English soil.

Charles' journey was of epic proportions. It resulted in biological and natural science breakthroughs that would forever change the way such sciences would be viewed in the future. Charles noted the following about his voyage: "As far as I can judge of myself, I worked to the utmost during the voyage from the mere pleasure of investigation and from my strong desire to add a few facts to the great mass of facts in natural science."

His work had major impacts on religion as well as on the social sciences, anthropology, geology, and psychology. He left as an amateur naturalist and returned triumphantly as a seasoned botanist, biologist, geologist, and naturalist. He became an instant celebrity in the scientific community. His father, originally skeptical about Charles making the voyage, arranged for business ventures such that Charles Darwin would be able to be a gentleman scientist.

The voyage of the *Beagle* was also highly successful for Captain Robert FitzRoy and the rest of the crew, who returned as heroes for the work they had accomplished in mapping the coastlines of South America. In May 1839, Captain Robert FitzRoy wrote a four-volume account of the two voyages of the *Beagle*; the first voyage was that of Commander Philip Parker King, and the second voyage was under his command. The title of this excellent book is Narrative *of the Surveying Voyages of His Majesty's Ships Adventure and Beagle.* Later in life, in recognition of all his naval accomplishments, Captain FitzRoy was promoted to Vice Admiral of the British Navy.

In May 1839, Charles wrote an account of his travels based on his abundant notes, titled *The Voyage of the Beagle*. His writings, travel notes, and scientific presentations were so well received internationally that its impressive acclaim overshadowed the work of Captain FitzRoy. This book made Darwin a popular author, and it impacted heavily on his other work *On The Origin of Species*, which was published in 1859. Over the years, the first book became one of the most widely known and discussed books on travel. It made Charles Darwin famous at age 29. Chapter nineteen of the book is devoted solely to his visits on the Galapagos Islands, which eventually led to his theories of evolution.

**Charles Robert Darwin, age 31**
(Biography of Charles Darwin: The
Theory of Evolution, 2015)

In his *Autobiography*, written in 1876, Charles acknowledged that his worldly trip on the *Beagle* had been, he wrote in his autobiography: "The Voyage of the *Beagle* has been by far the most important event in my life and has determined my whole career. I have always felt that I owe to the voyage the first real training or education of my mind. I was led to attend closely to several branches of natural history, and thus, my powers of observation were improved, though they were already fairly developed."

In 1839, Charles married his first cousin, Emma Wedgwood. Typically, he made a list of the pros and cons of marriage, including such items as not being lonely in later life and included such comments as "...object to be loved and played with...better than a dog anyhow." While the comment might seem unduly harsh out of context, it was well-known that he loved and adored his two dogs. His life from that point on became devoted to his research and studies at his home and he fathered ten children, seven of which survived to adulthood.

Much of his continued research included time reviewing his notes from his travels, especially the time spent investigating bird life on the Galapagos Islands. Eventually these studies and his work with Alfred Wallace, a researcher who had similar ideas, led to his bestselling book on the theory of evolution: *On the Origin of* Species. This document still sparks controversial debates throughout the world.

Charles' books on evolution were widely accepted by the scientific community and the general public. Early on, though, even when his research and evidence made clear that all species of life evolved over time from common ancestors, there was condemnation of this concept by most Christian religious sects. Most religions believed that life in all its detail was created by God, with no room for species to evolve into different shapes and sizes. Charles, the early student of theology, was accused of being anti-God and anti-religion, he had become an agnostic.

Later in life, Charles Darwin became more famous; the father of modern biology, a famous author, the most renowned evolutionist, and a noted world traveler. Who would have thought that Charles, who suffered throughout his life from various illnesses, would explore the most remote regions of the world? From getting seasick frequently during his voyages on the ship, *HMS Beagle*, to succumbing to differing ailments in far off places in South America, Charles continued his journeys and his work as a naturalist with few delays. The beauty of the areas he visited and the new plants and animals he discovered uplifted his spirits and infused new energy to his body, allowing him to continue his travels. These experiences and acute observation of the environments constantly inspired him, changing his life, leaving a legacy of new ideas to challenge views of the universe. This worldly traveler had, over the years, achieved a major impact on world views with respect to naturalism.

It is interesting to note that when he died in 1882, he was buried in the famous Collegiate Church of St. Peter at Westminster, which is usually referred to as Westminster Abbey.

**Charles Darwin**
(McNamara, 2019)

The worldly travelers discussed so far in this book had a certain curiosity and persistence that carried their spirits and bodies through perilous travel. Their minds were always full of ideas, always curious to know what the next part of their trip would deliver.

Had Charles not taken the journey on the *Beagle*, it's almost certain we would never have heard of him. But he did, and his experiences as a worldly traveler significantly impacted the world. His legacy not only included his research and immensely popular books, but it also his cherished image as one of the renowned scientists of England. There are many geographical features and species named after him. He was elected as a Fellow of the prestigious Royal Geographical Society in 1838, a learned world-renowned society for science. Later, Charles' son became a member of the Society, and he became its president in 1908.

Appreciating his amazing work as a conservationist always interested in the sustainability of the flora and fauna, a hot topic in today's world. In the Galapagos Islands, the Charles Darwin Research Station exits, supported by the Charles Darwin Foundation. Ironically, the Galapagos, so important to the work of Darwin, these days, have been under heavy siege by the world's travel community. Ecuador is faced with the need for tourist dollars to support their economy, and at the same time, must sustain and protect the natural life on the Galapagos for future generations of visitors to enjoy.

**Monument to Charles Darwin on
the island of San Cristobal**
(Charles Darwin – The Man Behind the Evolution, 2015)

As a worldly traveler, Charles noted in the conclusion of *The Voyage of the Beagle* that "…it appears to me that nothing can be more improving to a young naturalist than a journey in distant countries. It both sharpens, and partly allays that want…and the chance of success, stimulate him to increased activity…as the traveler stays but a short time in each place, his descriptions must generally consist of mere sketches, …But I have too deeply enjoyed the voyage, not to recommend any naturalist…to take all chances and to start on travels by land if possible, if otherwise, on a long voyage…In a moral point of view, the effect of traveling ought to be to teach the traveler good-humored patience, freedom from selfishness, the habit of acting for himself, and of making the best of every occurrence… Travelling ought also to teach him distrust, but at the same time, he will discover how many truly kindhearted people there are, with whom he never before had or ever again will have any further communication, who yet are ready to offer him the most disinterested assistance."

While Charles' worldly travels lasted only five years, he experienced a lifetime of adventures. His books, *The Voyage of the Beagle* and *On the Origin of the Species*, created international interest in nature, culture, geography, and in the conservation of all-natural resources. His scientific writings that all species of life have descended over time from common ancestors became the foundation of the theory of evolution universally accepted in today's world. While he received numerous international awards, his receipt of the famous Copley Medal, the most prestigious scientific award in Britain, in effect notes his ability to change the world through his international travels. The award further confirms that Charles Darwin was truly a great worldly traveler.

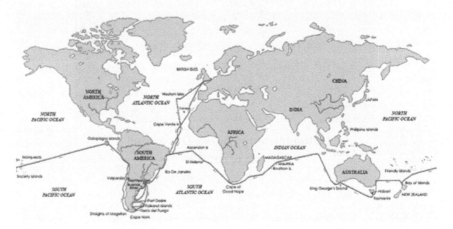

**A map depicting the "Voyage of the *Beagle*"**

# CHAPTER NINE

# MARK TWAIN
# INNOCENT WAYFARER

"...In a moral point of view, the effect of
traveling ought to be to teach him, the traveler
good-humored patience, freedom from
selfishness, the habit of acting for himself, and
of making the best of every occurrence..."
-Charles Darwin-

*Jane Clemens was not feeling well at all and called for her
husband, John, to come to her bedside. "John, I think I'm
going to give birth tonight."*

*"But," said John, "It's too early; you aren't due for another
two months."*

*That night, a premature baby joined the world, and he
was baptized as Samuel Langhorne Clemens. He was so
fragile neither parent thought he would live. He barely
survived, and was mostly bedridden until age four. He
continued in his frail condition until he was seven. Later,
as a grown- up, he challenged the proverbial expression
"a cat has nine lives" in his many close encounters with
death; especially a few times as a non-swimmer wading
in the Mississippi River.*

*As Sam grew older and became physically able, he explored the rural countryside near home. Full of life, enthusiastic, and anxious to play games with siblings and other friends, he became a real prankster, in and out of trouble at home, church, and school. He couldn't understand why his teacher sent him to the blackboard to write a hundred times that, "I, Sam, will not do that again," just because he dipped the ends of the ponytail of the girl in front of him in his inkwell. Sleeping in church seemed a good use of his time until his snoring got him in trouble. Later in life, he used his early childhood experiences, embellishing them a bit, to write "The Adventures of Tom Sawyer".*

\* \* \*

One of the most interesting, humorous, and unique travelers and travel writer ever to travel the globe is none other than our Mark Twain. No one could make travel facts and stories come alive with greater excitement, which he accomplished in many books and lectures on travel. His jocular humor, often sarcastic remarks, and unusual prose made the descriptions of world travel come alive. As much as any traveler before him or since him, he ignited an American passion for foreign and domestic travel in the nineteenth century. He truly had a "gypsy soul" and never had to psych himself up to travel. He was born to wander, possessing the strong urge to explore the world.

The middle of the United States of America in the early part of the nineteenth century was a wonderful time and place for young Mark Twain to grow up. Fascination with frontier life and the allure of nearby forests and rivers was especially attractive to this bright, curious lad. Most of the Midwest of America was still primitive. For the woodsmen and the frontiersmen, there was plentiful game to shoot and opportunities for moving about to trap animals to supply the large demand for furrier products in Europe. For farmers, ample rich land could be gotten for very little money. Other people interested in starting a new life and those who valued their privacy and independence were clearly welcomed to the frontiers of America. Also, adventurers and entrepreneurs could be found throughout the region seeking their fortunes.

The first eleven years of Mark Twain's life offered him an environment that lent itself to adventures in the woods and bluffs along the Mississippi River. He traversed nearby areas to play, fish, and run with his boyhood friends. Even as a young boy, he enjoyed telling stories of his exploits, and occasionally added a few tall tales to make the story more exciting.

It was from his early boyhood that his sense of humor evolved. First, it was childhood pranks played on his friends. Later on, he found that stretching the facts a bit and adding humorous anecdotes often attracted an admiring audience, whether they attended his lectures or read his books. Some of Mark Twain's childhood characteristics and experiences on the rural frontier of America emerged through certain characters in his books, such as *The Adventures of Tom Sawyer* and *The Adventures of Huckleberry Finn*.

*   *   *

During Mark Twain's lifetime, 1835-1910, the world was experiencing many changes. Some of these were mentioned in the previous chapter about Charles Darwin. Just two years prior to the birth of Mark Twain, the British Empire abolished slavery. The "slave issue" and its consequences in the United States would be of concern to Mark Twain for many years.

By 1835, the Spanish, Portuguese, Chinese, Holy Roman, and Mughal empires had collapsed. In its stead, the British Empire emerged as the dominant global force, controlling a quarter of the world's population and a third of the land area. The British Empire was constantly challenged by other nations seeking to establish or maintain their colonial holdings.

The Dutch Boer farmers were now entrenched in the British Empire's Cape Colony in South Africa, as they disliked the British governance and the British laws abolishing slavery. In 1836, between 10,000 to

14,000 Boers began what was to be known as their Great Trek away from British rule and towards new lands to occupy. In order to make the move, they battled the natives in the area who were led by King Ndebele. At the Battle of Vegkop, in October 1836, the Boers overpowered King Ndebele and settled in an area of Africa away from the British.

Also in 1836, in a different part of the world, the famous in U.S. history "Battle of the Alamo" in the Mexico Territory of Texas took place. The Army of the Republic of Mexico besieged a revolutionary group of Texans in the Territory of Texas in the San Antonio de Valero Mission, known simply as the "Alamo." The entire garrison of Texans, including the famous frontiersman and former United States Congressman from the U.S. State of Tennessee Davy Crockett, were killed. Later that year, on April 21, 1836, at the Battle of San Jacinto in the Territory of Texas, a decisive battle of the Texas Revolution took place. The Texan Army, led by General Sam Houston, engaged and defeated Mexican President and General Antonio López de Santa Anna's Mexican army. The Texans gained their independence from Mexico and in 1836 became an independent country: "The Republic of Texas."

Also in the 1830s, during the administration of U.S. President Andrew Jackson, who had been a U.S. hero during the war with Great Britain in 1812, the United States Congress passed the Indian Removal Act (1830) at the behest of President Jackson. This terrible Act within the history of the United States of America led to the removal of over 60,000 Native American Indians from their homelands east of the Mississippi River to territory west of the Mississippi River designated by the United States Government as "Indian Territory" between the years 1830-1850. So many thousands of Native American Indians died along the trails from the east to the west during this removal, causing this removal to be known as the "Trail of Tears."

By 1845, the U.S. Congress adopted a resolution for the annexation of The Republic of Texas to become part of the United States of America. This move by the U.S. Congress led to the Mexican-American War (1846-1848). In 1846, the U.S. Congress voted overwhelmingly to approve a declaration of war against Mexico. By the war's end in 1848, Mexico had lost nearly half its territory. Under the Treaty of Guadalupe-Hidalgo, the Rio Grande became the southern boundary between the U.S. and Mexico.

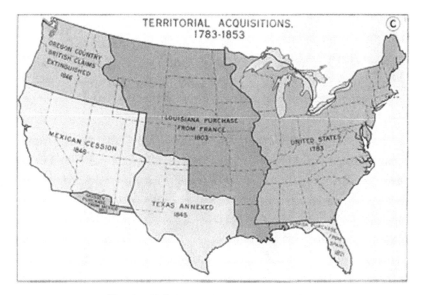

**Territorial Acquisitions: 1783 – 1853**
(The Great Debate: The Annexation
of Texas, 1845-1846, n.d.)

One of the greatest tragedies within the nineteenth century is the lesser-known Taiping Rebellion, also referred to as the Taiping Civil War in China. This civil war occurred in China from 1850-1864 between the established Qing dynasty and the so-called Taiping Heavenly Kingdom religious group. The rebels were led by Hong Xiuquan, a self-proclaimed "brother of Jesus", who called himself "Tianwang" or "Heavenly King". The rebellion failed with the deaths of more than 20 million people.

The Crimean War that took place from 1853-1856 proved to be a domination test between European Powers and Russia over disputed lands made available from a declining Ottoman Empire. It was fought with the Russian Empire and Bulgarian Legion on one side and the French, Ottoman, and British Empires and the Kingdom of Sardinia on the other; in the end, the pairing of the Russian Empire and Bulgarian

Legion were defeated. The war clearly pointed to Britain and France as the superpowers of that era.

In 1860, Abraham Lincoln was elected President of the United States of America which, among other political happenings, led to the United States becoming engaged in the devastating Civil War in 1861. This event had considerable impact on the life of Mark Twain. By 1865, the United States Civil War ended as the country re-emerged as a union. In the same year, U.S. President Abraham Lincoln was assassinated, and slavery was abolished in America.

In 1863, the formation of the International Red Cross was co-founded by Henry Durant and Frederic Passy. It was adopted by the First Geneva Convention in 1864. As a result, Henry Durant and Frederic Passy received the first-ever Nobel Peace Prize, given in 1901.

In 1868, the "Glorious Revolution" in Spain took place, and Queen Isabella II was deposed. The revolutionary leaders recruited Italian prince Amadeo of Savoy as king. Two years later, he was replaced by the first Spanish Republic. But in 1875, another change was made, and Queen Isabella's son was named King Alfonso XII of Spain.

The Franco-Prussian War of 1870-1871 led to a major defeat of France and was an important victory for the unification of the German states under the leadership of Prussia. One principal result was the elimination of French influence over Germany. This war gave Germany considerable prestige and set in motion Germany's powerful influence in European affairs.

The latter part of the nineteenth century saw many political changes taking place in Europe, the first of which occurred when Humbert I, Count of Savoy, was crowned King of Italy in 1878. Other major changes included William II, the "Kaiser", becoming emperor and King of Prussia in 1888 and Nicholas II being proclaimed the Czar of Russia in 1894. Toward the end of the century in 1898, the United States declared war on Spain over its inhumane treatment of the people of Cuba. The United States easily defeated Spain and emerged, in the eyes of the world, as a world power with a new stake in international politics. In addition, the nineteenth century saw America change from a basic agrarian society to one encompassing the Industrial Revolution that had begun in Europe.

Closing out some of the important events taking place in the nineteenth century, it is befitting to mention the re-introduction of the Olympics in 1896. As noted earlier in this book, in the chapter introducing our worldly traveler Herodotus, the Olympic Games were begun in Greece in 776 B.C.E. After several hundred years, the Olympic Games were dropped. However, the Olympics were revived in 1896 with the 1896 Summer Olympics, which became known as the Games of the I Olympiad. Properly so, the Olympics were held in Athens, Greece. They have been held every four years since, except for World War I and II, and each time located in different countries throughout the world.

By the end of the nineteenth century, with the advent of the expansion of travel by improved rail cars, more efficient and extravagant steamships on the oceans, and the development of the automobile, the travel industry was transformed into a major worldly commercial activity. This fueled the greater movement of people and goods and increased urbanization throughout the world. Inventions and technological changes were rapidly taking place, further adding to a dramatically changed world in the nineteenth century.

\*     \*     \*

Samuel Langhorne Clemens was born November 30, 1835 at the time when Halley's Comet was closest to earth. This reference to Halley's Comet would be a special memory to him for the rest of his life, and among the last things he thought about when he was dying seventy-four years later.

Here's another view of his life offering an important, different look. His birthplace was a log home in the very small rural community of Florida, Missouri, in the mid-west of the United States. Sam, his name used by family and friends, was the sixth of seven children. Despite suffering a premature birth, he survived and grew up to be a healthy young man. His father, John Marshall Clemens, tried many different careers including farming, business ventures, and investment speculation and basically failed in all of them. His mother, Jane Lampton Clemens, came from a well-educated family and had a significant impact on Sam for much of his life. By the time Sam was four, the family had moved 35 miles from Florida, Missouri to the small town of Hannibal, Missouri located on the Mississippi River.

**Samuel Clemens, age 15**
(Nix, 2014)

Sam attended school when he could, in a one-room schoolhouse, where it was difficult to find teachers willing to live in such a remote rural environment. Most of his early education came from a care-free life exploring the surrounding area near his home, occasionally getting into minor trouble. In 1847, when Sam was eleven years old, his father died of pneumonia. Deaths were commonplace on the frontier. For example, of the seven children born into the household, only Sam and three siblings survived to adulthood.

Around the time of his father's death, Sam spent time living and working on a large farm owned by his aunt and uncle. He loved this experience, and it is among the fondest of his childhood memories. Slavery was common in much of Missouri at the time, and his uncle's farm had many slaves. Many of Sam's young friends were slave children. As a child, he did not really understand what slavery was all about. Later, early in adulthood, he came to believe that ownership of slaves was terribly wrong. This realization hit him especially hard when he saw slave men and women chained together waiting in port cities along the Mississippi River to be shipped down river and sold in the slave market in New Orleans. Later he wrote: "Those were the saddest faces I have ever seen."

By age twelve, Sam became a printer's apprentice to his older brother, Orion, who owned a small local newspaper called the *Hannibal Journal*. Sam always admired his brother who was older by ten years. At that time, apprenticeships in the trades were common for mature boys and young men in both Europe and America. Sam quickly became enamored with the newspaper, learning new skills in his brother's business. He began to submit articles and humorous sketches for the newspaper; this, of course, was the aspect of the job he loved the most.

At age eighteen, Sam left home to become a beginning printer in the cities of New York, Philadelphia, St. Louis, and Cincinnati. During this period of his life, he became self-educated, which meant his education was dependent on visits to the libraries in the cities he worked and lived in. When his brother, Orion, Orion's wife, and Sam's mother moved to Keokuk, Iowa, he joined them. He went to work in the print shop for his brother's paper, the *Keokuk Post*. His wages as a printer were very low and to supplement his income, he wrote interesting letters for the *Keokuk Post* under the pen name Thomas Jefferson Snodgrass. This was one of many monikers he used throughout his life.

After Sam became twenty-two, he took a voyage down the Mississippi River to the city of New Orleans. On this trip, he chanced to meet a steamboat pilot who took a liking to him and convinced him to seek a career as a riverboat pilot. Steamboat pilots were highly skilled individuals. They needed to understand every nuance of the river in order to navigate the treacherous and ever-changing Mississippi River. Much of the attraction to becoming a pilot was the extremely high pay. By 1859, after two years of intense study and traveling up and down the river, he received his pilot's license.

Sam convinced his younger brother, Henry, to work with him. Later, while employed on another steamboat, Henry was killed when the boat exploded. Sam was devastated by his brother's death, blaming himself for the tragedy. However, he continued on as a steamboat pilot until 1861 when the United States Civil War broke out and traffic along the Mississippi River was temporarily halted. On a lark, Sam joined a rebel Confederate militia, the Marion Rangers, but the circumstance was more akin to an adventure than to a serious commitment and only lasted two weeks before he quit and traveled to the West. He described the Civil War as: "A blot on our history [United States], but not as great a blot as the buying and selling of Negro souls [slaves]."

His Mississippi experiences stayed with him for life, providing much material in enhancing his writing career. Had the Civil War not interfered, he might have had a long career as a river boat pilot. For him, the river had a spirit and language all its own that only a boat captain could understand.

His most popular pen name, "Mark Twain", came from a Mississippi River steamboat term. Leadsmen on steamboats measuring depths of the river would call out measurements as "quarter twain", "half twain", and, when reaching a safe depth, "mark twain". From the first time he used the pen name "Mark Twain", it stuck, and from that point on in his career, he was most often referred to as Mark Twain. And so shall we.

**Clemens piloting a steamboat**
(King, 2015)

When Mark Twain's steamboat pilot career on the Mississippi River came to an end, he again joined his brother Orion. This time, Orion was no longer connected to a newspaper. Instead, Orion had just been appointed secretary to the new Nevada territorial governor, James W. Nye.

The two brothers traveled to Nevada by overland stagecoach across the Great Plains and Rocky Mountains. Along the way, they had fascinating and exciting adventures. Mark Twain made notes of these interesting travel experiences, which led to two successful travel articles titled "Roughing It" which was later expanded into a book, and "The Celebrated Jumping Frog of Calaveras County." The latter article was published in the *New York Saturday Press*.

Even with the mild successes as a writer, Mark Twain did not yet embrace writing as a career. He wasn't sure what to do other than he wanted to earn money at whatever occupation he chose. He tried his hand as a Nevada silver miner and failed miserably. When he was offered an opportunity to work for the Virginia City, Nevada newspaper, the *Territorial Enterprise,* he jumped at the chance. He continued to have success as a writer and decided it was time to venture to the cosmopolitan city of San Francisco, California to further his writing career.

Shortly after arriving in San Francisco in 1866, Mark Twain accepted a travel writing opportunity that took him to Hawaii, which was not yet a United States territory, under the sponsorship of the *Sacramento Union* newspaper, a California newspaper. His assignment on this trip was to write interesting letters about his travel experiences for publication in the newspaper as human-interest stories. He loved Hawaii and stayed for four months, sending back twenty-five letters. With its laid-back nature, it reminded him of the rural environments where he had grown up, except, of course, for the wonderful weather, exotic flowers, and beautiful scenery. He was often reminded of Hawaii later during his many trips to the British territory of Bermuda.

His humorous letters for the *Sacramento Union* were of such great interest that the San Francisco newspaper *Alta California* dubbed him a travel correspondent and hired him to send back stories on a trip from San Francisco to New York City. These two trips, to Hawaii and New York, were the beginning of his career as a popular travel writer.

In early 1867, Mark Twain's newspaper writing successes led the *Alta California* to fund a five-month voyage abroad for him on the first transatlantic pleasure party vessel called the *Quaker City*. This extensive journey took him through much of Europe and the Middle East and his agreement with the newspaper was to write and send back publishable travel letters.

The ship finally set sail from New York in June of 1867. On board were 79 passengers, most of whom were religiously inclined and had booked the trip to learn more about the Holy Land and to visit the great cathedrals of Europe. Initially, Mark Twain tried to fit in with the church crowd. However, the church services and other observances were not compatible with his character and interests. Well, he found a few good old boys on board, and spent much time drinking, carousing, playing poker, and occasionally swearing. A few passengers let it be known they did not appreciate such activities. That did not stop him from continuing his partying.

On this trip, Mark Twain became a true worldly traveler. The ship proceeded first to the Azores, islands in the North Atlantic Ocean that were 900 miles off the coast of Portugal. It continued on to Gibraltar, a peninsula between Spain and Morocco. Then the ship visited the Italian cities of Genoa, Leghorn, Naples, and Palermo, the Greek cities of Athens and Corinth, and Marseilles, France. From there, it was on to Constantinople, Sebastopol, Russia, Smyrna, Turkey, Beirut, Lebanon, Jaffa, Israel, and Alexandria, Egypt. On the return voyage, the vessel stopped in Bermuda, a beautiful British island territory in the North Atlantic Ocean that was 500 miles due east of the U. S. state of South Carolina. Mark Twain fell in love with Bermuda and eventually made several visits to this wonderful destination.

Once the ship arrived on the distant shores of Europe, at each port, Mark Twain's keen wit, satiric charm, and engaging laughter overcame the tour group's objections to his earlier pranks and other mischievous activities. He became the consummate unofficial tour guide and amusing commentator to the joy and excitement of those who surrounded him. He had a fine time and not only observed the great historic buildings and artworks, but also took in the characteristics and movements of the people he saw and met along the way. In his many speeches and writings, he reveled in human folly and hypocrisy. He mocked and lampooned European customs and manners, and on occasion, made facetious and tasteless remarks about their culture. However, he always did so in colorful prose with humorous intentions and for the benefit of his listeners. At the same time, he made fun of the American travelers to Europe. His fellow travelers were in constant mirth with Mark Twain's humor.

He noted: "The human race has only one really effective weapon, and that is laughter."

Because of a cholera epidemic in Italy, on the ship's arrival to Greece, all passengers were forced to be quarantined for eleven days. Under penalty of being jailed, Mark Twain and three cohorts slipped away one night during the quarantine period to visit the Acropolis. While stealing grapes in a nearby vineyard, they were almost caught. The group rushed back to the boat just in time to enjoy the sunrise.

His travel excursions led to other trips and, eventually, he moved to Europe for several years. He was impressed with many of the sights and sounds throughout any journey. In some cases, he was totally depressed with the poverty and living conditions of the country or area, describing Palestine as "a hopeless, dreary, heart-broken land."

Like the worldly traveler Herodotus centuries before, Mark Twain was awed by the construction of the pyramid. He often made fun of important works of art or statues, but never about the Great Pyramid of Giza or the Sphinx, even with its nose broken off. It held certain serenity, noted in his words: "The Sphinx is grand in its loneliness; it is imposing in its magnitude; it is impressive in the mystery that hangs over its story...The great face was so sad, so earnest, so longing, so patient. There was a dignity not of the earth in its mien and in its countenance a benignity such as never anything human wore."

The Pyramid and the Sphinx left a lasting impression on him. It wasn't that the rest of the magnificent ancient sites in Egypt were lesser feats of architecture and engineering; the Pyramid and the Sphinx awed visitors who saw them, often left them speechless.

His wit, humor, and sarcasm came through loud and clear with his descriptions of the passengers during a voyage. "They were to sail for months over the breezy Atlantic and the sunny Mediterranean; they were to scamper about the decks by day, filling the ship with shouts and laughter – or read novels and poetry in the shade of the smoke-stacks, or watch for the jelly-fish and the nautilus over the side, and the shark, the whale, and other strange monsters of the deep; and at night they were to dance in the open air, on the upper deck, in the midst of a ballroom that stretched from horizon to horizon, and was domed by the bending heavens and lighted by no meaner lamps than the stars and the magnificent moon-dance, and promenade, and smoke, and sing, and make love..."

This voyage became the basis for his most successful travel book *The Innocents Abroad,* published by the American Publishing Company in 1869. A humorous account of American visitors in Europe, he wrote: "This book is a record of a pleasure trip. If it were a record of a solemn scientific expedition, it would have about it that gravity, that profundity, and that impressive incomprehensibility which is so proper to works of that kind, and withal so attractive." He went on to say: "It [the voyage] would be well if such an excursion could be gotten up every year and the system regularly inaugurated. Travel is fatal to prejudice, bigotry, and narrow-mindedness, and many of our people need it sorely on these accounts."

Well, it almost didn't get published. Mark Twain had a contract that said he must deliver the manuscript in July of 1868. He wrote the book in 60 days and met the deadline, but for months after, nothing happened. He immediately went to Hartford, Connecticut, to see his agent. The agent said the directors of the company were afraid to publish the book; they thought the book had too much humor in it and was a complete departure from any previous books they published. However, the publishing company was in deep financial trouble, and when Mark Twain warned them about breaking the contract, they reluctantly published a few copies. It immediately became popular and sold so many copies it took the publishing company out of debt. The result was that Mark Twain became very famous and rich beyond his dreams, which led to the publishing of many more books.

Of his five books on travel, *The Innocents Abroad* was his bestselling travel book. In its first year, this book sold three times as many copies as the initial edition of *The Adventures of Tom Sawyer,* a book also well-known in American literature.

The fact that *The Innocents Abroad* became so popular actually caught his imagination in such a way, that he was enticed to travel and write for the next thirty years. He loved to travel, write, lecture, and live well. In 1867, during the voyage of the steamship *Quaker City,* he met Charles Langdon, the younger brother of Olivia Langdon. Legend has it that Charles showed Mark Twain a miniature painting of Olivia Langdon on ivory, and Mark Twain fell in love with her the moment he saw the painting. In 1968, he courted Ms. Olivia Langdon through correspondence. She was a lady from a wealthy family with liberal ideas and a love of social equality. Her father was not impressed with Mark Twain initially, and he was against the courtship. However, as one might guess, the ever-clever conversationalist Mark Twain was able to win over most everyone he met. Thus, in 1870, Mark Twain and Olivia Langdon were married in Elmira, New York. With her, he met abolitionists, socialists, atheists, and activists of women's rights and social equality. They had multiple children, including three daughters and a son who died of diphtheria at the age of 19 months.

In 1872, he expanded his notes from the 1860s on his travels across the western part of the United States into a book called *Roughing It*. This book followed some of the same patterns of travel writing that he had produced in *The Innocents Abroad*, except that *Roughing It* was a recollection of early land trips in the western part of the United States, which was taken from notes and memory before he became so popular.

In the beginning of *Roughing It*, he noted: "This book is merely a personal narrative and not a pretentious history or a philosophical dissertation… Still, there is information in the volume; information concerning an interesting episode in the history of the Far West, about which no books have been written by persons who were on the ground in person and saw the happenings of the time with their own eyes…"

One of the characters in this book was the well-known western desperado named Jack Slade. Mark Twain became enamored by the stories of Jack Slade, and he noted in an article called "Stagecoach Tales and Slade's Untimely Death" which was later included in *Roughing It*, that "…Day or night, now, I stood always ready to drop any subject at hand, to listen to something new about Slade and his ghastly exploits…" Mark Twain did encounter Jack Slade at a stagecoach stops and noted that, in his presence at least, Slade was cordial and polite. Phew!

Mark Twain wrote about Jack Slade in two chapters of *Roughing It*, partly because he was fascinated by this famous gunslinger and because he was eager to share the details of their interactions from the one occasion in which they met. Before Wild Bill Hickok became well-known as a western gunslinger, Joseph Alfred "Jack" Slade was the gunfighter everyone in the West feared. He wasn't as vicious as he was made out to be unless he was drunk. At one point, he worked as a stagecoach division superintendent for the Central Overland stagecoach line. The stagecoach line was having constant problems with outlaws attacking the stagecoaches until they hired Jack Slade to supervise that part of the route. Since he had a reputation as a tough guy, suddenly, under his supervision, the attacks stopped. Jack Slade was also associated with the Pony Express and hired a young rider named William F. Cody, later to be known as Buffalo Bill. Jack Slade was generally an excellent employee until he got drunk, at which time he degenerated into a brawling, dangerous man. His drinking and outlandish behavior eventually got him fired, which led to his own death. There were many myths about him having killed several people, but the records seem to confirm only two such events. Mark Twain, not yet famous, read about the stories about Jack Slade and imagined him a tough guy – until he met him on a stagecoach trip.

**Jack Slade**
(Desperado Jack Slade, 2020)

In his book *Roughing It*, Mark Twain described his meeting with Jack Slade in 1861 at a rest stop of the stagecoach this way: "The coffee ran out. At least it was reduced to one tin-cupful, and Slade was about to take it when he saw that my cup was empty. He politely offered to fill it, but although I wanted it, I politely declined. I was afraid he had not killed anybody that morning and might be needing diversion. But still, with firm politeness, he insisted on filling my cup and said I had traveled all night and better deserved it than he – and while he talked placidly, he poured the fluid to the last drop. I thanked him and drank it, but it gave me no comfort, for I could not feel sure that he would not be sorry presently that he had given it away and would proceed to kill me to distract his thoughts from the loss. But nothing of the kind occurred…Slade came out to the coach and saw us off, first ordering certain rearrangements of the mailbags for our comfort, and then we took leave of him, satisfied that we should hear of him again someday and wondering in what connection…"

Mark Twain heard of him a few years later after Jack Slade went on a drunken shooting spree in Virginia City, Montana and was lynched by local vigilantes on March 10, 1864.

In 1880, Mark Twain wrote *A Tramp Abroad*, relating his travels throughout Germany and Austria in 1878. By the time he visited Europe the second time, he was already famous and could no longer travel as an unknown tourist. So he experienced the sights and sounds of tourism as a celebrity. Sometimes he appeared to be providing a history of an area, and it's only after one recognized that it was a humorous mockery of the location or event that it became apparent that the facts were irrelevant. He enjoyed adding his own interpretations and humor to local legends in the countries he visited to make them more enjoyable to his audience.

In *A Tramp Abroad*, a reader may make many interpretations of what was intended with the title. Was it a story about a vulgar promiscuous woman who flouted propriety as she traversed the continent? Or interpreted as a vagrant wandering around aimlessly to make a living among tourists? Or was it a journey on foot throughout Europe? As Mark Twain put it: "One day it occurred to me that it had been many years since the world had been afforded the spectacle of a man adventurous enough to undertake a journey through Europe on foot. After much thought, I decided that I was a person fitted to furnish to mankind this spectacle. So, I determined to do it. After a brief rest at Hamburg, we made preparations for a long pedestrian trip southward in the soft spring weather, but at the last moment we changed the program, for private reasons and took the express train."

In 1883, Mark Twain wrote *Life on the Mississippi*, recounting his days as a river boat pilot on the Mississippi River. This book is autobiographical in that it reflects his many adventures on and along the Mississippi River. A different twist on travel from his earlier books as his experiences on the Mississippi River are described as travel adventures; although, he was really at home in the sense that it related to his youth on the Mississippi River and as a pilot on the river later in life. He didn't have to search for the facts or descriptions of the area because he lived and breathed them on the river. Traveling the river presented him a new scenario from the eyes of the traveler. Yet, he had difficulty differentiating his new experiences from his memory of twenty years ago on the river.

Mark Twain's last travel-related book was in 1897 when he wrote *Following the Equator: A Journey Around the World*. Based on his lecture tours in 1895 and 1896, he wrote about the trip that included stops in Australia, New Zealand, India, and South Africa. By this time, he was a mature traveler; yet on this trip, and particularly in India, he saw new sights in a different way as an observant tourist---maybe with less humor. In India, as his carriage passed a young Indian woman, he noted: "She is so straight, so erect, and she steps with such style and such easy grace and dignity; and her curved arm and her brazen jaw are such a help to the picture – indeed, our working-women cannot begin with her as a road-decoration." He did not explain why he described her in this way and leaves it to the reader to make his or her own judgment.

His acerbic approach in *Following the Equator* was closing out the *Gilded Age* in fine style, writing: "All the territorial possessions of all the political establishments in the earth – including America, of course – consist of pilfering from other people's wash. No tribe, however insignificant, and no nation, howsoever mighty, occupies a foot of land that was not stolen. When the English, French, and the Spaniards reached America, the Indian tribes had been raiding each other's terrestrial clotheslines for ages, and every acre of ground in the continent had been stolen and restolen 500 times."

Mark Twain enjoyed some special international destinations more than others. He loved the picturesque British colony island of Bermuda, which he visited eight times in his life. This beautiful island's charm completely enraptured him. He thought that Bermuda was one of the most delightful islands in the world, and had this to say about his last trip to Bermuda: "You go to heaven if you want to; I'd druther stay here [Bermuda]."

**Mark Twain in Bermuda**
(The Bermuda Adventures of Mark Twain, 2011)

Over his lifetime, Mark Twain made twenty-nine separate trips outside the continental United States, spending time in such waters as the Atlantic, Pacific, and Indian Oceans: the Mediterranean Sea, Caribbean Sea, Black Sea, Caspian Sea, and Aegean Sea. Additionally, he visited destinations that included India, the European Alps, and such cities as London, Paris, Berlin, and Vienna.

Mark Twain became the consummate traveler, and at one point, he wrote in a letter to his mother: "I am wild with impatience to move – move – move...My mind gives me peace only in excitement and restless moving from place to place. I wish I never had to stop anywhere."

In 1909, Mark Twain is quoted as saying: "I came in with Halley's Comet in 1835. It is coming again next year, and I expect to go out with it. It will be the greatest disappointment of my life if I don't go out with Halley's Comet. The Almighty has said, no doubt, 'Now here are these two unaccountable freaks; they came in together, they must go out together.'"

His prediction was near correct as, in 1910, Mark Twain died of a heart attack while at home in Redding, Connecticut within a day after the passing of Halley's Comet.

In our time, Mark Twain is certainly the most humorous author to write about travel and tourism. While Americans are most familiar with his novels, it was the writing of *The Innocents Abroad* that first caught the attention of the world. This book, more than the others, is most probably the reason he wrote on the back of an envelope: "I like history, biography, travels, curious facts, and strange happenings, and science."

Mark Twain was an extensive reader and owned hundreds of travel books, including country travel guides describing travels to various countries. His books and references included some of the worldly travelers mentioned in this book. For instance, he read the book written by Herodotus, and in one of his own books, he included direct quotes from Herodotus. Of course, he had to read the travel tales from Marco Polo's book, but it is unlikely that he read Ibn Battuta's *Rihla* (Journey) or knew about Zheng He's travels, as neither man was well-known at the time. His bookshelves contained Charles Darwin's travel book *The Voyage of the Beagle*.

Travel was the thread that stitched together Mark Twain's life as a printer, reporter, humorist, writer, lecturer, and adventurer. No one before or since has been able to write about travel in such a casual, humorous, and interesting way. His ebullient personality and ability to conjure up interesting happenings, when most travelers were narrowly focused on a specific site or sound, allowed him to extract more from his travels. He knew his audience well in the lectures he gave, and was able to gage his readers and their interests in the books he wrote.

Some of his contemporaries thought him indecent, vulgar, and irreverent. Yet he simply wrote things as he saw them, not worrying about critics and highbrow writers. For example, in his book *The Innocents Abroad*, he had this to say: "The gentle reader will never, never know what a consummate as he can become until he goes abroad. I speak now, of course, in the supposition that the gentle reader has not been abroad and, therefore, is not already a consummate ass. If the case be, otherwise, I beg his pardon and extend to him the cordial hand of fellowship and call him brother. I shall always delight to meet an ass after my own heart when I have finished my own travels."

With titles about travel such as these, The *Innocents Abroad*, *A Tramp Abroad*, *Roughing It*, *Life on the Mississippi*, and *Following the Equator: A Journey Around the World* are all so witty that you wanted to know what he had to say. In *A Connecticut Yankee in King Arthur's Court*, he captured our imaginations with time travel, following a person who traveled back in time and, in so doing, changed history.

Lecturing became most profitable for Mark Twain. At age 59, when most men thought of retirement in his era, he found himself deep in debt due to some bad investments. He had failed as a businessman and in dire need to raise money to pay off his debts. Even though he declared bankruptcy, which relieved him of certain debts, he was unable to stand the disgrace and took on a long lecture series, which had always been the easiest way for him to make money. He eventually paid off all debts as a result of these highly successful lecture tours. While the actual lecturing was easy and enjoyable for him, it was the logistics of getting from place to place on time that eventually wore him out.

**Mark Twain, the lecturer**

In *The Innocents Abroad*, his profundity of feelings, in terms of the impact travel had on the way one viewed life, he philosophically wrote: "Travel is fatal to prejudice, bigotry, and narrow-mindedness, and many of our people need it sorely on these accounts. Broad, wholesome, charitable views of men and things cannot be acquired by vegetating in one little corner of the earth all one's lifetime." Further on, he wrote; "We wish to learn all the curious, outlandish ways of all the different countries so that we can 'show off' and astonish people when we get home. We wish to excite the envy of our untraveled friends with our strange foreign fashions which we can't shake off."

While Mark Twain often made fun of Europe and Europeans, he and his family chose to live in Europe for several years because he did love the history and culture of the Europeans.

By the end of the nineteenth century, international travel had grown immensely; Europe was the most popular destination. Europeans included tourism experiences as part of their education. Gradually, Americans travelled abroad in large numbers. His amazing stories relating his own journeys certainly helped to usher in the age of tourism growth in America. He, more than any American before him, saw the value of enjoying the history, heritage, and culture of the places he visited as well as the impressive structures. His was the age when many Americans were traveling to Europe, and he was as excited as the next tourist about the prospects of what he would see and learn from his travels.

In *The Innocents Abroad*, Mark Twain wrote: "I basked in the happiness of being, for once in my life, drifting with the tide of a great popular movement. Everybody was going to Europe – I, too, was going to Europe." He often looked at other tourists through the eyes of an interested bystander, wondering what or why such people were traveling. His trio of books about his world travels, *The Innocents Abroad, A Tramp Abroad,* and *Following the Equator,* put him into a special category that no one before him or since him.

But did Mark Twain's humor and outrageous prose unwittingly contribute to the phrase of the "Ugly American", introduced in the media in 1948. In 1958 a book with the title *The Ugly American* was published.

The "Ugly American" at this time could be defined as "a male or female who was a brazen, unapologetic, and boisterous individual who traveled abroad with very little appreciation for the local culture or an understanding of the history and heritage of the destination visited."

In a major speech in 1868, Mark Twain introduced "The American Vandal Abroad" this way: "I am to speak of the American Vandal this evening, but I wish to say in advance that I do not use this term in derision or apply it as a reproach. I use it because it is convenient; and duly and properly modified, it best describes the roving, independent, free-and-easy character of that class of traveling Americans who are not elaborately educated, cultivated, and refined, and gilded and filigreed with the ineffable graces of the first society...for your genuine Vandal is an intolerable and incorrigible relic gather..." He describes the Vandal's opinion of a celebrated old painting of "The Last Supper" in this way: "The Vandal goes to see this picture – which all the world praises – looks at it with a critical eye and says it's a perfect old nightmare of a picture and he wouldn't give forty dollars for a million like it, and I endorse his opinion, and then he is done with

Milan..." After having fun with a dose of sarcasm with the travel of the "Vandals" and he coyly admits he is a leader of the "Vandals", he closes his speech "The American Vandal Abroad" with this message: "If there is a moral to this lecture, it is an injunction to all Vandals to travel, I am glad the American Vandal goes abroad. It does him good. It makes a better man of him. It rubs out a multitude of his old unworthy biases and prejudices..."

He was another of the worldly travelers to change the world as a result of traveling. Antecedently, in his book *The Innocents Abroad*, he introduced to the world of the mid-nineteenth century a new approach to international travel never realized until he came along. His three books on international travel not only tracked his personal views of travel, but they formed an image of a new concept of Americans traveling abroad.

As Mark Twain grew in stature through his international travel experiences and as he engaged in more conversations with many of the world leaders, he became a true internationalist who gave us a broad, new view of the world during the Industrial Revolution. Whether the issues at hand were local, national, or international, he readily gave his views on the topics being discussed.

"When I finished Thomas Carlyle's book, *The French Revolution, A History* in 1871," he wrote, "I was part of the French moderate republican party called the Girondins. Every time I have reread this book, I've read it differently – being influenced and changed, little by little, by life and environment...and now I lay the book down once more, and recognize that I am a Sansculotte, a member of the French Revolution militant partisans! And not a pale, characterless Sansculotte, but a Marat like Jean Paul Marat, the French revolutionary leader."

His legacy through his travels and writings also gave the world a view of Americans who traveled abroad in the mid-nineteenth century.

Mark Twain's celebrity status allowed him to meet many international leaders throughout the world and to gain insights into the politics, cultures, and heritages that would appear in many of his writings and lectures. He is truly a *worldly traveler* who changed the world as a result of his sense of humor, his writing and his international travels. And we keep smiling.

**Mark Twain**
(Nordquist, 2020)

# CHAPTER TEN

# HEROIC EXPLOITS TO THE FORBIDDEN LAND WITH NAIN SINGH

"Travel is fatal to prejudice, bigotry, and narrow-
mindedness, and many of our people need it sorely on
these accounts. Broad, wholesome, charitable views
of men and things cannot be acquired by vegetating
in one little corner of the earth all one's lifetime."
-Mark Twain-

*The Indian pundit, Nain Singh, slipped past the border
guards, noiselessly crawling on the ground to cross,
brilliantly, from India into Tibet. Who was he and how
could he do this?*

*Terrified, silent, Nain Singh knew one false move
would land him in prison, and likely result in his death
sentence. His assignment, as a highly skilled explorer and
nineteenth century secret agent as a British surveyor,
mapper, and seeking information on the hinterlands of
Tibet, had been full of unknown perils. Acutely aware
that he was the only person the British trusted for this
mission, he was disguised often as a carefree wanderer
or sometimes as a trader or holy man. So far, he was able
to travel throughout Tibet and reach its capital, Lhasa,
without being discovered.*

*Nain Singh hurriedly gathered information in Lhasa, moving on to other dangerous and intriguing travels throughout Tibet. A highly skilled spy, he had been carefully trained by the British military to map out the vast unchartered areas of Tibet. Nain Singh became an expert at developing codes for recording secret information, which defied logic and detection. Young, clever, strong, and healthy, he loved hiking in mountains. He walked long distances tirelessly in the beautiful grit of his existence.*

*Why did Nain Singh risk so much for his British superiors? He was intelligent, resourceful, strong and capable of a promising career elsewhere in less dangerous lines of work. Was it the excitement of these wayward explorations and perilous missions throughout India, and China and drove him to spy on the Russians in Tibet?*

\* \* \*

Of the worldly travelers presented in this book, this Indian citizen, Nain Singh is the least known. Yet his travels boast him as an important mid-nineteenth century explorer-traveler-adventurer of enormous interest.

At the time of Nain Singh's travels, India was part of the British Empire. After the British defeated the French at the Battle of Waterloo early in the nineteenth century, they became the world's leading power, controlling one quarter of the world's population and one fifth of the total land area. The common expression was, *in the British Empire, the sun never sets.* British civilians and military personnel traveled throughout their empire to increase trade, provide security for their country's possessions, explore new areas for potential commercial opportunities, and simply for leisure pursuits. The capital of the world became London, where decisions were made that impacted every part of the globe.

World affairs changed rapidly in the nineteenth century. The Anglo-Russian rivalry over trade routes in and through the countries of

Afghanistan, Nepal, China, Tibet, and other nearby regions had bearing on later activities connected with Nain Singh's work and travel for the British in India. The Russian Empire and the British Empire became engaged in the Crimean War that ended in 1856 with Russia's defeat by an alliance of Britain, France, and the Ottoman Empire. While Russia was left in a weakened state, the Russians continued to protect their trade routes, which led to their special interest in Afghanistan, Nepal, China, and Tibet. The British, on the other hand, wanted to expand their trade routes that included utilizing a passage through Tibet. At the same time, China sought to protect her tenuous control of Tibet against intrusions by the Russians and the British. Each power – China, Russia, and Britain – became suspicious of the other country's intent over happenings in Tibet.

Tibet had been at the crossroads of international intrigue for several hundred years. The earliest conquering of Tibet was rumored to have taken place in the thirteenth century by the great Mongol leader Genghis Khan. We know that Genghis Khan's grandson, Kublai Khan, the ruler over the Mongolian Empire, had authority over Tibet, noted in the *Travels of Marco Polo*. It was under the rule of Kublai Khan that Buddhism developed as the principal religion in Tibet. Later, the Mongolian elite introduced the well-known title "Dalai Lama" as the leading disciple of the Buddhist religion. Tibet's capital city Lhasa was looked upon as the provenance of Buddhism in Tibet.

Wanting to develop new trade routes in China, Tibet and Nepal, the British needed to thoroughly explore the areas of Tibet and nearby states. The British base in India was the perfect place to conduct surveys and spy missions into Tibet. Russia, on the other hand, did not want the British interfering with their trade rights in Tibet and the surrounding region. This rivalry continued throughout the lifetime of Nain Singh. In addition to this rivalry, the British and Chinese fought over certain areas and policies regarding China's territories. Ultimately, the British won a major conflict with China, and the two nations signed "The Treaty of Nanking" in 1842, which, among the provisions, included Great Britain receiving the island of Hong Kong. The Chinese resented the Treaty and continuously tried to keep all countries out of China and Tibet, especially Great Britain and Russia.

The British Indian Empire was the perfect place to host a series of British and Indian surveyors and spies traveling into Tibet. Prior to the nineteenth century, India was always in a state of chaotic flux with many kingdoms forming and then falling due to internal conflicts and wars. For the most part, the country was backward, partially utilizing the Hindu caste system that separated the population into four major hereditary classes: 1) Brahmins (priestly people), 2) Kshatriyas (also called Rajanyas, who were rulers, administrators, and warriors), 3) Vaishyas (artisans, merchants, tradesmen, and farmers), and 4) Shudras (laboring classes). Women were treated like chattel: illiteracy was high as education was denied to them. The purdah system was in vogue, requiring Hindu women to wear a veil and keeping them out of the sight of men and strangers.

The British East India Company had been in India since the 1600s, and by the 1700s, the merchants of the company, backed by its own army, controlled trading relations in the country. Seeking even greater trade advantages with India over her competitors, the British invaded and conquered much of India just before the nineteenth century began. Britain saw an opportunity to replace the panoply of Indian customs, cultures, and heritage with their system of government and a society based on their ideals.

In effect, in the nineteenth century, India was considered the crown jewel of the huge British Empire. The British Indian Empire included what are now the four countries of the Republic of India, Islamic Republic of Pakistan, People's Republic of Bangladesh, and the Republic of the Union of Myanmar.

Exotic tales of life in India depicted in newspaper accounts and books fascinated the British population in London. The British realized in the mid-1840s that Indians in many parts of India heavily resented the rule of the country by the British East India Company. This resentment led to the so-called "First Anglo-Sikh War" of 1845-1846 between the Sikh Empire of India and the British East India Company. It ended with the partial subjugation of the Sikh kingdom and cession of Jammu and Kashmir as a separate princely state under British rule. This conflict laid the groundwork for even greater resentment of the British by 1850.

In the 1850s, the powerful British East India Company employed British military officers and Indian soldiers to assure control of the Indian trade economy. This continued British exploitation of the Indian natives led to a second Anglo-India conflict, the Indian Mutiny of 1857. In May 1857, soldiers of the Bengal Indian army shot their British officers and marched on Delhi, which was incorporated in 1857. This rebellion against the British East India Company and British authorities was a bloody affair sending shockwaves throughout the British Empire.

By 1858, the British were successful in putting down another rebellion and instigating what became known as "The Raj" which in the Indian language word means "rule". This established recognition that the British Crown ruled India, under the rubric Raj, that the British ruled India from 1858-1947. The Crown had complete dominance over life throughout the country. However, what the rebellion did accomplish was to weaken the British resolve to make India into a model British colony. Yet, the British still wanted to expand her trade routes by utilizing a passage through Tibet. At the same time, China sought to protect its control of Tibet against intrusions by Russia and Britain.

While little was known to the outside world about Tibet before the mid-point of the nineteenth century is that Tibet lay between the heart of the areas of the ancient civilizations of China and India. These major mountain ranges to the east of the Tibetan Plateau denoted the border with China, and the soaring Himalayas of Nepal and India separated Tibet from India. Tibet is often called "the roof of the world" and while it seemed that no one would ever be interested in traveling to or visiting the difficult mountain routes of Tibet in the nineteenth century, Britain, Russia, and China, each seeking to expand their economic opportunities and trade routes through Tibet, became interested in this mountainous country.

Certainly, a part of the interest in Tibet was due to hearsay, curiosity, intrigue, mystery, and mythical perceptions about Tibet. One source of the fanciful tales about Tibet was written by our historian Herodotus in the fifth century B.C.E. Other notes on Tibet came from Marco Polo, who, during his journey in the country, was particularly impressed with a special breed of horses that resided in Tibet. For the British and Russians, it was a matter of possible imperialistic gain and a desire for increasing trade routes. For China, it was a matter of trying to keep foreigners at bay from encroaching on China's territories.

Tibet and its capital, Lhasa, were of special interest to the British and Russians during the mid-to-late nineteenth century. Tibet's rugged mountain terrain was a destination that defied the most adventurous and hardiest of explorers and travelers, causing it to be an increasingly alluring, difficult challenge. As a vassal state of China, Tibet was under her protection. But China was not strong enough to ward off interests by the British and Russians. By the mid-1850s, Tibet, acting independently of China, banned all foreigners from entering the country. It became highly dangerous for outsiders to visit the country.

The British, fully ensconced in India, saw Tibet as providing not only overland trade routes but maybe even an opportunity to steal the lucrative Tibetan tea market from the Chinese. Meanwhile, the Russian Empire was moving south into Central Asia, suspicious of British interest in Tibet. As the most powerful empire at the time, the British simply ignored the Russians.

By the 1860s, the British in India began to secretly study the terrain, government, economies, and religion of Tibet, seeking information about the isolated hinterlands of Tibet in an effort to broaden its trade routes throughout the country. The idea of being the major trading partner with Tibet resonated with the British trading system for expanding its territorial interests.

The British began to train Indian surveyors, explorers, and special traveler-spies, such as the famous "Pundit" Nain Singh, to covertly infiltrate Tibet. "Pundit" was a word used in India to define a man of certain learning and respect, and the British used "pundit" as a code name for secret spy travelers like Nain Singh. "Pundit" became the generic name which the British used to keep from revealing the real names of their surveyor-spies. Later "pundit" was used by the British as a general term for a native of India trained and employed by the British to survey inaccessible regions beyond the British frontier.

\* \* \*

Nain Singh, as a representative of the British Empire, began a major mission to gather information about Tibet and nearby regions. His native India, controlled by the British, was enmeshed in domestic turmoil and, at the same time, engaged in international intrigue because of its location next to China, Tibet, Afghanistan, and Nepal.

India, as part of the British Empire, became the prime instrument for implementing British foreign policy in the region. A weakened China sought to keep Tibet under its grasp; it had neither the power nor the will to battle the British Empire or Russian Empire, while both countries made independent moves to infiltrate Tibet.

The British developed a desperate need to know the terra incognita beyond the Tibetan mountains. They were aware they knew almost nothing about the government, economy, religion, and social structure of Tibet, and they weren't sure if it was worth fighting the Russians and Chinese for dominance over this strange land. They needed information and maps about Tibet before London could decide on any political, economic, and military strategy for the area. Yet, due to Tibet's anti-foreigner policies, the British and all other foreigners risked their lives if they traveled to Tibet. They needed to develop alternative approaches to obtain new intelligence about Tibet.

In the 1850s, a British military engineer-surveyor, Thomas George Montgomerie, initially a British army Lieutenant who was later promoted to Lieutenant-Colonel. He was given the responsibility of mapping all of India. In 1845, at the age of 15, Thomas Montgomerie had joined the East India Company's Military Academy where he was a brilliant student. Six years later, when he arrived in India in 1851, he joined the Bengal Engineers. Shortly thereafter, he was assigned to the British Great Trigonometrical Survey of India.

The Superintendent of the British Great Trigonometrical Survey of India was Major James Thomas Walker, an Anglo-Indian Surveyor General of India, who later became a General in the British army. British political authorities often spoke and wondered about the greater glories of a positive future of Tibet trade, if the country could be fully surveyed and mapped.

By 1860, an Indian, Abdul Mejid, had limited success in his effort to gather information about certain parts of Central Asia which he then passed on to British authorities, but he did not have the appropriate instruments for a comprehensive survey of the area.

In 1861, British explorer-surveyor Major Edmund Smyth attempted to reach Tibet by traveling up the Yangtse River. While he had traveled widely on the Indian side of the Himalayas, he failed on this mission for several reasons. In his newly created appointment as inspector of the Kumaon Circle Public Instruction Department to establish Indian vernacular schools in the Kumaon highlands, Smyth took time off to try additional attempts to reach Tibet between 1861 and 1863, but he again failed.

However, in an 1861 letter to James Walker, Smyth recommended Nain Singh, a schoolmaster in Kumaon, to become a possible surveyor. James Walker personally traveled to Kumaon to recruit Nain Singh and his cousin Mani Singh as potential surveyors for the British Great Trigonometrical Survey team. They agreed to do this and were sent to the survey headquarters in the city of Dehra Dun in the district of Dehradun and were placed under Montgomerie's command.

In the meantime, Thomas Montgomerie was promoted to captain and ordered to expand his mapping of India and to also include surveying plus mapping of Tibet. Montgomerie had maintained good relations with Gulab Singh Jamwal, the Maharaja of Jammu and Kashmir, the second largest princely state in British India. This state was created after the defeat of the Sikh Empire in the First Anglo-Sikh War, and Gulab Singh had helped the British against the Sikhs. Afterwards, he was awarded all the lands in Kashmir for 7.5 million Nanakshahee Rupees. This relationship between Captain Montgomerie and Gulab Singh proved valuable during the organization of surveys of Kashmir, Central Asia and Tibet. It was during the Kashmir Survey in 1864 that Montgomerie named the mountain Karakorum as K2, the second highest mountain in the world. The Royal Geographical Society of Britain awarded Montgomerie with the *Founders' Gold Medal* "...for his great trigonometrical journey from the plains of the Punjab to the Karakorum Range..."

**Captain Thomas Montgomerie**
(Loney, n.d.)

In 1863 at a base camp in Kashmir, Captain Montgomerie began to train a local Indian, Abdul Hamid, in the intricacies of mapping and spying techniques using unorthodox methods approved by his superiors. Then Montgomerie sent Hamid on a mission to explore and survey areas of Central Asia beyond the Indian frontier. Specifically, Hamid was to survey the road to Yarkand, capital of East Turkestan, which is now the Xinjiang Uyghur Autonomous Region of China. Yarkand had difficulties due to uprisings by the Moslems against the Chinese. Disguised as a merchant and traveling with a caravan, Hamid began his journey along one of the most difficult trade routes in existence. Because he was a Moslem, like most others in the area, he was better able to carry concealed instruments that enabled him to map the geography of the area. With two servants and a pony, he crossed the Karakorum and Kunlun ranges. Hamid took daily observations to determine his position and measure distances. For safety purposes, he joined a caravan headed for Yarkand, and after two weeks of difficult travels, the caravan arrived there.

Abdul Hamid lived in Yarkand for several months, making continuous observations of the area. Through a friend, he met the Moslem governor of Yarkand, learning more about the people, customs, geography, and political factions. He sent back reports, maps, and information on northern China, including valuable reconnaissance disclosures of Russian activities in the area. A highly successful expedition.

In the meantime, certain Chinese officials became suspicious of Hamid's activities, but before they could arrest him, he joined a caravan heading to Leh and was able to pass through the most dangerous section of the route and get back to British protected territory. Shortly thereafter, he became ill and died. Fortunately for the British, there happened to be a British surveying camp not far away, and a British surveyor, William Johnson, was able to obtain Hamid's survey notes. Based on Hamid's success, Captain Montgomerie's superiors asked him to develop a formal program of recruiting, training, and directing local Indians in mapping and gathering sensitive geographical and political information on China and Tibet.

In 1863, Captain Montgomerie became more creative in his training techniques to avoid having the Chinese accuse him of outright spying. Noting that Indians could traverse more easily across borders in the region than the easily recognized British were able to do, he suggested that crude surveying instruments could be hidden on the Indian traveler, disguised as a trader, a wandering merchant, or as a Buddhist pilgrim. London and British India, anxious to learn more about Tibet and the Russian presence, formally approved Montgomerie's program in 1863. So he became the lead British officer for training Indian "pundits" as surveyors and spies.

Two of his first trainees were cousins Nain Singh and Mani Singh from the Johaar Valley of Kumaon, India. Nain Singh and Mani Singh spoke Tibetan, and had explored many areas within the country for years on their own. Mani Singh was from a wealthy family, and though he contributed materially to the Tibetan explorations, he was not as willing as Nain Singh to undergo the rigors and deprivations associated with such travel. Nain Singh, on the other hand, thrived on the arduous and rough conditions of the journeys. He became a true explorer exhibiting perseverance, energy, and courage, highly important qualities for traveling into unknown territories.

Nain Singh Rawat is generally considered to have been born on October 21, 1830 in the Milam Village in the Johaar Valley of Kumaon, a district of Uttarakhand, high up with an altitude of ten thousand to thirteen thousand feet in the Himalaya Mountains of northern India and twenty miles from the Tibetan border. Nain Singh's family had a strong association with the Tibetans, spoke the language and were accustomed to hard work and travel at high altitudes. Nain Singh could both read and write Tibetan, as well as having a good command of the English language. Important from the British survey administrator's viewpoint was that the people of this region already had a long-term trading relationship with Tibet. This association with the Tibetans made Nain Singh and Mani Singh ideal candidates for Montgomerie's survey team.

Nain Singh's grandfather, Dham Singh Rawat, was an important landlord who was rewarded land in both the Golma and Kotal villages in 1735. The family were members of the Uttarakhand tribe and known to lead a nomadic life traveling with large flocks of pack goats, sheep, and ponies. Their annual migrations in caravans took place along established trade routes that crossed into Tibet. As a result, they had long formed strong trade relationships with the Tibetans. Yet journeys into Tibet were often hazardous due to bad weather and frozen mountain passes, causing many men and animals to perish. The Singh family knew the area well, having traversed the trails for years as traders with Tibet and later, as employees and surveyors of the British government.

**Nain Singh**

Nain Singh became a small landlord who farmed fields he inherited from his father. While he farmed part of the year, he also spent time as a trader in Tibet. By small village standards where he grew up, he was considered to be well educated, speaking Hindi, Persian, English, and Tibetan. By 1855, he was recruited by three German brothers-geographers, Adolf, Hermann, and Robert Schlagintweit, to be part of their survey team in India. In 1854, the famous German physical geographer, naturalist, and explorer Baron von Alexander Humboldt recommended to the British East India Company that these German scientists make scientific investigations in India and Central Asia territory to study the Earth's magnetic field.

So between 1855 to 1857, with permission from the British survey office, Nain Singh helped the Schlagintweit brothers conduct their surveys. He traveled with the three scientists through the Deccan, a large plateau in western and southern India, and then up into the Himalayas, Karakoram, and Kunlun Mountains. While Nain Singh had traveled to these areas before, Hermann, Adolf, and Robert Schlagintweit were the first Europeans to cross the Kunlun Mountains. This expedition helped to establish Nain Singh as a future explorer, traveler, and surveyor for the British East India Company.

Nain Singh's education, with his practical knowledge of geography and social conditions through his travel experiences, led to him being chosen as a schoolmaster in the Indian village of Milam in 1858. During the next years, the British were so impressed with his intellect, that he became the schoolmaster in the larger village of Kumaon. Then, in 1863, British Captain Thomas Montgomerie recruited him to be trained as a native Indian surveyor. Giving him the title of *pundit*, Captain Montgomerie employed Nain Singh to conduct dangerous spy missions for the British.

Now the British trained Nain Singh in surveying and mapping using uniquely improvised tools. They knew that the Tibetans would be highly suspicious if Nain Singh entered the country with the practiced instruments needed for accurate surveying. So Captain Montgomerie made innovations in the training to allow Nain Singh and his expedition party to travel with just enough equipment to accomplish the mission by hiding the surveying tools in secret compartments in their luggage and clothing. Notepaper was put in Tibetan prayer wheels on which secret coded messages could be written. We're fascinated to learn that Nain Singh was trained to walk in all types of terrain with the same pace, so distances he traveled could be measured. One system used was to keep track of his paces using Buddhist prayer beads that had been reduced from 108 normal prayer beads to 100 for an easy recorded count of his paces, with 2,000 paces equaling one mile. In his expeditions for the British Great Trigonometric Survey team, he *walked* several thousand miles over some of the most difficult terrain in the world. Prayer wheels and beads were items never examined by officials at the border. In addition, Nain Singh was given the code name "Number 1".

After a year's training in 1863, Nain Singh, his cousin Mani, and a few helpers left Milam heading for Lhasa in 1864. Though they had crossed the border many times as traders to Tibet, on this occasion they were denied entry. Tibet had become suspicious of all travelers entering along the normal trade routes, because of previous troubles with China, British India, Russia, and even explorers from Germany. Nain Singh returned from this unsuccessful trip suggesting the itinerary be changed with an entry into Tibet from Nepal rather than India. He had heard from other travelers that Nepal was on better terms with Tibet than India; it would likely be easier to cross the border and proceed to Lhasa. Yet travel in the high mountains and over nearly impassable terrain was constantly difficult and exhausting. .

In 1865, Nain Singh, Mani Singh, and a few helpers again left India traveling to the capital of Nepal, Kathmandu. They explained to anyone who questioned their travels that they were traders and also making a Buddhist pilgrimage. This time at the border, they were initially stopped by Chinese guards. Their luggage was searched and nothing unusual was found. The equipment had been hidden in secret compartments. But the Chinese recognized them as Indians and turned them away. As they regrouped in Kathmandu, Nain Singh was greatly troubled by the possibility of another failed mission. While he wanted to try again, no one else from his party would accompany him, including his cousin. They simply saw the mission as being too dangerous. Mani no longer wanted to be a part of future expeditions. As a result, the cousins separated. While Mani and his cohorts managed to get across the border and travel through western Tibet and back to India, Nain walked alone to Lhasa.

Nain Singh found a merchant that had access to Tibet who was willing to allow him to join his party, providing Nain Singh gave him a monetary contribution. But, because of delays by the merchant, Nain Singh decided to disguise himself as a trader and travel by himself. Along the way, he came across a merchant caravan that welcomed him to join them. Thanks to his shrewd nature and training in deception, he was later able to separate himself from the caravan, again, at a place where he could dodge Chinese border guards and sneak across the border. It meant crossing a dangerous river where he had just seen three men drown, but this time he was successful in getting inside Tibet.

As Nain Singh approached Lhasa, he made a visit to a Buddhist monastery to demonstrate he was also on a pilgrimage. He was able to accompany or rejoin the caravan when he needed assistance, but then left quietly to secretly conduct surveys. He ventured into uncharted areas using his knowledge to map, taking notes of everything he saw and heard along the way. He measured the longitude, latitude, and altitude of Lhasa, the first person to do so, and traced the important Yarlung Tsangpo River basin throughout the area.

All the time traveling, he kept track of the distances, patiently recording his millions of paces or hundreds of miles, using his compass and taking notes, averaging 10 to 15 miles a day as he approached Lhasa. In 1866, he entered the fabled city of Lhasa where he secretly remained for three months.

Nain Singh was able to traverse the city without being molested. This allowed him to make observations with his sextant, which Montgomerie had taught him to use. He listened and learned about Lhasa's politics, geography, economy, and religion. Lhasa was a fascinating major trading center with merchants from China, Bhutan, Nepal, and Kashmir.

Always wary of being discovered, he stayed quiet and he hoped, undiscovered. One reason for his anxiety; when he was present during an investigation of another individual who was found to be misrepresenting his reason for being in Lhasa. The man was beheaded. The governor of Lhasa's justice system was not to be toyed with.

After three months in Lhasa, Nain Singh rejoined a caravan as they prepared to leave along the main east-west trade route toward Lake Manasarovar. He was relieved to be heading back to British territory and home, but before they reached the lake, the caravan was attacked by robbers. Using ability to seemingly just disappear, Nain Singh was able to quietly escape without being confronted by the bandits.

After seventeen months of perilous travel, Nain Singh returned to British headquarters with an incredible, exhausting report; he had walked 1,200 miles on this expedition and his surveys of the rough terrain and treacherous mountain trails were the first ever made. These reports gave the British important intelligence about the route taken as well as a vivid description of the terrain along the way. And his account of life in Lhasa were fascinating and invaluable. Later, when the British were able to send additional emissaries to Lhasa, the official statements mentioned that the new reports did not improve upon what had been provided by Nain Singh.

While in Tibet, Nain Singh picked up rumors about gold mines in a remote area of Tibet. This news excited Captain Montgomerie to the extent that he immediately began preparing an additional expedition for Nain Singh to find these gold-bearing alluvial fields in Tibet.

In 1867, for an additional secret expedition, Nain Singh joined a group of Khampas, accomplished sportsmen and horsemen, where he was able to explore western Tibet, always mapping, and recording what he saw. He was able to visit the legendary Thok Jalung gold mines and Gartok, Tibet's largest western city. He even bribed the chief of the goldfield, and managed to stay five days to note how rich the mines were. The living and working conditions for the miners were formidable at the elevation of sixteen thousand feet. The life-threatening cold conditions and difficult terrain made mining extremely difficult, but there was enough gold to be found in veins and in alluvial deposits to cause prospectors to stay in the area. He found that the workers only dug for gold near the surface; their superstitions led them to believe that to dig deeper was offensive to the earth and would lead to infertility. On this trip, he was identified by other travelers as being from India, but with an appropriate payoff, he was able to continue. He was always in constant peril of being recognized or being attacked by bandits, which happened on three separate occasions, but he was able to get away safely, and continue his travels.

After these incredible, adventurous trips, Nain Singh went into semi-retirement as a British agent. In the meantime, his trainer and supervisor, Captain Thomas Montgomerie, left India and was replaced by his colleague Captain Henry Trotter. Yet in 1873, Captain Trotter requested that Nain Singh please return to the British mapping service for an expedition disguised as a visit to Chinese Turkestan. While Nain Singh and Captain Trotter feigned the impression that he was returning to Yarkand for increased surveying of the area, the real reason of his mission was to make one last mapping journey into Tibet. This time they traveled to the north area of Tibet. His previous surveys had been conducted in Southwestern Tibet. He was told this would be his last trip, and afterward, he'd receive a British pension and a land grant.

In July 1874, Nain Singh journeyed from the city of Leh in the Himalayan kingdom of Ladakh to Lhasa by a northerly route along the Tsangpo River. For centuries, Leh was an important stopover on trade routes along the Indus Valley between Tibet to the east, Kashmir to the west, and between India and China. On this adventure, Nain Singh was joined by four companions to assist him, all disguised as Buddhist monks. This trip was precarious as, by now, Chinese officials on the border knew about Nain Singh and his service to British India. Yet the disguises worked; the party traveled throughout the area and mapped much of the mountainous terrain that was relatively unknown at the time and where very few inhabitants lived.

Nain Singh's party arrived in Lhasa in November of 1874, but they only stayed a few days, as Nain Singh was recognized by a local merchant who he thought might turn him in. He immediately gave all his mapping equipment and notes to other members of his party and sent them on their way back to India. He then faked a visit to a monastery and circled back to begin his own trip back to India without jeopardizing the other members of the team. On the way back to India, he was captured at one point, but he escaped and finally arrived back in India in 1875. Now he had walked over 1,400 miles. This mission was highly successful as far as the British were concerned. He had mapped important new areas not known to the British.

At this point, Nain Singh went into real retirement, exhausted and suffering from several ailments due to the hardships of his journeys. His last duties were to train new and younger groups of pundits for untold missions in the future. He continued teaching until 1879.

His unique efforts had been earlier recognized by the prestigious British Royal Geographic Society through their gift to him of an inscribed gold chronometer watch in 1868 for his outstanding surveying and explorations for the British Empire. Shortly after Nain Singh received this irreplaceable gold chronometer watch, it was stolen, which caused him great grief. This was a special kind of gift that recognized important explorations by individual explorers. Then Nain Singh's achievements were published in the *Geographical Magazine* of the *Royal Geographical Society* in 1876, a highly recognized honor in England. In 1876, the former president of the *Royal Geographical Society*, Sir Henry Rawlinson, wrote to the *Society* calling Nain Singh "the Pundit of Pundits", comparing him with such giants of explorations as David Livingstone and Lieutenant Colonel James Grant.

In 1877, Nain Singh received the *Society's* highest award, the Patron's Gold Medal. This last award was for "…great journeys and surveys in Tibet, and along the Upper Brahmaputra [Himalayan Mountain range], during which he has determined the position of Lhasa …" It was also mentioned that "…his journals formed an exceedingly interesting book of travels."

In addition, The *Society of Geographers* of Paris honored Nain Singh by awarding him a specially inscribed gold watch. Finally, a gold watch! The British *Great Trigonometrical Survey* of India, the sponsoring organization for Nain Singh's travels, gave him a special surveying instrument with the inscription *"The Great Trigonometrical Survey of India and Tibet 1867 Expresses Gratitude to Pundit Nain Singh for*

*Bravery and Devotion.* Later, on June 27, 2004, an Indian postage stamp featuring Nain Singh was issued commemorating his role in the *Great Trigonometric Survey.*

In 1877, the British Government of India awarded him a pension and a sizable land grant to commemorate his retirement from service. He continued to train new pundits for the British and spent time developing the land he received for his service to the British Government. He died in 1895 from a heart attack while working on his land.

Nain Singh's adventurous travels were never equaled by future *Pundits.* Through his perseverance, he accomplished everything that was asked of him by the British authorities. His unique and dangerous three trips into Tibet at a time when Tibet was off limits to foreign travelers, made him the most knowledgeable person in the world about this mysterious mountainous country. He was the first to accurately measure the altitude of Lhasa as well as many of the surrounding Tibetan mountains. In fact, the mountains south of Lake Pangong are now called the "Nain Singh Range." He mapped a large section of the most important body of water in Tibet, the Tsangpo River. He started at its source at Lake Manasarovar and followed it all the way into India, which provided the British with much needed information.

While Nain Singh is mostly remembered for his adventurous travels into Tibet, he also traveled and mapped areas of India, China, Nepal, and Kashmir. He traveled to Bhutan, Kashmir, Pakistan, and Afghanistan. His energy, intellect, courage, curiosity, explorations, and geographical endeavors in the unknown territories surrounding India led to changes in that part of the world. He was truly a worldly traveler of great curiosity and bravery who stood out among the many travelers to India before and after him.

He is remembered as the man who mapped the forbidden land of Tibet.

The last words about Nain Singh's many contributions to discoveries he made for the British Empire came from a letter written to the Royal Geographic Society by the great geographical scholar Colonel

Henry Yule, who noted: "…Nain Singh's observations have added a larger amount of important knowledge to the map of Asia, then those of any other living man." Through his travels and explorations, the worldly traveler Nain Singh changed the world in which we live. And we are inspired.

**Nain Singh on a 2004 stamp of India**

# CHAPTER ELEVEN

# CHARLES A. LINDBERGH FAMOUS AVIATOR BECOMES AN ENVIRONMENTALIST

"Do not go where the path may lead, go instead
where there is no path and leave a trail."
-Ralph Waldo Emerson-

*Even before the time of mythical Icarus' attempted flight,
man has dreamed of flying.*

*On this foggy, rainy morning of May 20, 1927, the thought
of flying seemed a simple fancy of the imagination. The
airplane, known as the Spirit of St. Louis, had been
checked and re-checked, and ready for flight. All that
was needed was a pilot crazy enough to risk all to be the
first to fly non-stop across the vast Atlantic, 3,600 miles
from New York to Paris.*

*The tall, handsome young man, Charles Augustus
Lindbergh, considered to be a dare-devil pilot of sorts,
was just the person to take up this challenge. Relying on
weather reports of dubious accuracy, Lindbergh stepped
into the cramped cockpit hoping his luck would hold for
the long flight ahead. Lloyds of London refused listing
his chances of making the flight, saying it was too risky
to predict. Lindbergh called down to the ground crew to*

*crank the engine. The propellers responded positively, and the motor hummed the right tune. Time for Lindbergh to go on a path no man had gone before and blaze a new trail in the sky.*

*At the last minute, he was advised that the unpaved runway was too muddy for a takeoff. It was doubtful under such conditions he could clear telephone wires at the end of the airport runway. Hell, no! Lindbergh was undeterred. He bumped along the landing strip, dodging deep holes, and lifted off the ground momentarily, then bumped back on the ground. Finally, enough lift to keep him in the air. He pulled the control stick back as far as it would go, and to the cheers of the crowd which had suddenly appeared, the Spirit of St. Louis cleared the telephone wires. Defying all odds, Lucky Lindy was on his way.*

**Charles A. Lindbergh dressed and ready to fly from New York to Paris in his plane, the *Spirit of St. Louis***

\* \* \*

Examining both sides of Charles A. Lindbergh's family lineage allows us to understand Charles A. Lindbergh himself. While Charles, the aviator, was sometimes referred to as "junior" to differentiate him from his father, this technically was not correct. Their middle names were different. The father's middle name was August, and Charles' was Augustus. In addition, Charles also had a son who did use junior in his name. To avoid confusion early on in this chapter, the designation of I and II is used here to differentiate the father and son. Later, simply Charles A. Lindbergh will be used to identify the aviator.

His father, Charles August Lindbergh I was born in 1858 in Stockholm, Sweden and became a Swedish immigrant to the United States. He was the child of politician Ola Mansson from the rural community of Smedstorp, Sweden, and his girlfriend, Lovisa Callen of Stockholm. Ola, a farmer, and father of several children became a powerful member of the Swedish Parliament, who befriended the King of Sweden. Along with this, other important people helped him to become an officer in the State Bank of Sweden. His farm, located more than 600 miles from Stockholm, was looked after by his wife Ingar Jonsdotter and their seven children when Ola was traveling to participate in the Parliament.

In his effort to support his wife and family and his girlfriend, Ola used his position as a bank officer to deliberately misappropriate funds for his personal use from the bank. This led to him being accused of embezzlement. As a result, he was stripped of his political position and in jeopardy of being convicted for the crime and of going to jail. But he had a passport, so he decided to leave the country to avoid prosecution for his crime. He asked his wife if she wished to accompany him, but being concerned for the welfare of their children, she refused.

So Ola quietly left the country with his girlfriend, Lovisa and their eighteen-month-old child Carl before he could be incarcerated. From Sweden, they went to England and then to Canada. Easily slipping across the United States-Canadian border, they arrived in Melrose, Minnesota in the United States. Ola then changed his name to August

Lindbergh; Lovisa became Louisa Lindbergh; and Carl was then named Charles August Lindbergh.

Now American, Charles August Lindbergh I was a strong, energetic man who was basically a farmer but educated as a lawyer. He bought land in Little Falls, Minnesota, and pursued a career as a rural lawyer and part-time farmer. He met a young, attractive girl from the area, Mary LaFond, and after a short courtship, they were married in 1887. They had three daughters, however, only two daughters, Lillian, and Evangeline, lived to adulthood. In 1898, as Mary was giving birth to the third daughter, she and their daughter both died. A widower, Charles Lindbergh I was devastated with his loss, and he turned his attentions and energy to the farm and his law practice.

In 1900, Charles I moved from his farmhouse into the Antlers Hotel in Little Falls, Minnesota. It was in the hotel where he met his future wife Evangeline Land Lodge. Evangeline was born May 29, 1876 in Detroit, Michigan and came from a highly educated family. She received her degree in chemistry from the University of Michigan. Her father was both a dentist and an inventor of dental equipment and other equipment. Later in life he became famous as "the father of porcelain dental art".

After graduation from the university, Evangeline accepted a teaching position in the rural area of Little Falls, Minnesota. There were few opportunities for a young, attractive, educated woman to meet suitors in such a farming community. But she did meet one of the town's best-known lawyers, Charles A. Lindbergh I, and soon she and Lindbergh were dating. Charles I, while much older than Evangeline, was impressed with her intellect, education, and general worldly knowledge, traits not easily found in single women in Little Falls. Evangeline married Charles I in March 1901. Aside from their intellectual interests, they had little else in common. He had grown up on a farm and settled in a rural area. She had grown up in the city and had trouble adjusting to a small rural town. These differences, as well as being two strong-willed individuals seeing life quite differently, led to their early divorce in 1909.

Charles I apparently inherited political genes from his father; in 1906, he was elected as a U.S. Congressman from the sixth congressional district in Minnesota. He served as a congressman from 1907 to 1917 until he ran for the U.S. Senate. A major issue in his senatorial campaign included his strong opposition to the United States entering World War I. He put forward cogent reasons against the United States being involved in a European war, but he was clearly in the minority on this position. While Lindbergh felt the odium of his position from fellow congressmen, he would not make a change in how he felt about the war. His opinions about the war were the reason he was defeated in the Senate election.

What makes his opposition to the war of particular interest is that after his son Charles A. Lindbergh II became a famous aviator, he too strongly opposed a war; this time it would concern the United States' entry into World War II.

Charles Augustus Lindbergh II was born to Evangeline on February 4, 1902 in Detroit, Michigan. Not wanting to deal with the birth of a child in a rural area, she went to her home in Detroit prior to February 1902 where she could be attended to by her uncle, a medical doctor. Charles I joined his wife in Detroit shortly after his son's birth. Within two months of Charles II's birth, his parents bundled him warmly for an 800-mile trip from Detroit back to the family's rural home in Little Falls, Minnesota.

When Charles II was three, a great tragedy struck the Lindbergh household. The family home caught on fire and burned to the ground. With help from the family maid, Charles luckily escaped the fire only to watch his home go up in flames. He remembered this tragic experience the rest of his life. While he lost a few favorite toys, his biggest loss was his upstairs bedroom that had overlooked the picturesque western banks of the Mississippi River, a joyful sight.

Because of his father's congressional position, much of our Charles's early boyhood was now spent in Washington, D.C. During the summers, he stayed in the rebuilt family home in Little Falls. After the divorce of his parents in 1909, his mother moved to California. Between a mother living in California, a father in Washington D.C., and a family home in Little Falls, Charles ended up attending more than a dozen schools in Washington, D.C., California, and Little Falls, where he graduated.

His education was frequently interrupted when his mother took him on what she considered educational trips, including a visit to Panama. He wrote in his book *WE*, published in 1927 after his famous flight, that "... Through these school years, I crossed and re-crossed the United States, made one trip to Panama, and had thoroughly developed a desire for travel, which has never been overcome..." With the interruptions in his schooling and differences in the educational systems he was exposed to, he apparently developed little interest in academics.

Although our Charles was barely able to graduate from high school, he became interested in subjects requiring mechanical skills and using various types of equipment. He became an expert mechanic, able to take apart and put back together, reasonably well, any machine, tractor, bicycle, or automobile. With encouragement from his mother, he enrolled as a mechanical engineering student at the University of Wisconsin at Madison in 1920. After a few unproductive years as a failing student, he left the University.

Yet the University years provided him with one lifetime interest; aviation. Charles wrote: "...While I was attending the University, I became intensely interested in aviation. Since I saw my first airplane near Washington, D.C. in 1912, I had been fascinated with flying..." He began reading articles about flying, a relatively new means of transportation in the 1920s. The more he read, the more interested he became in wanting to fly. He was fascinated by the account of two bicycle makers from Ohio, Orville and Wilbur Wright, who had designed a plane that could stay in the air, even if it was airborne for only a few moments. He read about their plane, the *Wright Flyer*, and how it had been tested on December 17, 1903 in the sand dunes at Kitty Hawk, North Carolina. Flying airplanes became Charles A. Lindbergh's métier for the rest of his life.

In 1922, young Charles headed to Lincoln, Nebraska where he enrolled as a student at an aviation school operated by the Nebraska Aircraft Corporation. Shortly after arriving, he took to the air as a passenger in a two-seated biplane. The biplane has two sets of wings stacked one above the other, and this hooked him on flying. He was a quick study as a student pilot. In no time, he was ready to fly by himself. But, the owner of the school wouldn't let him fly alone unless he posted a bond, in case he crashed. Since Charles had never been in the workforce, he had no money to pay the bond. He had to wait for a later time to make his solo flight.

Charles' next concern was how to earn a living in this new era of aviation. To keep connected to flying, he signed on as a *barnstorming "wing walker" and parachutist,* both dangerous avocations in the early 1920s. As a *wing walker,* he had to stand or move around on the wing of a biplane while the barnstormer pilot maneuvered the aircraft through various stunts. To create more excitement for the spectators, he sometimes jumped off the wing and parachuted to the ground. As a tall, handsome, risky, and reckless individual, Charles attracted a great deal of attention. He barnstormed in Nebraska, across Kansas, Colorado, Wyoming, and Montana, appearing at air shows, local fairs, and any event where outlandish flying was part of the entertainment.

From his barnstorming earnings, Charles scraped together enough money and bought a Curtiss JN-4 "Jenny" biplane for $500. It was this plane that he used for his first solitary flight. His first solo flight took place in 1923 in Americus, Georgia, at a former World War I aviation training area. Once he was flight certified, he became known as a stunt pilot, ever willing to risk his neck for the entertainment of others. He barnstormed throughout the area of Georgia and beyond, earning the nickname Daredevil Lindbergh. He was also known as Slim due to his slender build, and then Lucky Lindy, after surviving a midair collision. Also as The Lone Eagle, because he preferred flying alone. These excitements became his main interest in life, and he endured numerous accidents while flying, but none of them were serious enough to keep him out of an airplane. In addition, his mechanical abilities allowed him to quickly repair his crashed aircraft.

**Charles barnstorming**
(Meitner, 2015)

After barnstorming for a year, Charles headed to Brooks Field, Texas, on March 19, 1924 to join the U.S. Army and complete a year of military flight training. There, he developed into an excellent military pilot. However, during a flight training maneuver a year later, he crashed into another plane in midair. Luckily, he was able to bail out in time. As did the other pilot. Graduating at the top of his class, where out of the original 104 cadets, only 18 graduated, Charles was commissioned a 2nd Lieutenant in the U. S. Army Air Service Reserve Corps.

In 1925, the U.S. army had only a limited need for peacetime pilots, so Charles, as a reserve officer, returned to flying as a civilian. He credited his military aviation experiences as most important in his development as a first-class aviator. Writing in his book *WE*, a book about his transatlantic flight, which became an instant bestseller, he wrote; "… But when he [cadet] receives the wings at Kelly a year later, he has the satisfaction of knowing that he has graduated from one of the world's finest flying schools…"

**Graduation, Second Lieutenant Charles A.
Lindbergh, U.S. Army Air Service, March 1925**

In 1926, Charles and several other aviators became the first pilots to deliver mail by air for the United States Postal Service. His route took him from St. Louis to Chicago with intermediate stops in Springfield and Peoria, Illinois. He flew, carrying the mail by plane in all kinds of weather. The science of predicting weather was not very accurate at the time, so he often found himself flying during unpredicted storms. In addition, the planes were not designed nor constructed for flights in bad weather. He had many harrowing moments that included parachuting from one aircraft just before it took a nosedive and crashed. On two occasions while delivering mail, he found himself in a crash situation causing him to bail out of the plane. As soon as his parachute hit the ground, he rushed to the crash sites to retrieve the mail.

By the late 1920s, aviation had caught the attention of the world. During the aftermath of flying military aircrafts used during World War I, a new breed of adventurous aviators was born. France became a haven for both highly decorated World War I military pilots as well as others simply seeking adventure. The major goal of French, English, and American flyers became a non-defined race to be the first to fly an aircraft nonstop across the Atlantic Ocean.

In 1919, a prize of $25,000 had been established by the French-born New York hotelier Raymond Orteig, to be given to the first person able to fly across the Atlantic either from New York to Paris or Paris to New York. If one adjusts for inflation, $25,000 in 1919 is equal to $402,893 in 2023. A substantial prize.

Initially, this incentive was available for only five years. But no one had yet won and his offer extended for another five years. Even though many qualified aviators had failed, many of them dying in their failed attempts, there was no loss of experienced and sponsored contenders ready to keep trying for the prize. The renowned French fighter pilot of World War I René Fonck tried unsuccessfully to fly from France to the United States in 1926. As well, a famous American, Commander Richard E. Byrd who had flown over the North Pole, was also unsuccessful in trying to reach Europe nonstop across the Atlantic. They all wanted to be the first pilots to fly nonstop across the Atlantic and, in doing so, win the $25,000 Orteig prize.

Not well known, on June 14, 1919, Captain John Alcock, an English pilot, and Arthur Whiten Brown, a Scottish aviator and Alcock's navigator and flying partner, flew nonstop across the Atlantic Ocean in a Vickers Vimy IV twin-engine bomber from St. John's Newfoundland to Clifden, Ireland. Both men had flown airplanes during World War I, and at one point, both had been captured and were prisoners of war. They left on their flight at around 1:45 p.m. on June 14, 1919, and at 8:40 a.m. on June 15, 1919, Alcock and Brown had flown 1,890 miles during the worst kind of weather. They flew through thick fog, rain, and a snowstorm for 15 hours and 57 minutes. They had carried a small amount of mail, making it the first transatlantic airmail flight. This flight was eight years before Charles Lindbergh flew solo from New York to Paris.

A late entry for the Orteig prize was our little-known "barnstorming" aviator and U.S. Air Mail pilot, Charles A. Lindbergh. With the help of two local St. Louis, Missouri businessmen, Charles convinced the St. Louis State National Bank to lend him $15,000 to purchase an airplane to be built In California. In mid-February 1927, he left for San Diego to oversee the design and construction of the plane in which he would attempt to fly across the Atlantic. He named it the *Spirit of St. Louis* in honor of the St. Louis businessmen and community who helped sponsor him. Charles, the mechanic and by then a knowledgeable aviator, insisted that the manufacturer, Ryan Airlines Corporation, build the plane as light as possible.

The Ryan Airlines Corporation contracted for $10,580 to deliver the single-engine monoplane within 60 days. Once the plane was finished, it was sent to New York so that final plans for the flight could be prepared. Even after receiving the plane, Charles further reduced its weight by removing the heavy leather pilot seat and substituted, instead, a lightweight wicker chair. Final preparations included loading 448 gallons of gasoline and 28 gallons of oil so he could avoid refueling during his flight. He included a week's worth of food and four quarts of water. Just in case he crashed in the Atlantic, among his emergency supplies were a rubberized boat, fishing wire, fishhooks, water, and canned food. By the time Charles was ready to attempt a flight across the ocean, six well-known pilots had lost their lives pursing the Orteig prize. This news did not deter him. He renewed his spirit, courage, and daring regarding all the challenges he knew he faced.

With difficulty, he took off for Paris from a rain-soaked, muddy Roosevelt Field in Long Island, New York in the *Spirit of St. Louis* at 7:52 a.m. on May 20, 1927. His thirty-three-and-a-half-hour flight from New York to Le Bourget Aerodrome, Paris, France, was replete with adventures as he knew he'd be facing difficult weather conditions, sleep deprivation, and other difficulties. An interesting sidelight to the flight that happened just before he landed in Paris, a prelude to his later interest in protecting the environment; at 9:20 p.m. he unwrapped a sandwich, and after eating it, prepared to toss the wax paper out the window. In a moment of reflection, he decided it would be bad manners for an American to litter the countryside just before landing at the airport. Finally, he arrived in Paris at 10:22 p.m. on May 21 after having flown 3,614 miles nonstop in thirty-three hours and thirty minutes.

Charles was immediately mobbed by a crowd of 150,000 spectators. This began his life as the world's most popular superstar. When the flight was over, Charles was completely exhausted, hardly able to enjoy the excitement he had created. The thrilled crowd pulled him from the plane and hoisted him above their heads while they circled the field for almost an hour. He felt sick, suffering from dehydration and dizzy from all the fanfare. Fortunately, he was rescued from the mob by a group of French military flyers, soldiers, and police who were able to put him in the hands of U.S. Ambassador to France Myron Herrick. The ambassador seeing how exhausted he was, whisked him to his residence where he could be fed and put to bed without any interruptions by the hounding press or others. Completely fatigued, Charles fell into bed and slept for ten hours.

In the meantime, Ambassador Herrick wired U.S. President Calvin Coolidge about Lindbergh: "Had we searched all America, we could not have found a better type than young Charles Lindbergh to represent the spirit and high purpose of our people." Later, in writing the foreword to Lindbergh's book *WE*, Ambassador Herrick wrote: "…Charles Lindbergh, not only as a brave aviator, but as an example of American idealism, character and conduct."

As soon as he awoke in the morning, Charles contacted his mother to let her know that he had arrived safely. The one request he had made the night before was that his plane be safeguarded. The mob that had greeted him at the airport included those certain souvenir hunters hoping to get a "piece of the plane".

After breakfast in the ambassador's residence, during which he met with some members of the media, he headed back to the airport to check on the *Spirit of St. Louis*. In the meantime, Ambassador Herrick made arrangements to meet with the President of France and other dignitaries. The President of France awarded him the country's most prestigious medal, the Cross of the Legion of Honor. From Paris, Charles made a few flights in the *Spirit of St. Louis* to other European cities. He was an instant world hero and celebrity, possibly the world's first superstar. Good looking, charming, and active, he had captured the world's imagination. But even with notoriety, fame, and the superstar treatment he had earned in Europe, he was anxious to return to the United States.

The United States Government sent the navy vessel *USS Memphis* to bring Charles and his plane back. Shortly thereafter, he met with U.S. President Calvin Coolidge in the White House. New York City honored him with their biggest parade of the century. Some of the media referred to him as the Columbus of the Air. He flew to more cities in the 48 U. S. continental states, receiving special honors wherever he landed. Two months after this American tour, he wrote a book about his transatlantic flight, which became an instant best-seller. Interestingly, it was published by George P. Putnam, who would later marry the most famous female pilot Amelia Earhart.

World leaders were anxious to meet and honor the charming Charles A. Lindbergh. He did a 7,800 mile Good Will Tour of Latin America and the Caribbean in the *Spirit of St. Louis* from December 13, 1927 to February 8, 1928. On this tour, he visited Mexico, Guatemala, British Honduras, El Salvador, Honduras, Nicaragua, Costa Rica, Panama, Colombia, Venezuela, St. Croix in the U.S. Virgin Islands, Puerto Rico, Dominican Republic, Haiti, and Cuba. Charles became the most famous world traveler in history. He was young, handsome, and photogenic. The ladies loved him; he received over 10,000 proposals for marriage.

Charles foresaw the day when regular passengers could fly throughout the world. While generally a shy person, he effectively used his celebrity status to advocate the development of U.S. commercial aviation and promote U.S. air mail service. He joined with others to begin to develop concepts for new aircraft that could fly further, faster, and with more passengers.

During his Latin America and Caribbean tour, he visited Mexico City in December 1927. It was there that Charles met his future wife Anne Morrow, the daughter of U.S. Ambassador to Mexico Dwight Morrow.

Until he met Anne, Lindbergh had not dated anyone seriously. His intense interest in flying left him with little time for romance. Anne was an exceedingly bright young lady who was most interested in a career in writing. When she graduated from Smith College, she won the prestigious Jordan Prize for writing. Like Charles, she was shy. However, they began to see each other as often as possible, and on May 27, 1929, two years after his famous flight, they married. They eventually had six children together.

**Charles and Anne Lindbergh**
(Author of the Week – Anne Spencer Lindbergh, 2010)

Shortly after Charles married Anne Morrow, he taught her to fly. In September of 1929, they flew together to Cuba, Haiti, Puerto Rico, Trinidad, Venezuela, Colombia, Panama, and Nicaragua. Every place they went, there were mobs of people to meet them and invitations from dignitaries to attend to.

For Charles, it was back to his many business interests and other activities that a celebrity had to participate in. Lindbergh had strong interests in science. In a meeting with Robert Goddard, a physics professor at Clark University, he became fascinated with experiments the professor had been conducting in rocketry. He quickly grasped the need for such experiments for the future of space travel. He believed so strongly in what Dr. Goddard was accomplishing that he arranged, through his wealthy friend Harry Guggenheim, for Dr. Goddard to have the financial assistance he needed to continue his experiments.

Dr. Goddard went on to be the U.S. father of rocket science. Charles continued throughout his life to support U.S. space travel efforts. In 1968, he was invited to lunch with the Apollo VIII crew just before they took off on the first voyage to the moon. Then, six months later Neil A. Armstrong invited Anne and Charles A. Lindbergh to attend the launch of Apollo XI, which led to the first man to walk on the moon.

In 1931, Charles and Anne Lindbergh took off on a ten-week journey through Alaska to the Orient. They proved that the shortest way to Japan and China was over Alaska. With Charles as the pilot and Anne as co-pilot and navigator, they became the first persons to fly from America to China. So that they could see and do more on the trip, the plane was fitted with pontoons, allowing the Lindberghs to land on lakes, rivers, and harbors. They were met in Japan by large crowds and feted throughout the country by officials and aviation personnel. When they arrived in China, the country was suffering from severe floods. Since they had the only plane in China that could travel beyond the flooded area, they offered their services to the government to fly food, medicines, and messages throughout the devastated area. China was so grateful that the President, Chiang Kai-shek, awarded them the National Medal of Honor. Then they received a telegram that Anne's father had died. They canceled the rest of their trip and headed home.

Anne Lindbergh had developed into an excellent pilot and navigator and participated equally in many of the decisions that such a journey to the orient entailed. She became highly proficient as a radio operator during the couple's many world flights. Although Anne often accompanied her famous husband on trips and shared in the flight responsibilities, she seldom received much credit for her contributions from her husband. However, the journey to China provided her with much information that became the basis for her first bestselling book called *North to the Orient*. In the book, she wrote: "One could sit still and look at life from the air; that was it. And I was conscious again of the fundamental magic of flying…Looking down from the air that morning, I felt that stillness rested like a light over the earth…flying… it will always remain magic."

While notoriety and fortune followed Charles after his famous flight, it had its drawbacks as well. He now began to shy away from fame. And just when things began to calm down, a major tragedy struck. What a shock! On the evening of March 1, 1932, their son, 20-month-old Charles Augustus Lindbergh, Jr., was kidnapped by an intruder. An intense 10-week nationwide search for the child took place. A ransom of $50,000 was paid in exchange for information about the boy. Eventually the child's body was found in the woods near the Lindbergh house. A year-and-a-half later, Bruno Richard Hauptmann was arrested as the kidnapper because he had a stash of money containing $13,760 of the marked ransom bills in his garage. Within six weeks, he was convicted of the crime and sentenced to death.

**Charles Lindbergh Jr.**
(Haddon, 2012)

After the dreadful crime and loss of their son, the Lindberghs tried to put their life back in order. In 1933, Charles and Anne took another long trip together, flying first to Greenland where they had several adventures. From Greenland, they went to Iceland where they circumnavigated the entire country. Then they spent a week in Denmark and voyaged on to Sweden where they visited the homestead of Lindbergh's grandparents. Visits to European countries followed, including Russia, Switzerland, Spain, and several others. On their return trip they flew to several locations in Africa and Latin America. After six months, they returned home to Long Island.

When they returned from their long trip they received word that Robert Hauptmann had been arrested for the kidnapping of Charles A. Lindbergh Jr. The media frenzy began once again. The trial put the Lindberghs back on the front page. They both testified during the trial.

With the spotlight still on the Lindbergh family after the trial, they decided to move to England in 1935, hoping for privacy. The peace and quiet they sought came true in a small town in England called The Weald of Kent. While they enjoyed the privacy of rural England, they regularly flew throughout Europe.

In 1936, the U.S. Embassy in Berlin, Germany, invited Charles to visit to discuss Germany's air strength. Germany, like every place he visited, greeted Lindbergh royally. The Germans were proud of what they were developing in new military aircraft and took him on tours through their factories, including their experimental centers that were considered highly secret. Charles and Anne considered living there at one point. The German Air Ministry was excited to have Charles fly some of their planes. He came away duly impressed with the advanced state of German aeronautical design, engineering, and production.

Charles met and socialized with Hermann Goering, Germany's Air Minister who was second only to Adolph Hitler in the Nazi hierarchy. Charles knew of the great feats of air combat Goering had displayed in World War I, earning Germany's highest honor, the Iron Cross First Class. Charles had also visited the Soviet Union three times in the 1930s, which had developed air power not even remotely close to that of Germany. He suggested to the U.S. Embassy that the United States Government and the fledgling U.S. private aviation industry needed to move more rapidly toward improving its capability in producing more and better planes.

In 1938, during a special dinner in Berlin that included high-level American, British, and German diplomats, Hermann Goering presented Charles with the *Service Cross of the German Eagle* in recognition of his aviation services to the world. Accustomed to receiving high-level awards, he didn't give it much attention. The French Ambassador and Henry Ford had both also received the award. Later during the war years, many American citizens thought he should have publicly denounced the award. He never did so.

**Charles Lindbergh in Nazi Germany
with Hermann Göring**
(Rhapsodyinbooks, 2014)

Even during Charles' visits to Germany, it was clear that Germany intended to aggressively dominate and eventually seek to conquer Europe and beyond. Charles advised American officials that it was a European affair and maybe the U.S. should let them deal with the crisis, strongly opposing possible U.S. involvement in a war outside the U.S. This was in a similar vein as his father had done with respect to World War I. For the first time, Charles took advantage of his fame for a cause, saying; "For five years, at home and abroad, I spoke, wrote, and argued..." forcefully against the U.S. being potentially involved in a war against the Germans. While not a peace activist, he advocated that the U.S. remain neutral. His position was one of isolationism and nonintervention. He wanted the U.S. to develop a strong military program but to use its forces only if the U.S. were attacked.

Col. Charles A. Lindbergh tells the House
Foreign Affairs Committee that a German air
invasion of the United States and the landing
of troops is "absolutely impossible"
(Rhapsodyinbooks, 2014)

His objection toward U.S. involvement in Europe put him in complete opposition to President Franklin D. Roosevelt's intent of having the U.S. support an allied effort against Germany. In Charles' meetings with the President, they discussed the need for a U. S. military buildup. Roosevelt used Lindbergh's help in this regard to get legislation passed to increase the defense budget. But on the contentious issue of the U.S. supporting England and Europe in their war efforts, he and Roosevelt had totally different positions. This difference of opinion developed into a deep animus between Roosevelt and Lindbergh. Roosevelt used the strongest language to impugn the legitimacy of Lindbergh's views on the war. Charles took umbrage at the President's remarks and launched a vitriolic attack on the President's remarks. Their debates became so bitter that, in 1939, Charles, after much cogitation, resigned his commission as an Air Corps reserve colonel writing: "…with utmost regret…for my relationship with the Air Corps is one of the things which has meant most to me in my life. I place it second only to my right as a citizen to speak freely to my fellow countrymen. I will continue to serve my country to the best of my ability as a private citizen." He remained intransigent in his neutral views on the war in Europe until the Japanese attacked Pearl Harbor.

When the Japanese attacked Pearl Harbor, Charles quickly switched his position saying: "I can see nothing to do under these circumstances except to fight." He asked to be reinstated in the Army Air Corps. President Roosevelt refused to allow his reinstatement, and in fact, sought revenge for Lindbergh's earlier positions against him. He made it clear that as Commander-in-Chief, he did not want Lindbergh connected in any way to the U.S. military establishment.

In the meantime, President Roosevelt asked the political and economically powerful Henry Ford, founder, and president of the Ford Motor Company, to sign a contract with the government to convert its auto manufacturing assembly line to build airplane bombers. The President was in desperate need of Ford's help. Ford then hired Lindbergh as a technical consultant and test pilot. Roosevelt could hardly refuse such an arrangement, as he needed those bombers in the worst way. And so, Charles was a civilian consultant and not a part of the U.S. Government. As compensation for his work, Charles could have had a lucrative contract, but he only asked for $666.66 a month, equivalent to the amount a colonel was paid in the Air Corps. He helped the Navy with their "Corsair" fighter plane and demonstrated special maneuvers. In that effort, at 40 years of age, he was still outperforming the young naval pilots.

In 1944, Charles met with Marine Corps Brigadier General Louis E. Wood. The General suggested Charles go to Asia to inspect what the navy was accomplishing with the Corsair airplanes that were presently flying over Japan. Charles replied that President Roosevelt would never approve. The General obtained permission if it was clear that while Charles was a civilian consultant.

Lo and behold, and with some difficulties, Charles, as a civilian, was able to fly fifty combat missions over Japan that included shooting down a Japanese airplane during an air duel in the sky. In 1948, he wrote about these experiences in his next book, titled *Of Flight and Life*.

Once the war was over, Charles continued his earlier efforts to improve opportunities for the civilian population to fly commercially throughout the world. From the aviation experiments made during the war, tremendous improvements were available in the construction and operation of aircraft. The need was to transfer the technical knowhow to civilian aircraft, and he was able to help make this happen. In addition, his business efforts gave him the financial wherewithal to allow him the freedom to pursue other interests, which included testing improved aircraft capable of flying to new destinations.

Even though Charles had lost his reserve status as a colonel, he continued to support the U.S. military in any way possible. He was able to test airplanes, suggest mechanical changes to improve military aircraft, and provide other services as requested. In recognition of such loyalty, in 1954, President Dwight D. Eisenhower restored his U.S. Army Air Corp reserve status and promoted him to Brigadier General. As a result, in 1954, Charles was served on the advisory panel that determined the location of the United States Air Force Academy near Colorado Springs, Colorado from possibly 582 sites.

Often, Charles' travel and business interests caused him to be away from his family for long periods of time. Anne was always supportive of his activities, but she too had ambitions. A highly competent pioneering aviator in her own right, she was a successful author and gained attention for publications that included popular books as *North to the Orient, Listen! The Wind, The Wave of the Future*, and *War Without and Within*. Because of Charles' immense popularity and celebrity status, there were social responsibilities that sometimes led to family conflicts. Charles and Anne were quite different; he was stoic and she was goal oriented. She was a woman who sought equality and assumed large responsibilities. She needed time to pursue her interests.

Anne Lindbergh enjoyed her writing successes. Yet, in various activities, she acknowledged that she received little emotional support from her husband. When he was authoring his book *The Spirit of St. Louis*, she helped him as a highly competent editor. When he received a Pulitzer

Prize for the book, an immensely popular volume, surely she felt jealous that her efforts were overlooked. Partially as a result of his inattentiveness, she sought attentions and interests outside the marriage. Beginning in 1956, she had an affair with her longtime physician and friend, Dr. Dana Atchley. Whether Charles knew of the affair is not known. He never addressed it publicly. It was only after his death that researchers learned of her affair and, in the process, found that Charles also had liaisons outside the marriage.

Charles, our celebrated worldly traveler, had his own foibles and shortcomings like others in society. Beginning in 1957, Lindbergh, then 55, had a dark secret he was able to keep from the press. Though it was never known by his wife nor his admiring public, he also had an affair with his private secretary in Europe. Her name was Valeska, and she bore him two children. He also had two long-time affairs with both a German hat maker, Brigitte Hesshaimer, and her sister, Marietta Hesshaimer. Brigitte bore him three children, and Marietta gave him two sons. His liaisons lasted from 1957 until his death on August 26, 1974 at age 72. Anne, lived to be 93, and she died in 2001, seemingly unaware of the affairs. Brigitte died the same year at age 74.

One of Charles' favorite adventures was living and traveling in Africa, especially in Kenya and Tanganyika. In 1962, he deliberately made a trip to Africa just to live among the Masai tribe to learn about their customs and culture. He visited again in 1964, and on this trip, he accidentally met the famous British archaeologist and anthropologist Dr. Louis S.B. Leakey. They had many conversations together. These trips to Africa and to other locations, solidified his interest in the environment and the protection of wildlife.

As Charles grew older, he continued to possess a strong interest in flying and seeing the world. In 1969, he flew around the world five times. Earlier, one of the places he enjoyed most was the Philippines. That year, he was there again for an extended period, particularly interested in the primitive cultures existing on the islands. For a while, he lived with one of the tribes.

On several of his trips, Charles stopped in Hawaii, where he particularly enjoyed the island of Maui. The Lindbergh family built a house there, which eventually became their principal residence. At the end of his life, when he was dying in a New York hospital from cancer, he asked to be flown to Hawaii where he would find peace of spirit.

Charles A. Lindbergh died on August 26, 1974 in Kipahulu, Maui, in Hawaii.

Of all the worldly travelers to date, none traveled as far nor as often as Charles. Once he became a pilot, he crisscrossed America and Europe many times, flying to the Orient, including Southeast Asia, South America, the Caribbean, and Africa. Most of his flight activities had to do with his various positions in and out of government and with goodwill tours. He said he most enjoyed those experiences that included many jaunts with his wife.

Charles probably received more medals and awards than any single person in U.S. history. The honors were from the U.S. government, the private sector, U.S. states, foreign governments, and nonprofit organizations. As a military person, he received the highest medal given, the *Medal of Honor* "...for displaying heroic courage and skill as a navigator at the risk of his life..." Congress gave him their highest civilian medal, the *Congressional Gold Medal*.

As the author of seven books, he received the 1954 Pulitzer Prize for *The Spirit of St. Louis*, published in 1953. He was *Time* magazine's "Man of the Year" in 1927; the first person to receive this honor. In 1968, the National Institute of Social Sciences gave him their Gold Medal Award. Also in 1968, he received an Honorary Doctor of Science from Georgetown University. Most U.S. states presented him with various awards. Foreign governments honored him with their highest medals of honor, usually reserved for citizens of their own countries. Schools, airports, and buildings across the country and abroad were named in his honor.

No aviator has been celebrated to the degree attained by Charles A. Lindbergh. In addition, no person had greater access to U. S. presidents than Charles, from President Calvin Coolidge to President Richard Nixon. The legacies from his historic flight and post-flight accomplishments remain incredible. After his historic transatlantic flight, he wrote a letter to the director of Longines Watches describing in detail a watch he thought would make navigation easier for pilots. The watch was manufactured to his design and is still produced today.

When Charles met the French born Nobel Prize winning biologist Dr. Alexis Carrel, thirty years his senior, they became good friends, joining with some medical ideas at the prestigious Rockefeller Institute for Medical Research in New York. Dr. Carrel's research in heart-related medicine fascinated Charles, and during several years of on-and-off research with Dr. Carrel, Charles used his mechanical aptitude and analytical skills in inventing a heart-related device.

As a staunch environmentalist, naturalist, and conservationist with interest in the sustainability of travel destinations, Charles observed: "The primitive was at the mercy of the civilized in our twentieth-century times…and nothing had made it more so than the airplane I had helped develop. I had helped to change the environment of our lives." This actually troubled him a great deal. Ironically, it caused him, the person who all his life had supported technological improvements in civilian aircraft, to oppose the supersonic passenger jets being developed by the airlines in the 1960s.

He observed that civilization often destroyed the development of birds and other species, as he remembered the sky being black with thousands of ducks in flight during his epic voyage in 1927. In an article entitled "Is Civilization Progress?" in the July 1964 issue of *Reader's Digest*, he wrote: "I realized that if I had to choose, I would rather have birds than airplanes." Later, in in a December 22, 1967 article in *Life* magazine, he noted: "In wilderness I sense the miracle of life, and behind it our scientific accomplishments fade to trivia. Real freedom lies in wildness, not in civilization."

While he had devoted his career to aviation, Charles embraced the concept of environmentalism much in the same way as Henry David Thoreau noted when he wrote: "…in wildness is the preservation of the world." Charles became a strong supporter of such organizations as the Nature Conservancy, the World Wildlife Fund, and the International Union for the Conservation of Nature and Natural Resources. He worked on environmental issues throughout the world, especially in Africa, the Philippines, and Peru. In the United States, he worked to protect Artic wolves in Alaska, to identify preservation concerns in Hawaii, and he helped to establish Voyageurs National Park in northern Minnesota.

For many years after his historic flight in 1927, he was the best-known celebrity in the United States and possibly the world. His airplane is enshrined in the National Air and Space Museum where his *Spirit of St. Louis* remains today. In 1948, Charles wrote: "I devoted my life to planes and engines, to surveying airlines, to preaching wherever men would listen the limitless future of the sky."

His portent for the future has been accurate. In 2004, there existed an "X Prize Foundation", a nonprofit organization based in St. Louis, Missouri, that offered $10 million to the first private group that could build and launch a manned craft into space and then repeat the feat within two weeks of the first flight. The framework for this prize was modeled after the Orteig Prize, the $25,000 received by Charles A. Lindbergh for making his New York to Paris trip. 2004 saw SpaceShipOne, designed by Burt Rutan and piloted by Mike Melville win the "X Prize" award.

Our aviator, author, inventor, explorer, environmentalist, and worldly traveler, impacted the world more immediately during his lifetime than any of his predecessors reported in earlier chapters of this book. All of our Worldly Travelers changed the world in one way or another, but in most cases, the dramatic impacts came after they were dead. Charles, through a variety of circumstances and because of his superstar status, left immediate legacies in whatever endeavor he tried. He contributed to the aviation industry, medical technology, and efforts in sustaining the environment. Fortune seemed to follow him.

The moniker "Lucky Lindy", more than any of his other many nicknames, fits this worldly traveler. While not academically well-educated, and with the help of his wife, he became a prolific writer.

This brief paragraph written by Charles is memorable: "The life of an aviator seemed to me ideal. It involved skill. It commanded adventure. It made use of the latest developments of science. I was glad I failed my college course. Mechanical engineers were fettered to factories and drafting boards, while pilots had the freedom of wind in the expanse of sky. I could spiral the desolation of a mountain peak, explore caverns of a cloud, or land on a city flying field and there convince others of aviation's future. There were times in an airplane when it seemed I had partially escaped mortality, to look down on earth like a god."

**Charles Lindbergh**
(Charles Lindbergh: An American Aviator, n.d.)

# CHAPTER TWELVE

# TRAVELING ON THE WINGS OF AMELIA EARHART, AVIATRIX

> "My own journey started long before I
> left and was over before I returned."
> -John Steinbeck-

*Flying over the Pacific Ocean on July 2, 1937 looking for a landing field on Howland Island, Amelia Earhart glanced at the plane's fuel gage to find it was on empty. Howland Island was so incredibly small that neither Amelia nor her navigator Fred Noonan was able to locate the island. Though not easily frightened, she now feared for her life. She turned and shouted her concerns to Fred, praying that he had a suggestion of a place for an emergency landing. Unfortunately, he had no idea where they were, since he had been unable to make radio contact with the support vessel, the United States Coast Guard Cutter "Itasca" for several hours. Amelia thought: "God help us – where is the safest place to ditch this aircraft in the ocean".*

*The right engine of Amelia's twin-engine Lockheed Electra stopped. The left one began to sputter, and shortly, it too died. The plane plunged violently towards the ocean. Amelia frantically tried to adjust the rudders in an attempt at righting the aircraft, hoping she might "glide" the plane to a successful water landing. Emergency bailing out from the aircraft was not an option as she and Noonan had not packed parachutes. Amelia turned towards Noonan and said her last goodbyes.*

*The plane crashed into the waves, floating a few moments and then disappeared into the depths of the sea. Amelia Earhart, Fred Noonan, and the aircraft sank in the vast Pacific Ocean. Search efforts by the U.S. Navy and Coast Guard were futile. The world was stunned.*

**Amelia Earhart and Fred Noonan**
(Hanes, 2012)

\*　　\*　　\*

Until the twentieth century, international travel was largely a man's world. Major travel expeditions and explorations were almost always accomplished by men. If women did travel, they were usually wives of missionaries or government officials, or they were on leisure travel with their husbands.

The 1920s set the tone for increased rights for women to travel, this mobility increased dramatically with the onset of travel by train and steamboat. Women had entered the work force in larger numbers, making up about 25 percent of the workforce, during and after World War I. In 1920, women were given the right to vote in the United States. Many women became active in the politics of the nation. Women began to wear more convenient clothing and stopped wearing long, cumbersome dresses. Definitely a change in attitude toward a woman's place in society.

Also by the 1920s, especially in the United States and Europe, many women who journeyed independently of their husbands or fathers were well-educated, had their own financial resources, and possessed an unquenchable curiosity about the world in which they lived.

However, the woman who had the courage to crusade for women's rights, gain respect for women pilots, and who changed the world of travel for more than half the world's population, women, was none other than our worldly traveler Amelia Earhart, America's best-known aviatrix. A remarkable and different story about life in flight for us.

**Amelia Earhart next to her airplane**

\*   \*   \*

Amelia Mary Earhart, daughter of Samuel "Edwin" Stanton Earhart and Amelia "Amy" Otis Earhart, was born July 24, 1897 in Atchison, Kansas at the home of her wealthy maternal grandfather Alfred Gideon Otis. The *Atchison Daily Globe* newspaper announced: "A girl baby was born to Mr. and Mrs. E.S. Earhart at the residence of Judge Otis on Sunday night." This brief mention in a newspaper was Amelia Earhart's first appearance in the media; it certainly would not be her last.

Amelia's parents had earlier decided to have their first child born at the home of Amy Earhart's parents. And possibly live there. At first, the independent minded Edwin was reluctant to do so. However, since he was not yet fully established in a career and had only recently graduated from law school, he bowed to his wife's wishes to be surrounded by her family when she was giving birth. Furthermore, the Otis' had in their employ servants capable of making living conditions quite comfortable for a new mother and child.

Amelia's grandfather, Alfred Otis, was a former federal judge, president of the Atchison Savings Bank, and a leading citizen in the community. Located on the Missouri River in the heartland of America, the small town of Atchison was an ideal place for raising children. It offered lots of open space and friendly residents. Young children moved freely and safely throughout the area. As a child, Amelia was nicknamed "Meeley". She had a younger sister, Grace Muriel Earhart – nicknamed "Pidge" – who was extremely close to her and someone with whom she could share her dreams and secrets.

Amy Earhart let her daughters roam throughout the neighborhood with few restrictions. Amelia, at least in terms of what was expected from a young girl at the beginning of the twentieth century, was a restless sort of "tomboy", always looking for boyish-type adventures. She liked to collect worms, toads, and other creatures, keeping them in her special secret indoor places. She also enjoyed climbing trees, playing basketball and tennis, and other activities that were typically reserved for young boys. Later she described her childhood in her grandparent's home in Atchison this way: "Throughout the grade school period, which was mostly spent in Atchison, I remember having a very good time. There were regular games and school and mud-ball fights, picnics, and exploring raids up and down the bluffs of the Missouri River."

Amelia's father, Edwin, basically an unsuccessful lawyer, struggled with different jobs throughout his life. He was always searching for a position that better suited his interests and abilities. During much of his career, he worked in various capacities for railroad companies, which caused frequent absences from his family. Depressed, lacking job satisfaction, and lonely, he began to drink excessively. His drinking did not bode well with his immediate family, especially with his in-laws. His actions impacted the whole family. He moved from job to job, often uprooting the family. Except for the early happy years spent in Atchison, Amelia would find herself moving many times.

In 1907, when Amelia was nine years old, her father was working as a claims officer for the Rock Island Railroad. The company transferred him to Des Moines, Iowa. Because he had railroad complimentary privileges, he encouraged Amelia to take train trips with him when he had the opportunity to travel, which stimulated her love of travel. The next year at the Iowa State Fair, Amelia's father tried to talk Amelia and her sister into taking a flight on an airplane. Aviation was new, having just come into being with the first flights by Orville and Wilbur Wright at Kitty Hawk, North Carolina in 1903. Since passenger aviation was just beginning in 1908, most airplanes were shabby, rickety-looking machines, and eleven-year-old Amelia wanted no part of flying in such a contraption.

During their father's many absences, Amelia's mother, Amy, and the two girls remained at their grandparent's home in Atchison. Initially, Amy home-schooled Amelia and Muriel. In 1909, they all joined Amelia's father in Des Moines, and Amelia entered school in the seventh grade at the age of twelve. Shortly after the move, Amelia's grandmother, whom she adored, unexpectedly died. Her grandmother left a substantial trust fund in her mother's name. The intention was clear that the inheritance was not to be shared with Edwin – a decision that greatly angered him, led to more intensive drinking, and added to a difficult marriage that was already in trouble.

In 1914, Amelia's father lost his railroad job in Iowa. He was forced to retire until he could rehabilitate himself from his alcohol abuse problem.

Even after rehabilitation, the Rock Island Railroad did not re-hire him. However, in 1915, he landed a job as a clerk with the Great Northern Railway in St. Paul, Minnesota. Another move took place, and Amelia entered Central High School in St. Paul as a junior. Again, Edwin's job did not last. This time Amy, disgusted with her husband, took the children to Chicago where they temporarily lived with friends. Amelia graduated in 1916 from Hyde Park High School in Chicago.

In 1917, Amelia left Chicago to join her sister, who was a student at St. Margret's school in Toronto, Canada. As part of the British Empire, Canada had joined Great Britain and its allies in 1914 to fight the axis powers during World War I. While some Americans independently joined Canada and Great Britain in their war efforts, it was 1917 before the United States became officially involved. During the war campaign, wounded Canadian soldiers were returning home in large numbers from the war zone. Seeing and reading about the plight of so many injured veterans touched Amelia's soul. She impulsively volunteered to become a nurse's aide at Canada's Spadina Military Hospital. This decision put her completely on her own for the first time in her life.

Amelia learned to ride and enjoy horses early in life. In contacts with the Canadian military, she met some air force officers who also loved to ride. After riding, they invited her to the airfield to watch their flying maneuvers. Strict military rules did not allow her to join them in flight, but she found herself fascinated just watching them go through their flight routines.

Also while in Canada, Amelia and a friend visited the Canadian National Exposition in Toronto, which also featured an air show. Amelia became quite excited watching one of the World War I pilots perform various antics in the air. The pilot was swooping down near the crowd to create excitement. He noticed Amelia and her friend had drifted off to one side, and he began diving in their direction. Amelia got a big rush from being so close to the plane. At that moment, she knew that sometime in her life she had to learn to fly.

In 1918, the Spanish flu pandemic reached Toronto at the Spadina Military Hospital where Amelia worked. This flu, also known as the 1918 influenza pandemic, was an unusually deadly influenza pandemic caused by the H1N1 influenza A virus. Lasting from February 1918 to April 1920, it infected an estimated 500 million people, or one-third of the world's population at the time – in four successive waves. The number of deaths was estimated to be 50 million worldwide with about 675,000 deaths in the United States. Amelia caught the flu and became very sick; her illness progressed into pneumonia and maxillary sinusitis. It wasn't clear why, but the flu apparently caused her to suffer from sinus headaches for the rest of her life. She had several operations to relieve the pain, but none were effective for any length of time.

In 1919, Amelia entered Smith College, but impulsively changed her mind and went to Columbia University. Even though she was a good student, a year later, she quit the university and joined her parents who had been reunited in California. In Long Beach, she and her father visited a nearby airfield. Seeing Amelia's interest in his plane, a pilot gave her a ride. That experience created an excitement in Amelia that she had never known before and became the impetus for her to earn enough money for flying lessons.

California in the 1920s was the mecca for individuals interested in flying. The mild year-round weather and suitable areas for building landing fields contributed to a fledging aviation industry. With few safety devices available, it was considered risky and dangerous to fly airplanes. Men, as well as a few women pilots, took their chances, and many died as a result. The planes, with wings made of linen panels sewed together, had no gas gauges or brakes. The use of parachutes had not yet entered the picture. While men dominated as pilots and instructors, there were a few adventurous females entering such careers. Amelia spurned a wonderful opportunity for learning to fly from a highly qualified male instructor perceiving that she would learn more quickly from a woman. In 1921, her teacher was Neta Snook, who was already a successful pioneer female aviator in California and just a year older than Amelia.

One characteristic about Neta that seemed to appeal to Amelia was her independent spirit and that she was not intimidated by her male counterpart aviators. In fact, Neta was the first woman to enter a "men's" air race and finished in fifth place. At the time, she commented to the media: "I'm going to fly as cleverly, as audaciously, as thrillingly as any man aviator in the world." The next year Neta married, became pregnant, and gave up flying. Her greatest claim to fame in later life was to be known as the instructor who taught Amelia Earhart to fly. She capitalized on this notoriety in a book titled *I Taught Amelia To Fly*.

**Amelia Earhart (right) and Neta Snook (left)**
(Amelia Earhart, n. d.)

Amelia was a quick learner; flying seemed to come naturally to her. After her successful lessons with Neta, she wanted desperately to buy her own plane. She worked at a variety of jobs, including as an office file clerk, and with some financial help from her parents, she saved enough money in 1921 to buy a second-hand plane. She bought a bright yellow Kinner Airster biplane, which she named "The Canary". By 1922, she was flying as often as possible, and, in so doing, she set an altitude record for female pilots. On May 15, 1923, Earhart became the 16th woman to be issued a pilot's license by the Federation Aeronautique Internationale --- quite an accomplishment in the 1920s.

Amelia was always her own person in the sense of making impromptu decisions. On a whim, she might have decided to do something new or seemingly unusual. In 1924, she sold her airplane and bought a bright yellow Kissel "Speedster", a two-passenger automobile, which she christened the *Yellow Peril*; she loved yellow and saw herself as a perilous driver. Following her parent's divorce in 1924, she put her mother in the *Yellow Peril*, and they made a transcontinental road trip from California to Boston. Instead of driving straight across the country, they drove hundreds of miles out of the way to visit national parks in the U.S. and Canada. They made many other side trips, causing the journey to be about 7,000 miles long before they reached their destination.

After arriving in Boston, Amelia continued to have problems with the sinus infections she developed in Canada, and she underwent more surgery. In 1925, she re-entered Columbia University, only to withdraw after one semester. Part of the reason for her withdrawal and lack of flying was due to monetary problems. Her mother's inheritance, which had provided some family support, was almost depleted. Amelia's mother had never worked before, so it fell to Amelia to support the two of them. She was able to find work as a teacher and social worker, and she began to save some money.

In 1927, like the rest of the nation, Amelia was excited when Charles A. Lindbergh made his solo flight from New York to Paris. That event re-stimulated her interest in a career in flying. She began to fly on a regular basis, wanting to emulate the example set by Charles A. Lindbergh. She also took advantage of her writing skills and wrote impressive articles on flying for *The Bostonian* newspaper, publicizing the ability of women to fly.

In one article, she wrote: "While women are hopelessly adventurous, they seem content to take their thrills vicariously and watch men do things a long time before they attempt to do them. I have the hope that this year will see many more women flying…There is no door closed to ability, so when women are ready, there will be opportunity for them in aviation."

Amelia increased her airtime, logging 500 hours of solo flying without any major incidents --- a milestone for women aviators during that era.

She became a serious record-setting and responsible pilot. Her strong will, positive attitude, and considerable abilities eventually led to her earning not only numerous aviation accolades but also to a career as a businesswoman, lecturer, and author.

In 1927, Amelia received a phone call from a Captain H. H. Railey asking if she would like to be a passenger in an attempt to fly in a seaplane from the United States across the Atlantic to England. The flight was billed as the "Friendship Flight". She was caught completely off guard with such a request and was a little suspicious. However, she showed up for the interview. Captain Railey was impressed with her. When asked if she would like to be the first woman to cross the Atlantic in a plane, she became excited. In her heart, she would have preferred to be chosen as the pilot. But she knew just being in a plane flying across the ocean would be good preparation for future oceanic flights by women.

After Amelia agreed to be part of the Friendship Flight, she was turned over to the flight promoter George P. Putnam. He was an outstanding marketer, book publisher, and publicist, who had been involved earlier with promoting and publicizing Charles A. Lindbergh as a pioneer pilot. Putnam was to have the final word regarding the choice of Amelia for the flight. In his first meeting with Amelia, he was immediately taken in by her charisma and infectious positive attitude about flying. Putnam had an uncanny eye for what would sell, and he immediately seized the moment to note this attractive, poised, well-spoken, five-foot eight-inch, 118-pound female had all the right attributes for molding into a celebrity. He would later manage her in such a way that she received the utmost media exposure and promotion. In effect, he molded her aviation exploits and parlayed her fiery, mediagenic personality and her business acumen so that, in effect, she would become the most famous woman in the world.

The planning for the *Friendship Flight* was solely the responsibility of Commander Richard Byrd, a renowned navy pilot who had flown missions in World War I. He was already famous for his flights over the North Pole, an area he would later explore. He was impressed with

Amelia and felt that as a female pilot, she'd be ideal to be the first woman to cross the Atlantic in an airplane, even though only as a passenger. Initially, she was to be responsible for the flight logbook. But the attorney drawing up the papers for the flight expanded Amelia's role such that she would be mostly in charge of the flight. She would accompany the pilot named Wilmer Stultz and his co-pilot/mechanic Louis Gordon. The *Friendship* was the first pontoon equipped plane attempting to cross the ocean. Their initial target was Ireland.

The flight team left from Boston Harbor and landed in the waters of Newfoundland, Canada. Weather delays kept them in Canada for several days. There were also difficulties because Wilmer Stultz was a heavy drinker. With a brief break in the weather pattern and Amelia's strong coaxing of Stultz, who was suffering from an alcoholic binge from the night before, the team was finally able to take flight again. It was foggy for most of the 20-hour flight, but they finally reached the coast of Wales, United Kingdom, just as the *Friendship* ran out of fuel. While they were unable to reach their destination in Ireland, the seaplane was the first such aircraft to successfully cross the Atlantic.

As the first female to cross the Atlantic in an airplane, Amelia received an enormous amount of media attention in England. Actually, she was recognized with far more publicity in the aftermath of this trip than were the male pilot and co-pilot. Part of the reason was the novelty of a woman on such an adventure in an aviation industry dominated by men. Also, George Putnam had sent a writer to England to promote Amelia and the flight. In addition, Amelia was more articulate and made a better appearance than her male counterparts. As a result, she was treated like royalty, while her colleagues were treated well, but not at the same level. When all three returned to the United States, they were honored by a welcome parade in New York where the mayor of New York presented Amelia with a key to the city. She was now a public figure, and with the help of George Putnam, she became a favorite of the media.

Quickly taking advantage of the notoriety and novelty of the flight, George Putnam asked Amelia to live in his house in Rye, New York while she completing writing a book about the flight. She did. He had accomplished something similar in 1927 with Charles A. Lindbergh. Putnam gave Amelia's book the title of *20 Hrs. 40 Min., Our Flight in the Friendship*. He immediately published the book while the trip was still in the limelight, making it a best-seller. An unbelievable publicist, media guru, and publisher, Putnam helped Amelia get her numerous books and poems and other writings published and launched to the public in America and abroad. At the same time, he encouraged Amelia to expand her flying career, and he introduced her to his powerful set of friends who would help her whenever needed.

The adventure on the *Friendship* whetted Amelia Earhart's appetite for more flying. She began establishing new flight records for women and receiving immense amounts of publicity. Because of her notoriety as an aviator, her tall height and thin frame, and her engaging smile, a press agent portrayed Amelia in the same limelight as Charles A. Lindbergh. She began to be dubbed, from time to time, as "Lady Lindy", a misnomer reference to Lindbergh's title of "Lucky Lindy". Amelia was uncomfortable with such comparisons because she realized she had not really accomplished much as an aviator and was certainly not in the same league with Charles A. Lindbergh. She also had other monikers such as the "Queen of the Air" and "Pilot in Pearls".

Amelia's proficient promoter, Putnam, arranged for numerous writing and lecturing opportunities. He made sure she was well photographed and her activities heavily publicized. A savvy marketer, he created a certain mystique about Amelia that captured the nation. He helped her to become more fashion conscious. As a result of such favorable publicity, and with Putnam's help, she successively developed and designed her own line of women's clothing, especially sportswear. He also arranged for her to earn money in endorsing many other products. In brief, she was one of America's first female superstars.

Furthermore, Amelia's celebrity status and endorsements helped her campaign for greater public acceptance of aviation in general, with a special focus on women pilots. In 1928, she was the first woman to fly solo across the North American continent and back. The next year she became a promoter of commercial air travel. Amelia encouraged women to fly whether as pilots or as passengers. Along with Charles A. Lindbergh, she represented the Transcontinental Air Transport airline that had begun to provide city-to-city air shuttle service. The company was particularly interested that Amelia was strongly advocating that women fly commercially. At the time, ninety-five percent of the commercial passengers were men, leaving a large potential market of women largely untapped.

In 1929, after a competitive women's air race, Amelia convinced some of her colleagues of the need for an aviation club for women. She worked with like-minded pilots to organize "The Ninety-Nines", an organization of female pilots. Amelia suggested the name of The Ninety-Nines based on the number of charter pilot members who had signed up. One of their principal objectives was to help provide moral support to women interested in flying. She was the Ninety-Nine's first president in 1930, an organization that still exists to this day.

**Amelia Earhart and members of the Ninety-Nines**
(Aviatrix, 2016)

Because Amelia was engaged in so many activities, there seemed little time left for her to enter into a serious romance. In 1921, she did meet and enjoy the company of a chemical engineer named Sam Chapman. While she was lukewarm with respect to a more serious relationship, Chapman fell head over heels in love with her. They became engaged in 1924. He was her confidant and supported all her activities. Even though they had been engaged for a long time, Amelia broke off the engagement in November 1928. He was devastated. He never married and remained a friend for the rest of her life.

For years, Amelia's closest male friend and benefactor was George Putnam. He was a handsome and interesting man, and for years, he and his wife had both become very close friends to Amelia. As a result of Putnam's constant travels and intense interest in his work, his marriage began to suffer. After he was divorced in 1929, and partly because they spent so much time together, a romance between Amelia and Putnam blossomed. He proposed to Amelia no less than six times. However, she was hesitant toward marriage, possibly because of her parent's embittered relationship and maybe also because women were still struggling for equality with men. Despite her hesitations, she did marry George Putnam on February 7, 1931.

Amelia referred to her marriage as a "partnership" with "dual control". In a letter handed to her betrothed on the day of the wedding she wrote: "I want you to understand I shall not hold you to any medieval code of faithfulness to me nor shall I consider myself bound to you similarly…I must exact a cruel promise, and that is you will let me go in a year if we find no happiness together. I will try to do my best in every way…" Such reference to sexual freedom was certainly an extremely bold and radical idea, breaking with most feminine conventions of the 1930s. To add fuel to the fire, she refused to ever wear her wedding ring. Later, she would have a lasting affair with the handsome flyer, athlete, and politician, Gene Vidal. She even became close to Gene's young son, Gore Vidal. George Putnam, aghast at such behavior, was so in love with her that he did his best to ignore the affair.

Between the years of 1930-1935, Amelia Earhart set seven women's speed and distance aviation records. In the meantime, Putnam had arranged another book deal for Amelia. The book, *The Fun of It*, was all finished except for one chapter. This chapter would only be finished, and the book published, after Amelia piloted a plane across the Atlantic Ocean. Other than Charles A. Lindbergh, no one else had flown across the Atlantic solo. So early in 1932, Amelia set her sights and made her plans to fly across the Atlantic.

On May 20, 1932, the same month and day as Charles A. Lindbergh's famous flight, but five years later, Amelia set off from Harbour Grace, Newfoundland with the intent of a solo flight across the Atlantic to Paris, France; she was, in effect, partially emulating the 1927 flight of Charles A. Lindbergh. After about 15 hours flying in severe weather, compounded with mechanical problems and a fuel leak, she found herself over land but could not find an airfield. All she saw below her was pastureland. She wondered for a moment if she would be able to bring the plane down safely in the grassy area and avoid rocks and ditches. Without hesitation, she made the decision to land and did so without difficulty. She wasn't sure just where she was, but a surprised farmer told her she was in Northern Ireland.

**Article published in the Cleveland News about**
**Amelia Earhart's solo flight across the Atlantic**
(Amelia Earhart Flies Solo Across the Atlantic..., 1932)

After a night's rest in a farmer's home in Ireland, she went on to London. She was immediately received as a world celebrity, wined, and dined by royalty and the rich and famous. She met and danced with the Prince of Wales, who was later King Edward VIII and who abdicated his throne in order to marry an American divorcee, Wallis Simpson. She also went to France, where she was royally received, Italy, where she had an audience with the Pope and met with head of state Mussolini, and Belgium, where she had dinner with the king and queen. Then it was on to New York where she was "bombed" with roses from three airplanes and given a tickertape parade.

As the first female to fly solo across the Atlantic Ocean and the first person to cross the Atlantic twice, Amelia was showered with additional honors. Such recognition included the receipt of the U.S. Congressional Distinguished Flying Cross, the French Cross of Knight of the Legion of Honor (received five years earlier by Lindbergh), the Belgium Cross of Chevalier of the Order of Leopold, and the National Geographic Gold Medal (like Lindbergh) as presented to her by President Herbert Hoover. Later, in Los Angeles for the opening of the Olympic Games with fellow Kansan U.S. Vice President Charles Curtis, he awarded her the Distinguished Service Cross. An interesting side note is that Charles Curtis, a U.S. Congressional Representative, and longtime U.S. Senator from Kansas who had also served as the Senate Majority Leader of the Republican Party was the first Native American Senator and only Native American Vice President.

Even though Amelia had always been somewhat reserved, she gained a great deal of self-confidence during this period, both in the air and on the ground. In 1933, she became friends with Eleanor Roosevelt, wife of President Franklin D. Roosevelt, and the two had long conversations at the White House about the role of women in society. She even took Mrs. Roosevelt for a spin in her plane, which greatly impressed the first lady. From that day on, whenever she was in Washington D.C., she stayed in the White House – quite a heady mark for a shy young lady.

**Pictured left to right: First Lady Eleanor Roosevelt,
Amelia Earhart, Scottish pilot Jim Mollison, his wife,
pilot Amy Johnson, President Franklin D. Roosevelt**
(Everett Collection, n.d.)

She also met with President Roosevelt, who informed her that if there was an issue she felt the President should know about, she merely had to contact his office and he would meet with her. One such issue was her request to the President to appoint her friend Gene Vidal as his Director of the Aeronautics Branch of the Department of Commerce, the highest-level aviation position in the U.S. Government. While there were 43 candidates, some of whom were very close to the President, Amelia's efforts paid off, and Gene Vidal got the job. In return, Amelia campaigned for the President's re-election, which he won.

Amelia continued to lecture, write, and attend public events promoting aviation and convincing more women to fly. She hoped that once more women learned to fly, they would enjoy just being in the air and seeing the beauty of the skies and stars. She noted: "I have often said that the lure of flying is the lure of beauty, and I need no other flight to convince me that the reason flyers fly, whether they know it or not, is the esthetic appeal of flying." At the same time, she advocated greater equality for women. While most of her aviator friends were male, Amelia was years ahead of such feminists as Betty Friedan and Gloria Steinem in promoting the causes of women. She once said: "Women must try to do the things as men have tried. When they fail, their failure must be a challenge to others." Her celebrity status brought her a request from the famous newspaper magnet William Randolph Hearst to visit Hearst Castle in California – an invitation which was considered an extreme honor at the time. Like Lindbergh before her, she accepted the invitation.

By 1934, Amelia was the most famous and best-known woman in the world. She no longer had personal privacy. As an aviation icon and wife of a great promoter, she now belonged to the public. Even foreign governments asked her for endorsements. In 1934, in an effort to promote goodwill and gain a larger tourist market, Mexico convinced her to help them develop a better relationship with the United States. It worked. It was as if she could, by some magic, increase the image of a person or country. Still, she was always looking for new challenges.

On January 11, 1935, Amelia became the first person, female or male, to fly solo across the Pacific from Honolulu, Hawaii to Oakland, California. The resulting publicity helped put Hawaii on the map as a major tourist destination. In addition, she was the first woman to fly an autogiro, an unconventional aircraft powered by a regular propeller and provided with lift in flight by a freewheeling, horizontal rotor. Of course, with all these experiences, George Putnam made sure she was always in the media. In a 1935 New York University poll, the best-known men were President Franklin D. Roosevelt and Adolph Hitler. And for the women, it was Eleanor Roosevelt and Amelia Earhart. Later in 1935, she joined the faculty of Purdue University as a visiting instructor to counsel women on careers and as a technical advisor to the University's Department of Aeronautics. It was during her presence at the university that she began planning a round-the-world flight.

Amelia enjoyed the university speaking circuit, especially when the audience included large groups of women. In 1936, she delivered a special lecture to a large body of over fifteen hundred persons (mostly female students) at East Carolina Teachers College (now East Carolina

University) in Greenville, North Carolina. At that time, the university was dominated by women studying to become teachers. The admission price for students to attend was forty cents (equivalent to a little over $7.44 in 2020), an amount during the height of the Great Depression not necessarily considered a paltry sum for an evening of entertainment. She regaled those in attendance with stories of her adventures in aviation. Her message to the female students was to expand their horizons whether by enjoying flying or stimulating career thinking beyond traditional jobs for women. *The Daily Reflector* (the local Greenville newspaper) noted: "...never has an audience responded so enthusiastically to a speaker..."

**Amelia Earhart sharing her knowledge of aviation**
(Discovery Channel, n.d.)

After a series of speaking engagements where she advocated for equal rights for women, she returned to the planning activities for her world trip. Her first need was to find an excellent navigator. She had learned from her earlier long-distance flights how difficult it was to navigate. (The term used in her day was *avigate*.) Her first choice was Captain Harry Manning, who had been the captain of the *President Roosevelt*, a ship that had brought Amelia back from Europe in 1928. Her second choice was another very experienced navigator, Fred Noonan. Fred had experience in both marine and flight navigation having flown for Pan American Airlines. He had flown the Pacific route many times for Pan Am and was considered an excellent choice for navigator. However, he had several personal problems including a recent difficult divorce, which he tried to forget by drinking excessively. Even though Amelia was aware of this situation, she ignored advice by others and kept him as her navigator.

As Amelia prepared for her trip, the newspapers and media began gathering in the area from which she was to leave. Women across the country were particularly excited as Amelia was living the dream that many others could only experience vicariously. Thousands of people began to appear for the proposed takeoff. Amelia was relying on both national weather reports and on flight information by Pan Am. At the time, Pan Am was the world's most important international airline, and their pilots carefully followed the weather reports. The company had offices in the Pacific, which provided the latest information on flying conditions.

**Pictured left to right: Paul Mantz, Amelia Earhart, Harry Manning, and Fred Noonan posed in front of Earhart's Lockheed 10E Electra prior to taking off from Oakland, California, for Honolulu, Hawaii, March 18, 1937**
(Smithsonian National Air and Space Museum, 1937)

The initial plans were for Amelia Earhart to leave from California for Hawaii and then on the trip around the world. She left California on March 18, 1937 with seasoned navigators Harry Manning, Paul Mantz, and Fred Noonan. After arrival in Hawaii and servicing the aircraft, with her navigators in tow, she began her next worldly adventure. For some seemingly unknown reason, the plane became erratic, with some said a tire was blown; others thought it was a pilot error. It crashed, severely damaging the aircraft. This left the flight plan in a quandary. Expensive and time-consuming repairs were necessary, causing delays. New plans were developed.

In the meantime, during the planning and preparations for her flight, her husband, George Putnam, tried valiantly to keep her from being distracted. There were some financial issues that had evolved with her mother and sister, which Putnam sought to resolve, sending money as needed. Because Amelia was so famous, there was the continuing need for Putnam to handle her correspondence, publicity, and other matters that she would have been personally involved in if she were not finalizing these flight plans.

Putnam was, of course, detail-oriented and helped to get permission from every country she would fly over so that she would not be deemed an intruder in their airspace. He worked with the U.S. Department of State and other offices. He even wrote a letter to Amelia's friend, Eleanor Roosevelt, asking for help. Eleanor was a willing supporter and helped with protocol arrangements. Actually, there were a few countries unwilling to cooperate, causing a need for changed routing of the flight. Arrangements had to be made for refueling along the way, which was a logistics nightmare. Pan Am had refueling stations along some parts of the route, but they were designed to refuel Pan American's sea planes; thus, not useful to Amelia.

U.S. Naval Operations became involved in the refueling needs thanks to the White House correspondence giving the right permissions. The U.S. Navy was willing to absorb the costs for their assistance with logistics, but it was Amelia's responsibility to reimburse them for fuel costs. The refueling remained a serious political and policy conundrum. The U.S. Bureau of Air Commerce headed by Amelia's friend Gene Vidal adjusted some of their policies to help with the problem of refueling. As other problems emerged, solutions were found.

After some careful thought, the initial plans were changed. Instead of leaving from Hawaii, the team felt it better to fly from the Caribbean. On May 21, 1937, Amelia departed from Los Angeles, California for Miami, Florida, in her newly repaired plane. Due to other career concerns during the time of the repairs, she lost the services of Harry Manning and Paul Mantz. Navigation would be left solely to Fred Noonan.

Fred Noonan's role as navigator was extremely important for the success of the mission. He was a very experienced pilot and navigator. He had been hired by Pan American Airlines, the major world air carrier at the time, as head of their navigation school. As flight preparations were being made, Fred Noonan had some personal problems as noted earlier, and he began a pattern of drinking too much. Pan Am let him go, and others advised Amelia that maybe he wasn't a good choice. But Amelia liked Fred, had confidence in his abilities, and kept him as her only navigator.

On June 1, 1937, Amelia Earhart and her navigator took off from Miami in a heavily loaded twin-engine Lockheed Electra aircraft to circumnavigate the globe. Her first stop was San Juan, Puerto Rico. From there, she flew along the edge of South America and across the ocean to Africa. From Africa, it was a non-stop flight to Karachi, India, the first time someone had flown that route non-stop, and then on to Calcutta, India, Rangoon, Bangkok, Singapore and Bandung, Indonesia. Bad weather in Bandung kept her on the ground for several days. It was a time to repair some of the communication instruments that had been causing trouble. In addition, Amelia was suffering from a severe case of dysentery.

By June 27, 1937, conditions were such that Amelia and Noonan could leave Bandung to head toward Port Darwin, Australia. Some minor repairs were made in Port Darwin, and their parachutes were left behind as there would be no place along the route to parachute to if that became necessary. They next flew to Lae, New Guinea on June 29, 1937. By then, they had flown 22,000 miles with 7,000 miles left to go on their trip around the world.

The next to last leg of the trip was from Lae to a tiny island in the Pacific, Howland Island, which would be the refueling station. Amelia's friend Gene Vidal suggested this island and had a special landing field constructed for her use. In addition, the Captain of the U.S. Coast Guard cutter *Itasca* was instructed to stay near the island to provide communication support. Howland Island was an uninhabited coral island southwest of Honolulu, about halfway between Hawaii and Australia. This small 450-acre island was about a half mile wide and a mile-and-a-half long. It was part of an unincorporated, unorganized territory of the United States. In retrospect, because it was so small – being just a speck in the ocean – it was not really a very good choice for a flight of this magnitude.

On Lae, Amelia talked with all the aviation personnel at the airport, and with the exception of problems with Fred's drinking and some complications with the communications gear, she felt quite positive about the upcoming flight to Howland Island. On the evening of July 1, before Amelia and Fred were to leave the next day, both had agreed to get a good night's sleep. Amelia went to bed early, but Fred went out drinking and arrived back the next morning just before takeoff. This was a bad omen, as both Amelia and Fred were already suffering from fatigue after flying so many days under difficult weather conditions and with poor communications. Amelia had to half drag him to the plane for boarding. Harry Balfour, the radio operator at Lae, had become somewhat of a friend with Amelia and let her know he was uncomfortable with her flight on July 2 due to confusion on the use of the radio equipment and her sick navigator. Neither Amelia nor Fred were strong with radio operations.

During the flight, for reasons still unknown, Amelia and Fred lost partial use of their radio navigation transmission equipment. From the beginning of their attempt to fly around the world, both Amelia and Fred did not fully understand the communication equipment and consistently had problems in reaching and speaking with crew aboard the *Itasca*. They were able to transmit to the *Itasca* but were not able to receive communications. The radio operator on board the ship kept sending messages, but he did not know if they were being received. Thinking they were near Howland Island, Amelia and Fred sent the message: "We must be on you but cannot see you...flying at 1,000 feet... Gas is running low." It was a clear day where the ship was located, but none of the sailors spotted the airplane. An hour later they sent a final full transmission stating their position and these words: "We are running north and south." Then there was a one-word message: "wait", and no more messages were received after that. Fred Noonan, a very experienced navigator, had earlier been suspicious of the accuracy of radio direction in navigation of aircraft. Amelia and Fred were either unable to locate Howland Island because of pilot error, lack of communications with radiomen on the *Itasca*, or due to miscalculations by the navigator. Amelia or Fred may have gotten mixed up and missed the island completely.

After receiving no additional radio communications from Amelia, the U.S. Navy conducted an extensive search of the likely areas for the plane to be found. Nothing related to the flight was located to suggest when or where they disappeared. What happened during the flight remains a mystery, and no one knows to this day what really took place.

By July 2, 1937, they were listed as missing, and on January 5, 1939, they were officially declared dead. Her disappearance shocked the world; her proposed flight around the world had captured audiences on virtually every continent. The news of her flights had been posted everywhere, and an anxious global public followed the news stories of her adventures.

Ever since Amelia's death, individuals, groups, and organizations have sponsored expeditions to the area where it is thought Earhart and Noonan might have disappeared. To date, no definitive evidence has surfaced even though the search continues. Theories as to where she crashed – or landed – abound to this day.

One theory that continues to be researched and talked about is that they crash landed on the Marshall Islands and were picked up by the Japanese who were occupying these islands. At the time, Japan was already on a war footing, having invaded and conquered Manchuria, and were preparing to invade China. This invasion took place just 5 days after Amelia Earhart's fateful air disaster. Politically, the United States had strongly opposed Japan's Pacific area encroachments. This situation added to the unsubstantiated rumors that Amelia Earhart and Fred Noonan had crash landed on a Pacific island occupied by Japan where they were taken prisoner by the Japanese and then accused of being U. S. spies before they died from dysentery or were executed. Presumably, native islanders in the area say they saw both Amelia and Fred being captured. A Japanese photo of very poor quality, taken in Saipan, supposedly identified them in port. The photo has since been discounted from several different perspectives. From the time of Amelia Earhart's disappearance until the present, there have been stories and books written about what *really* happened to her. Their disappearance is still one of the great mysteries of all time.

Amelia Earhart's career as the most celebrated aviatrix in history, as a great international traveler, and champion of women's rights kept her in the spotlight throughout her career. Her love of travel, spirit of adventure, and numerous achievements were reflected in her actions, lectures, and writings. Certainly a woman ahead of her time. While only 40-years-old when she died, she packed in more aviation accomplishments and adventures in her short life than any woman before or after her.

Amelia Earhart left a rich legacy to the travel industry, her recognition international in scope with honors from across the globe. Academic scholarships in her name have been made available. Also attached to her name, are schools, roads, parks, festivals, airports, buildings, stamps, and countless other facilities. Many plays, books, movies, television shows, and music renditions have an Amelia Earhart theme. She became a role model for millions of women and men throughout the world.

Amelia's list of "firsts" for women pilots included receiving pilot certification from the National Aeronautics Association, flying across the Atlantic (as a passenger), flying solo across the Atlantic, flying nonstop across the United States, flying the autogiro across the United States, flying from Hawaii to the West Coast, and numerous national and international honors and awards. Undoubtedly, Amelia Earhart is the most celebrated aviatrix in history and was one of the most famous women of her time.

Her greatest legacy, however, was her contribution to the equality of women, both in the air and on the ground. Amelia had a strong social conscience and fought for international peace. She became a role model for young women seeking to enter a world dominated by males, with her actions inspiring women to take on challenges they might not have otherwise assumed. It has taken the airline industry time to accept women pilots in the same vein as men, but in the twenty-first century, that has finally changed.

Amelia's courage and fortitude have been imitated more recently by women flying into space. During her lifetime, starting from a very early age, she would write poems, often depicting how she felt at the time. In 1927, she wrote the following poem titled *Courage*:

> "Courage is the price that Life exacts for granting peace,
> The soul that knows it not, knows no release
> From little things.
> Knows not the livid loneliness of fear,
> Nor mountain heights where bitter joy can hear
> The sound of wings.

> Poem appeared in Marion Perkins's "Who is Amelia Earhart?" (*Survey* magazine, July 1, 1928).

Her efforts to obtain recognition for women flyers have helped open the door so that women pilots today are now seen as pilots in country air forces, in commercial airlines, as flight instructors, as academic professors of aviation, and as astronauts traveling to the international space station.

Amelia Earhart, like Charles A. Lindbergh before her, had many interests besides just being a popular pilot. She was an effective lecturer, a writer, a humanitarian, a supporter of wildlife endeavors, and an educator as well. A few selected highlights from hundreds of lifetime recognitions of her honors and tributes suffice to demonstrate her wide latitude of interests: Amelia Earhart Centre and Wildlife Sanctuary, The Purdue University Amelia Earhart Scholarship, Amelia Earhart Airport, Amelia Earhart Commemorative Stamp, Earhart Foundation, and the list goes on and on.

As noted at the beginning of this book, most of the great worldly travelers introduced in the text are men; Amelia Earhart's travels and her exceptional life left an impressive legacy to the world at large for men and women in the wake of her extraordinary accomplishments. She was one of the great worldly travelers who has changed the world as a result of her travels.

**Amelia Earhart**
(Amelia Earhart Mystery Could Be Solved at Last, 2018)

# CHAPTER THIRTEEN

# YURI GAGARIN, THE FIRST SPACE COSMONAUT/TOURIST

"There is a peculiar pleasure in riding out into
the unknown. A pleasure which no second
journey on the same trail ever affords."
-Edith Durham, *High Albania* (1909)-

*Five-year-old Yuri Gagarin meandered slowly across the
meadow. The beauty of the landscape, the butterflies
flitting nearby, and the smell of the wildflowers added
to his happiness. He noticed a faint rainbow stretched
across the welkin. A deer walked along the forest's edge
of the farm momentarily capturing Yuri's attention. The
serenity of his environment was interrupted as he heard
an unfamiliar sound. Just in time, looking skyward, Yuri
saw an airplane disappear into fluffy white cumulus
clouds. He imagined for a few moments how wonderful
it might be to fly beyond the visible heavens.*

*He hustled back to the farmhouse before he was missed by
his older sister who took care of him while his parents were
working. This was a difficult time to grow up; the world
economic depression of the 1930s had reached almost all
corners of the global economy. The farm where he lived,*

*though, yielded plenty of food to eat but produced little money for other necessities.*

*His father, a skilled carpenter, doubled as an agricultural worker. His mother, self-educated in the literary arts, was also a field hand on the farm. Every night, before Yuri went to sleep, his mother read to him. His favorite stories were about airplanes, adventure, and travel. Jules Verne, a nineteenth century science fiction writer, became one of his favorite authors.*

*Yuri remembered a saying from Jules Verne: "I see that it is by no means useless to travel if a man wants to see something new." As young Yuri drifted off to sleep, his dreams took him around the world and into the heavens above.*

\* \* \*

I nformation about Yuri Gagarin is somewhat limited. Sadly, he had a short life of only 34 years. Those years, from 1934 to 1968, were a time when events of great magnitude were taking place throughout the world. During his lifetime Yuri was a countryman in the secretive Union of Soviet Socialist Republics. Before his birth, the world had been re-adjusting from the results of World War I, which saw the Allies of the British Empire, France, Russia, Italy, and the United States defeat the Central Powers of Germany, Austria-Hungry, the Ottoman Empire and Bulgaria. In addition, the Great Depression was well under way, creating economic havoc and high unemployment rates throughout the world.

In 1922, the Russian communist revolutionary, politician, and political theorist Vladimir Lenin formed the Union of Soviet Socialist Republics (Soviet Union). At its height, the Soviet Union included fifteen countries: Russia, Ukraine, Georgia, Belorussia, Uzbekistan, Armenia, Azerbaijan, Kazakhstan, Kyrgyzstan, Moldova, Turkmenistan, Tajikistan, Latvia, Lithuania, and Estonia. The Soviet Union was by far the biggest collective nation in the world. The Communist regime of the Soviet Union was well-established by 1934, and it continued throughout Yuri's lifetime.

The Soviet Union was dissolved in 1991, and it is now simply the Russian Federation (Russia). Size-wise, today Russia is the world's largest country by land mass. It is nearly twice as big as Canada, which is the world's second largest nation, and Russia covers all of northern Asia and much of Europe. Interestingly, the United States (Alaska) and Russia share a maritime border – narrowly separated by the Bering Strait in the Bering Sea.

By 1934, Germany was already flexing its muscles. Led by German Chancellor and dictator Adolph Hitler, Germany was anxious to move to expand the Nazi regime by invading Austria in 1938. This was followed the next year by Germany's invasion of Poland on September 1, 1939. Almost immediately after Germany's invasion of Poland, her allies, France, and England, declared war on Germany on September 3, 1939. Germany was better prepared for war than most any nation of the world at the time, and by May 10, 1940, she had not only defeated Poland, but France had fallen as well. Economic conditions had not improved, and the world was at wits end to determine what economic policies should be instigated to move in a positive direction.

By 1935, the great English economist John Maynard Keynes suggested a new economic theory, which had a significant impact on economic thought for generations to come; however, it did not lead to immediate solutions in the short term. Hitler took advantage of the dismal economic conditions in Germany at the time and sought to improve conditions by beginning to build an advanced army, air force, and navy, which began to employ millions of workers to produce armaments for the military. He was able to test some of his war materials in 1936 during the Spanish Civil War, a harbinger of World War II.

Adolph Hitler noted that if he could keep the United States and the Soviet Union at bay while he invaded Europe, his military plan would work. Hitler's Germany had had a non-aggression peace pact with the Soviet Union, which was signed in 1939. Yet that agreement was only to buy time until Germany felt strong enough to invade the Soviet Union. In the United States, there was great opposition to becoming involved with the seemingly endless wars that had taken place in Europe for hundreds of years.

By 1934 when Yuri Gagarin was born, the roots of World War II had already begun to take shape, and Yuri and his family suffered greatly during this new war. Economic conditions had not improved, and the world was at its wits end to determine what economic policies could be instigated to move in a positive direction. By 1935, the great English economist John Maynard Keynes suggested a new economic theory, which, as noted earlier, did have a significant impact on future economic thought, but not in the short-term in the 1930s.

Germany's war strategies seemed to be working as she easily annexed Austria in 1938 and invaded and defeated Poland in 1939; all the while, the country faced only limited opposition from England and France. By 1940, Germany had successfully invaded Denmark, Norway, France, Luxemburg, Belgium, and the Netherlands. Germany maintained a "Blitzkrieg" of bombers over London to weaken the British Royal Air Force. Except for England, Germany had little major opposition. Then Japan launched a surprise attack on the U.S. military base in Pearl Harbor, Hawaii, which brought the United States into the war against Japan, Italy, and Germany.

Some historians suggest that Germany's biggest mistake of World War II was launching an invasion of the Soviet Union on June 22, 1941. While no country would suffer more losses in terms of humans being killed during World War II than the Soviet Union – some twenty-six million civilians and military – the Soviet Union fought back valiantly. With limited strategic and military assistance from her allies such as the United States, Great Britain, and others, the Soviet Union was able to drive the Germans out of the country and later shared in the allied victory over Germany in 1945. Shortly thereafter, in 1945, the United States dropped two atomic bombs on Japan. This counterattack by the United States caused Japan to surrender, and finally, soon after, World War II was over.

By 1946, it was clear that the Soviet Union and the United States were the world's two most powerful superpower nations. However, both countries had major differences in their political structures, their economic strategies, and their opinions on what constituted a progressive society. This situation was exacerbated in 1947 as the World War II allies, the United States, and the Soviet Union, became locked in what would become known as a geopolitical-economic "Cold War". This term was used because there was no actual fighting going on between the United States and the Soviet Union even though both nations were politically and diplomatically opposed to each other.

The Cold War continued to escalate in 1948 with the United States leading the "western democratic nations" in Europe and elsewhere in the world against the Soviet Union of the "eastern bloc" communist nations. In 1949, the United States and eleven other western nations formed NATO, the North Atlantic Treaty Organization, an intergovernmental military alliance to act as a buffer zone to confront the Soviet Union. Later, in 1959, the Soviet Union and its affiliated communist nations in Eastern Europe organized a rival alliance called the Warsaw Pact. Also in 1949, Mao Zedong established a communist regime in China leading to the establishment of the Peoples Republic of China. This move challenged U. S. policies in East Asia and the Pacific. The Cold War intensified as the United States and the Soviet Union increased their spy missions in each other's country. The famous Soviet Union spies in the U.S., Julius and Ethel Rosenberg, were caught in 1950. They were put to death in 1953.

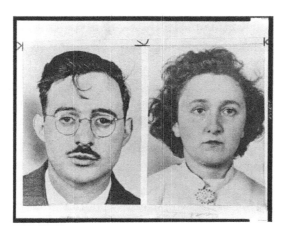

**Soviet Union spies, Julius, and Ethel Rosenberg**
(Wellerstein, 2014)

Also taking place in the Soviet Union in 1953 was the death of the de facto ruthless dictator of the Soviet Union, Joseph Vissarionovich Stalin, who was replaced within six months by Nikita Sergeyevich Khrushchev. Khrushchev led the Soviet Union throughout the Cold War with the western nations. In 1956, he began the de-Stalinization of the Soviet Union, releasing millions of political prisoners and liberalizing Soviet politics.

Another major event pitting the United States against the Soviet Union took place in 1959 when a revolution in Cuba, situated within 90 miles of the US. Cuba produced a leader, Fidel Castro, who opted to make the nation a communist country. The Cold War intensified as Cuba aligned itself with the Soviet Union, and in 1960, the Soviet Union shot down a U-2 high altitude spy plane that had been employed by the United States. To make matters worse, Cold War allies of the Soviet Union – the East German communist country – built the Berlin Wall in 1961 to keep East German citizens from escaping to the west.

In 1962, the Soviet Union was intent on installing its missiles in Cuba, and the Cuban Missile Crisis took place. Fortunately, near a possible brink of war, Nikita Khrushchev backed down. This Cold War lasted until 1991 when the Soviet Union was finally dissolved.

After World War II, both the Soviet Union and the United States had begun to recruit German scientists, engineers, and technicians who had worked on advances in rocketry in Germany, to help boost their respective interests in space exploration and travel. The two countries became highly competitive in developing programs for eventual travel in space. This phenomenon became known as the United States-Soviet Union "Space Race". Some 1,600 German scientists, engineers, and technicians voluntarily came to the United States; while, under considerable coercion, 2,000 similar individuals ended up in the Soviet Union. By 1957, the Soviet Union launched the first artificial satellite, Sputnik, to orbit the earth, which clearly put the Soviet Union ahead of the United States in the Space Race.

**WEATHER**
Sunny and cool today.
High today 64.

**CLEVELAND PLAIN DEALER**

GREATER
CLEVELAND
FINAL

116TH YEAR—NO. 278          CLEVELAND, SATURDAY MORNING, OCTOBER 5, 1957          1801 Superior Ave, N. E.          42 PAGES          SEVEN CENTS
MAIn 1-4500

# SATELLITE FIRED BY RUSSIA; CIRCLING US 15 TIMES A DAY

## Polish Rioters Stone Militia at Reds' HQ

Warsaw Police, Outnumbered by
Thousands of Demonstrators,
Fire Tear Gas; Center of City
Finally Cleared

WARSAW, Poland, Oct. 4 (Reuters)—Citizens
stoned police militiamen tonight as an angry demonstration erupted in front of Polish Communist party
headquarters.

The police—completely outnumbered by thousands
of demonstrators—retaliated with tear gas bombs and
charged the crowds several times.

In this other hour for the
Polish government and Communist Party, the milling demonstrators angrily chanted "Go-

Scholastic

## U. S. Tracks It in Space Orbit 560 Miles Out

185-Pound 'Moon' Visible With
Glasses, Moscow Says in Claiming IGY Victory; Launched by
Rocket; Radio Signals Heard

By HAROLD K. MILKS

MOSCOW, Saturday, Oct. 5 (AP)—The
Soviet Union announced today it has the
world's first artificial moon streaking around
the globe 560 miles out in space.

A multiple-stage rocket launched the earth satellite yesterday, the Russians said, shooting it upward
at about five miles per second.

They said the satellite, a globe described as 23
inches in diameter and weighing 185 pounds, can be
seen in the orbit with glasses and followed by radio

The Space Race began when the Soviet
Union launched Sputnik
(Pettinato, 2017)

The U.S. response in 1958 was to establish the National Aeronautics and Space Administration (NASA) to lead the U.S. space programs. In 1959, the Soviet Union launched an unmanned Lunar rocket that reached the moon. Then in 1961, the Soviet Union successfully launched the first man into space, cosmonaut Yuri Gagarin. This feat was followed in 1962 when the United States astronaut John Glenn became the first American to orbit the earth. These two successful space events led to a new facet of the Space Race – a two-nation race to see which nation would be the first to land on the moon. This race was won by the United States in 1969 when American astronauts Neil Armstrong and Buzz Aldrin landed and walked on the moon's surface. At this point, the United States became the leader in space. After the collapse of the Soviet Union in 1991, the United States and Russia began to cooperate on their respective space programs.

\*   \*   \*

**Yuri Gagarin (bottom middle) and his siblings – his
older brother Valentin (top left), his younger brother
Boris (top middle), and his older sister Zoya (right)**
(Little Known Facts about Life of a First
Man in Space Yuri Gagarin, n.d.)

Yuri Alekseyevich Gagarin was born on March 9, 1934 in the village
of Klushino, near Gzhatsk in the Russian Republic of the Union of
Soviet Socialist Republics. His father, Alexey Ivanovich Gagarin, was a
carpenter, bricklayer, and farmer, and his mother, Anna Timofeyevna
Gagarin, was a milkmaid and farmhand. They had four children; Yuri
was the third. His older brother, Valentin, was born in 1924, and by the
time Yuri was born, his brother was already helping with light chores on
the farm. His sister, Zoya, was born in 1927, and she helped take care of
her brother, Yuri. The youngest sibling was Boris; he was born in 1936,
and he was a boyhood companion of Yuri's.

Yuri's family lived and worked on a collective farm in an area 100 miles west of Moscow, Republic of Russia. From 1930 to 1992, the Soviet Union, a socialist-communist regime, organized the collectivization of agricultural production throughout the twelve core republics. In effect, the government shared with the farmer the produce and livestock from the land and was responsible for setting quotas for the agricultural workers depending on the nature of their jobs and the size of their family. Most often, the people who worked under such circumstances were referred to as peasants.

**Yuri Gagarin as a six-year-old boy**
(Little Known Facts about Life of a First
Man in Space Yuri Gagarin, n.d.)

When Yuri was six, he began attending the local school. Yet within a few weeks, his education was disrupted; the entire area was put on alert because of the German invasion of Russia during World War II. Klushino, his town, was directly in the path of the invaders as they marched toward Moscow. By November 1941, Klushino was invaded by the German army. A Nazi military officer took over the Gagarin's home, but he allowed the Gagarin family to stay on their land behind the house. Like millions of Soviet Union citizens, Yuri's family suffered under the partial occupation of the Soviet Union by Nazi Germany during World War II. The family built a small mud hut, measuring about 10 by 10 feet, away from the family house, where they lived for a year and nine months. The family grew vegetables to keep from starving. Yuri's older brother and sister had planned to leave Klushino to avoid being captured by the Germans. Unfortunately, they were not so lucky and were captured and deported as slave laborers to Germany.

During World War II, the Soviet Union suffered over 26 million deaths, more than any other single country. Fortunately, Yuri's family survived, including his elder siblings, and they were all reunited in Klushino after the war. The war experience left an indelible mark on Yuri; a childhood nightmare that was never forgotten.

Prior to World War II, Germany, under the leadership of Adolf Hitler, developed the most sophisticated and advanced military-industrial complex the world had ever seen. The Germans experimented with new weapon technology, including rocket-powered missiles. By war's end, German scientists were more advanced in rocket-engine science for military purposes than either the Soviet Union or the United States. As a result, in order to expand their own programs after World War II, the wartime allies of the Soviet Union and United States both sought to employ the German scientists, engineers, and technicians who had worked on rocket technology during the war.

After the war, Yuri's family encouraged eleven-year-old Yuri to seek as much education as was available. Education and communist party affiliation were prime movers for obtaining the best jobs and a better life in the Soviet Union. In 1950, Yuri became a student and foundry man at a technical-vocational manufacturing trade school and steel plant in Lyubertsy, a town outside of Moscow. These vocational schools were designed to produce workers in various industrial trades. Yuri proved to be intelligent and a hard worker. He applied himself to the tasks at school and graduated with high marks. At the same time, he joined the communist party.

**Yuri Gagarin in 1954**
(Little Known Facts about Life of a First
Man in Space Yuri Gagarin, n.d.)

Yuri was sent for technical training as a metalworker in 1951 at the Saratov Industrial Technical School in Saratov, Russia, southeast of Moscow, where he studied information about tractors. One of his teachers had been a pilot during World War II, who fascinated our young soon to become a worldly traveler with his stories about flying.

While in this school the high energy and intelligent Yuri, among many other activities, joined the "Aero Club", and he learned to fly a light aircraft. Flying came easy to him, and in a short time, he became a licensed pilot. He was moving forward with his life and career based on his successes as a student, an athlete, and as a pilot. He became known at school for his wit, erudition, and personality. Chosen to enroll in the Soviet Union air force cadet training center in the Orenburg Aviation School in 1955, he successfully applied himself to the rigors of training and education. In 956, he became an aviation cadet. After some difficulties in landing the small two-seater trainer airplane, he finally qualified to fly solo in 1957. He had dreamed of flying the famous Russian MIG jet fighter, and during his cadet training, he was able to do so. It was during a 1957 May Day, also called Worker's Day or International Worker's Day, a nonworking holiday to celebrate the labor movement, celebration with festivals and dancing in Red Square in Moscow that he met a shy young lady, Valentina Goryacheva, whom he married on November 11, 1957, the very day of his graduation from flight school. Valentina was well-educated, and she had graduated from Orenburg Medical School and was working as a medical technician.

Valentina gave birth to their two daughters: Yelena Yurievna Gagarin, born in 1959 and who became an art historian, and Galina Yurievna Gagarin, born in 1961 who became an economics professor. After his flight training, Yuri was commissioned as a lieutenant in the Soviet Union Air Force and was stationed at the Luostari Air Base near the Norwegian border in Murmansk Oblast for a two-year assignment.

**Yuri Gagarin with his wife Valentina**
(Little Known Facts about Life of a First
Man in Space Yuri Gagarin, n.d.)

**Yuri Gagarin with his two daughters**
(Little Known Facts about Life of a First
Man in Space Yuri Gagarin, n.d.)

During the time Yuri was being educated and developing his keen interest in flying, major changes were taking place with respect to the Soviet Union and the United States. Both countries had become recognized as the most powerful nations in the world with completely different political systems. As noted earlier, this became known as the Cold War competition between the two nations. On May 15, 1957, the Soviet Union launched the world's first intercontinental rocket. As new developments in weaponry and rocket-science technology took place, both countries became highly competitive in the field of space technology.

On October 4, 1957, the Soviet Union launched Sputnik, an artificial earth satellite, into orbit. This most remarkable achievement galvanized the attention of the world and confirmed the Soviet Union's leadership in space technology. The United States-Soviet Union space race was on. These successes gave the Soviet Union complete confidence in their ability to move more quickly in their space program than that of the United States. Shortly before Yuri was married, the Soviet Union went a step further, and on November 3, 1957, the country sent Sputnik 2 aloft with the first living mammal on board, with Laika, the famous space dog. Although Laika died a few hours into space, the experiment proved that a living passenger could survive the rigors of rocket-powered vehicle movements. In effect, Laika paved the way for humans to travel in space. It was in this military-political-space oriented environment that Yuri came of age. With the great triumph of the Sputniks as the benchmark for space programs, it took another three-and-a-half years of successes and disasters before the first man could be launched into space.

Yuri Gagarin expressed a strong interest in the Soviet Union space program, and in 1959, after mental and physical examinations were conducted, he became a cosmonaut candidate. In 1960, by the time Yuri was 26, he and 19 others were chosen by the Central Flight Medical Commission overseen by Major General Konstantin Fyodorovich Borodin of the Soviet Army Medical Service for the cosmonaut training program. The chief designer of the Soviet Union space program was the indomitable Sergei Pavlovich Korolev, the most influential space scientist during the space race between the United States and the Soviet Union in the 1950s and 1960s. Under his tutelage, the cosmonaut students studied newly developed courses ranging from space navigation to rocket propulsion. The group of students were put into a special training regimen which involved long periods of vigorous exercise. They also underwent parachute training, a process that required them to make numerous jumps at the training site in Saratov Oblast.

**Yuri Gagarin (pictured in the center of the first row) and his fellow cosmonaut students training at the Central Flight Medical Commission to be selected to travel into space**
(Little Known Facts about Life of a First
Man in Space Yuri Gagarin, n.d.)

When the final group of six out of the twenty cosmonauts were chosen, which included Yuri, they underwent intense physical and psychological examinations, as well as numerous other tests at Central Aviation Scientific-Research Hospital in Moscow. Colonel A. S. Usanov served as commander, and he was also a member of the Central Flight Medical Commission. Yuri underwent specially designed oxygen starvation tests, during which he was locked in an oxygen isolation chamber with the air being slowly pumped out. There were also tests to determine a reaction to "g-forces" in a specially designed laboratory device. Possibly the most difficult test was being isolated in a small chamber for ten days. After all these tests, one of the air force doctors, name unknown, evaluated and reported on Yuri's personality as follows: "Modest; embarrasses when his humor gets a little too racy; high degree of intellectual development evident in Yuri; fantastic memory; distinguishes himself from his colleagues by his sharp and far-ranging sense of attention to his surroundings; a well-developed imagination; quick reactions; perservering: prepares himself painstakingly for his activities and training exercises; handles celestial mechanics and mathematical formulae with ease as well as excels in higher mathematics; does not feel constrained when he has to defend his point of view if he considers himself right; appears that he understands life better than a lot of his friends."

Everything about the cosmonauts' training was aimed toward simulated flight into space. They trained in their regular spacesuits and participated in mock-ups of spacecraft undergoing simulated space travel. They talked incessantly about every aspect of the program and were constantly questioned by their trainers and supervisors.

Out of the twenty who started the program, the selection of an individual for the proposed manned space flight was narrowed first to six and then to two, Yuri Gagarin and Gherman Titov. Interestingly, when the 20 candidates were asked anonymously to vote for who they thought should be the first to fly into space, all but three voted for Yuri. These two cosmonauts went through additional intensive physical and psychological training, medical examinations, and related tests. While Yuri was the final choice to go into space, his colleague, Gherman, was fully prepared for the flight in case a last-minute change was needed. One advantage both these cosmonauts had was that they were not big persons. The small cockpit in the spaceship did not allow much room for a cosmonaut. Yuri was short, about five feet two inches tall, which allowed him to easily get in and out of the limited room in the cockpit.

**Yuri Gagarin (left) and Gherman Titov (right),**
**Gagarin's alternate on the Vostok 1 mission**
(The Man: Yuri Gagarin, the First Cosmonaut, n.d.)

We can perhaps imagine what must have been on Yuri's mind as he prepared for this flight. He knew that if he was successful, he would go down in history as the world's first man in space. If not, he'd be totally forgotten. On the surface, he seemed relatively calm for someone about to be launched into space, casually engaging in conversations with the support personnel immediately surrounding him. Obviously, he was quite aware of how dangerous this trip might be, but there was no past record for comparison. He dismissed such concerns. Other than a small group of cosmonauts and technicians, Yuri had few people to discuss the intricacies of space travel with because of the high degree of secrecy involved and because only a few individuals understood the concepts of space travel. However, he did have conversations with Vladimir Suvorov who was a distinguished chief documentary cinematographer, and who eye-witnessed and described, in his top-secret diary, the Soviet space program from 1959-1969, including many of the events related to Yuri Gagarin.

The day chosen for the flight at the Bailkonur Cosmodrome near Tyuratam, Kazakhstan was April 12, 1961. That morning, physician Colonel Yevgeniy Anatoliyevich Karpov, also a member of the medical commission, came to examine both cosmonauts. Also part of the medical team included Colonel Vladimir Ivanovich Yazdovskiy, the head physician for Yuri's flight, and Major-General Aleksandr Nikolayevich Babiychuk, a physician flag officer on the Soviet Air Force General Staff to the Commander in Chief of the Air Force. They all went through several exercises, cleaned up, and ate a light breakfast. The pre-launch preparations were performed, and both cosmonauts were ready. Like any manned space launch back in 1961, as well as today, the technicians, flight engineers, administrators, and astronauts were somewhat nervous and on edge. However, by the time Yuri was to launch into space, he had been so well trained and tested that he was both excited, calm and ready for the flight into space.

**Yuri Gagarin in his cosmonaut suit just
prior to traveling into space**

Dressed in his spacesuit, Yuri ascended the stairs to the launch pad. He climbed into the space vehicle, Vostok 1, and signaled that he was ready to go. As the flight director, technicians, and program heads huddled around the launch site, there was total silence, except for a dialogue between the space capsule coordinator and engineer, Sergei Korolev, and Yuri, that went like this: Korolev: "Preliminary stage…intermediate…main…Lift-Off! We wish you a good flight. Everything's all right." And a response from Yuri Gagarin: "Off we go! Goodbye, until soon dear friends."

At 6:07 a.m., the flight director punched the launch button, and Vostok 1 soared into the cosmos; Yuri aboard. Cheers were heard throughout the building – "*he's successfully on his way*". The world's first human to fly in space, Yuri circled the earth once and ushered in the age of manned spaceflight. A new threshold had been crossed; humankind could now fly in space.

Yuri's flight lasted 108 minutes, and then he parachuted to Earth, landing in Soviet-controlled Kazakhstan. During the time in flight, he was able to maintain good radio contact with the ground crew. At one point, Yuri reported: "Flight is proceeding normally. I feel well." Later he reported: "I am withstanding state of weightlessness well," as items in the spacecraft floated in midair. Although he had an emergency key to take control of the operation of Vostok 1, it was not needed. The entire trip was well-controlled from the ground. He parachuted from the capsule on reentry, since early on in space travel, it was not yet possible to land a spaceship. Yuri's space flight demonstrated to the world the strength and depth of the Soviet Union space program. During his historic orbiting of the earth, he was promoted to a major in the air force.

Throughout the flight, all radio stations in the Soviet Union and in most countries of the world interrupted their broadcasts to announce the sensational news that the Soviet Union had successfully launched a man into space. The news sparked a wave of euphoria across the world. The stunning news caught most people and governments by surprise since there was no advanced notice about the flight. In Moscow, crowds of jubilant citizens celebrated this great feat in any way they could. Red Square hadn't seen such celebrations since the end of World War II.

Once the world learned of Yuri's venture into space, people were mesmerized by the magnitude of such a happening. In every corner of the globe, they listened to their radios hoping to learn of the latest details of this amazing event. The name Yuri Gagarin became known in almost every household throughout the globe. A clearly tremendous scientific, political, and diplomatic coup for the Soviet Union. As the first human in space, Yuri, like Charles Lindbergh, after his sensational flight in 1927, became an instantaneous universal celebrity. From April 12, 1961 forward, space travel caught the imagination of scientists, politicians, and the general public. It was a clear call to action for the slower moving United States space program.

A few days after the space flight, Yuri flew to Moscow. His large plane was escorted by friends flying the same fighter jets he had flown a few years earlier. After landing, military bands began to play as he stepped from the plane. The crowds were excited, and a festive spirit was felt everywhere as he moved toward the platform where Nikita S. Khrushchev, First Secretary of the Communist Party of the Soviet Union and Premier, waited for him. Yuri saluted Premier Khrushchev and reported that his mission was successfully accomplished.

The people went wild greeting their hero as he left in the convertible limousine with his wife, Galina, and Premier Khrushchev. The crowds cheered, clapped, and whistled as the car passed by, providing a cacophony of excitement in the air. Gagarin and Khrushchev stood and waved to the tumultuous crowds that were trying to follow the procession. Flowers were strewn everywhere along the route. Young boys were hanging from tree limbs and lampposts, hoping to get a glimpse of the first cosmonaut to travel in space. The world diplomatic community was caught up in the celebrations, and at once, they acknowledged that the Soviet Union was ahead in the race into space.

**Yuri Gagarin greeting the crowds in
celebrating his successful flight**
(Little Known Facts about Life of a First
Man in Space Yuri Gagarin, n.d.)

Gagarin, Khrushchev, and the rest of the entourage arrived at Red Square hearing the loud paeans of praise: "Ga-ga-rin! Ga-ga-rin!" They listened to the speakers and popular patriotic songs that were often interrupted by cheers. The fanfare continued as Yuri was awarded the Gold Star of the Hero of the Soviet Union (highest honor possible), the Order of Lenin, the newly minted Pilot Cosmonaut medal, and the Honored Master of Sport medal. This was heady stuff for a farm boy from middle Russia who had dreamed of flying but had surely never imagined being a Soviet hero. Through it all, he appeared calm, collected, and in complete control of himself. The celebrations were capped with a fantastic display of fireworks.

**Yuri Gagarin, a bemedaled space hero**

For several years after his historic flight, Yuri Gagarin traveled the world to speak about the progress of the Soviet Union's space program. He had an engaging smile and pleasant personality that allowed him to easily meet all kinds of officials, the media, and regular Soviet citizens. He handled the international press with ease, and received medals and all kinds of awards from the many countries he visited. The world celebrated with him his pioneering efforts in outer space travel. Other than the customary official country tours in more than 30 countries, he did not spend much time on his worldly jaunts visiting the tourism sights at the destinations. The United States, being the world's most anti-communist country, did not invite Gagarin for a visit to the United States. However, he did meet U.S. Vice President Hubert Humphrey at the 1965 Paris Air Show.

Yuri was excellent at discussing the technical aspects of his adventure, but he became bored and frustrated with ceremonial life. There were rumors that he had begun drinking heavily. Part of this rumor came as a result of social drinking during his many tours, international functions, and speaking events. Increasingly, he wanted to get away from the limelight and back to what he liked most, which was flying.

Once his world ceremonial duties were mostly over, Yuri returned to the Soviet Union in the role of deputy training director for the cosmonaut program. He received a promotion to the rank of colonel in the process. He was imbued with a desire to be a test pilot again and to help further the space program. The government was reluctant to have him flying untested aircraft, afraid to lose their hero in a flight mishap or accident.

Yuri was such a popular hero in the Soviet Union that he literally had carte blanche to do whatever he wanted, with no restraints. His first love was flying, and he took to the skies whenever he had the opportunity. He re-qualified as a fighter pilot and was re-admitted to the cosmonaut program. In that respect, he was designated as part of the backup crew for Soyuz 1, and he was a leading candidate for the planned Soviet piloted lunar landing. Sadly, the Soyuz 1 mission ended in a fatal crash that killed Gagarin's friend and fellow cosmonaut Vladimir Komarov. After this mishap, Gagarin was not allowed to continue in the cosmonaut program, nor was he allowed to pilot a plane solo. The Soviet Union needed to protect its great space hero.

On March 27, 1968, Colonel Yuri Gagarin, and chief training director Colonel Vladimir S. Seryogin were flying a MiG-15 on a routine training exercise from the Chkalovsky Air Base when their plane crashed. Both men died. Yuri Gagarin was 34 years old. Many rumors circulated as to reasons for the crash, but no one had a credible answer. Official reports by the Russian Committee for State Security organization, the KGB, the main security agency for the Soviet Union from 1954 until its break-up in 1991, suggested that the most plausible answer was that the air base personnel provided the pilots with outdated weather information, which caused the pilots to be caught in a severe storm. Some individuals believed the plane was not carefully checked before the pilots went in flight and that the pilots' hatch was not properly secured. Others put forward that the pilots may have hit a bird causing a malfunction of the aircraft. Another opinion was that a large experimental Soviet plane got too close, causing a wake that upended Yuri's plane, putting it into an uncontrollable spiral. There were even some who thought Yuri may have been intoxicated when he took off. Early on, there were a few conspiracy theories bruited saying that an international plot had been hatched aimed at killing Yuri. Whatever the cause, the world lost one of its most notable worldly travelers.

Yuri Gagarin was given a state funeral, and his ashes were interred in the Kremlin wall in Moscow.

**Kremlin Wall in Moscow, the location
of Yuri Gagarin's ashes**
(Little Known Facts about Life of a First
Man in Space Yuri Gagarin, n.d.)

In spite of his early death, Yuri's life was impressive. He had been honored in a multitude of ways by the Soviet Union, received the country's highest honors, and had been inducted as a deputy of the Soviet parliament. He also had become a member of the Young Communist league and honorary member of the International Academy of Astronautics. His honors, awards, and special medals certainly matched those of America's famous pilot, Charles A. Lindbergh.

The British Interplanetary Society honored Yuri with their special gold medal. He also received a gold medal from the International Aeronautics Federation. In addition, he won the Galabert International Astronautical prize. The Soviet-Cuban Friendship Society had honored him as did other communist countries and non-communist countries throughout the world.

In 1968, the town where Yuri was born, near the town of Gzhatsk, was named Gagarin in his honor. Many buildings, streets, and other sites carry his name, including the training center where he started preparations for his space flight. In addition, Gagarin Square was named in Moscow, including a special monument to honor him. Each year, Russians celebrate Cosmonautics Day on April 12 in honor of his flight. In 1968, the Russian Air Force Academy was renamed the Gagarin Air Force Academy.

As mentioned earlier, Yuri Gagarin had re-entered space training and was in line as a possible candidate for a lunar mission. In this respect, to honor her husband's interest in becoming a lunarnaut, Gagarin's wife requested that American astronauts Neil Armstrong and Buzz Aldrin leave one of Gagarin's medals on the moon during their lunar landing on July 20, 1969. The request was honored by the Americans as a special tribute to the first human to fly in space. A crater on the moon was also named for him.

The United States had conceived the idea of reaching the moon under the Apollo Program during the administration of President Dwight D. Eisenhower. The program was moving forward yet needed a strong incentive to speed up progress. Yuri's success challenged the United States to accelerate its policies and programs for a more serious outer space effort. In 1961, U.S. President John F. Kennedy announced a new, comprehensive American space program that later surpassed many of the space efforts made by the Soviet Union. If not for Yuri's space ventures, United States Astronaut Neal Armstrong may not have walked on the lunar surface in 1969.

Yuri Gagarin's legacy continues to this day as space tourists, astronauts, and cosmonauts have regularly flown in Russian spacecraft to the universally supported international space station, a practice that has continued over the past few years. The United States temporarily abandoned its spaceflight program in 2011, although it has now resumed space flights, resulting in the need for its astronauts to fly on Russian spacecraft to get to the space stations. After the Soviet Union was dissolved in 1991 and the Russian Federation replaced it, new directions in their space program have taken place. The Russian "Roscosmos State Corporation for Space Activities", commonly known as Roscosmos, is a state corporation of the Russian Federation responsible for space flights, cosmonautics programs, and aerospace research.

Like the other worldly travelers, Yuri Gagarin was curious, courageous, and daring. He had the fortitude and commitment to go where others might not tread and to face dangers of the unknown without trepidation. His travels changed the world in which we live. He was truly the early hero of the space age. While his life was short and there is not much documentation regarding his impressive feat, our worldly traveler Yuri Gagarin will always be remembered as the first space traveler of our universe.

**Yuri Gagarin**
(Little Known Facts about Life of a First
Man in Space Yuri Gagarin, n.d.)

# EPILOGUE

"Experience, travel – these are
education in themselves."
-Euripides-

*The storyteller paused to catch his breath. He perceived the agitated state of mind in his audience. The hushed crowd, their stillness, suggested the story was not yet over. They glanced at one another, their eyes misty with emotion. He smiled and began to speak anew.*

*"You have heard the fascinating stories of these worldly travelers of the past and how their lives have changed the world. You may be the future travelers who may very well journey to the far reaches of the universe and leave a new exciting and different kind of legacy for mankind. It is up to you to portend a glimpse of what's ahead; your imagination will reveal the rest."*

*There were excited murmurs from the crowd. The visitors leaned forward, eager to know what else this soothsayer might say. The room became profoundly still. A sigh from a young woman in the audience filled the otherwise quietness that all shared.*

*"We've learned how deeply traveling brings forward a certain harmony, knowledge, and understanding of humanity," the storyteller continued. "Reach out and embrace your future. Does any traveler know the fate the Father of the Universe has in store for him? All our journeys remain secret until taken, and then weave into our future destiny."*

*"Future travel is that additional dimension to our bodies, mind, and soul that taxes the imagination and goes beyond the limits of today's knowledge*

*into longing for what is beyond the next horizon." He smiled knowing he had inspired every single person listening to him to be interested in travel. The audience slowly left the premises realizing that the story of travel was never over, and that the future of travel belonged to them.*

*AND TO YOU, DEAR READER...*

# AFTERWORD

"Two roads diverged in a wood, and I-
I took the one less traveled by,
And that has made all the difference."
-Robert Frost, *The Road Not Taken*-

A difficult decision in preparing to write this book was selecting the characters we would write about. History is replete with great worldly travelers who added so much wealth of knowledge to the world and who have left behind impressive contributions to mankind. We were challenged with the task of searching through stacks of documents to finally arrive at selections for our characters. There was a conscious decision on our part to research different time periods and regions of the world in order to share the cultures and discoveries made by a broad variety of worldly travelers. All the worldly travelers were curious, brave, and courageous as they risked their lives to journey to distant lands and return with knowledge of their discoveries to impart to the world at large. We hope you have decided these choices of our worldly travelers are justified.

An important connection to early travel was its strong affinity to religions. Religions, religious holidays, and religious pilgrimages were, in the past and continue to be, major reasons for travel. Travel for religious purposes, whether it was the Egyptian religious festivals, special events related to the Greek gods, the Christian era movements, the Muslim journeys to Mecca, Jewish peregrinations, or other pilgrimages, is so comprehensive and encompassing as to be beyond the scope and interests of this book, even though two of the worldly travelers mentioned in the book had strong connections to religious communities.

Another piece of the ancient travel puzzle is the impact of military conquests on geography, history, and travel. Military leaders, for their own purposes, added much to travel, transport, road construction, facility developments for accommodations, eating establishments, safety, security, and other important attributes necessary for travel. Their contributions to travel are adequately chronicled elsewhere and were not major topics in this book.

Commerce was a major motivator for travel as well. Traveling merchants and international traders charted the course and directions for certain types of travel. This motivation for travel is mentioned many times in the book, but it is not a central theme.

Political leaders, likewise, contributed significantly to the growth and development of travel. Occasionally, we mention the importance of political leadership in travel and explorations, but it's only mentioned in reference to its association with the worldly travelers. In many respects, our worldly travelers, as a result of their travels, were more powerful in shaping the world than monarchs, heads of state, and legislative bodies.

Who were these men and two women and why were they willing to leave their families to travel into the unknown? What were they thinking about that excited them so much to explore uncharted and dangerous destinations? How did they view the world around them at the time of their travels? When did the world acknowledge their accomplishments? We have considered these questions as we delved into the lives of these unique individuals.

The word "travel" is usually associated with leisure excursions, scenic expeditions, visits to friends and family, business trips, a pilgrimage, safari, trek, or cruise. In *Webster's II New College Dictionary* (2001) section titled "word history" as travel is defined: "The hardship of making a journey in earlier times is reflected in the etymological identity of the words *travel* and *travail*. Both are derived from the Old French word *travailler*, which originally meant 'to torment, to trouble,' and later came to mean 'to be troubled, to be in pain, to work hard.'" Early travel was certainly "painful" and often unpleasant and difficult. While most of us as travelers anticipate a "pleasant" trip, many might feel, from time to time, that today's "air travel" more closely resembles the earlier definition.

This book also reflects on the impact the worldly travelers have had on the way we view travel, tourism, and cultures throughout today's world. Occasionally, we comment on the influence the worldly travelers had on the philosophy of today's travel. For instance, sustainable tourism, popularized in the twenty-first century, was also noted by early travelers. Marco Polo might fit the title of the "father of sustainable tourism", as he often viewed tourism from a broad social, cultural, geographical, and historic perspective. Likewise, Charles A. Lindbergh saw the importance of nature travel and could easily be associated with the advancement of eco-tourism.

*   *   *

While we, Dr. Edgell and Ms. Kogos are not professional biographers or historians, we attempted to utilize the research and information available to us in the best way possible. We took literary license throughout this writing about the worldly travelers to make the stories more interesting. We perused the Internet frequently to obtain information and to locate certain books and articles we wished to read in connection to the worldly travelers. Any errors or omissions of historical fact and judgment of what to include in the book are ours alone.

There were many people, colleagues and friends, who helped on this project even though they may not have realized it at the time. We wish to acknowledge with sincere thanks and gratitude their assistance.

Much of the pertinent research we sought on Zheng He is housed in China. However, a friend and colleague of Dr. Edgell's, Dr. Huili Hao, was willing and excited to help us to obtain information from China about Zheng He. She translated information and patiently explained background about China that relates to this very important worldly traveler.

We had difficulty in researching the worldly traveler Yuri Alekseyevich Gagarin, as there is not much information about this interesting space traveler. His travel took place during the Cold War between the

United States and western nations and the Union of Soviet Socialist Republics. The USSR maintained tight security on knowledge about their space development programs. However, it happens that a friend of Dr. Edgell's, Dr. Alexander Sabelnikov, co-authored with his uncle, Vladimir Suvorov, the book *The First Manned Spaceflight: Russia's Quest for Space*. This book provided Dr. Edgell with intelligence and insights about Yuri Gagarin that were not available from any other source. Dr. Sabelnikov's co-author and uncle was the late Vladimir Suvorov, the distinguished chief space documentary cinematographer for the USSR, an eyewitness to the space program, and a friend of Yuri Gagarin. Fortunately, Vladimir Suvorov kept detailed notes on the USSR's space program, and when he died, his wife gave the notes to Alexander. Alexander generously shared his information with Dr. Edgell.

Dr. Edgell also wants to thank Bryna Coonin at East Carolina University's Joyner Library for helping in the research phase of the book. She directed a few key sources that Dr. Edgell would likely not have found on his own. If the Library did not have the research publications he was interested in, she arranged to borrow it from other libraries.

Dr. Edgell especially wants to mention Dr. Steve Creech, who graciously gave Dr. Edgell his many edits and comments on the book. Another who helped edit the book and who researched pictures for the book was Ms. Amber Kay Whitley.

Ms. Kogos especially thanks Ms. Susan Shagrin Pitkowsky, who kindly, courteously and carefully helped us edit this book.

Dr. Edgell is fortunate to have a wonderful and supportive wife, Sarah, who believes in him and his work and who was willing to provide him with constructive criticism and advice during the writing of this book.

Ms. Kogos is, as well, grateful to have an amazing constituency of friends and readers throughout her years as a travel agent and writer, novelist and a newspaper columnist. What an amazing goal it has been, to care, coordinate, create and curate these amazing stories with Dr. Edgell, whom she has known professionally in the travel and tourism field for many years.

# A GUIDE TO FURTHER READING

"We have not inherited the Earth from our ancestors,
we have only borrowed it from our children."
- (Anomalous)-

Research about the characters in this book included reading and digesting numerous books, articles, Internet references, hearsay, and movies about the worldly travelers. Research and information sources reviewed with respect to the characters in this book are too numerous to completely name and identify but this "Guide to Further Reading" section and the "General References" segment which follows includes some of the references that were consulted in writing this book. The range of references include books, articles, biographies, memoirs, movies, hearsay, legends, and a liberal perusal of the Internet. The information in this "Guide to Further Reading" and "General References" is developed to assist the reader to locate research materials and information more easily on the various characters in the book.

There were a number of books reviewed to simply get a better understanding of what was happening during the time period when the worldly were traveling and information on the characters themselves. A book consulted frequently, especially with respect to early travel, was *Unknown Lands: The Logbook of the Great Explorers* by Francois Bellec. Another highly useful general book on travel, *The Norton Book of Travel* as edited by Paul Fussell was most helpful. Also of importance was *The Worldly Philosophers: The Lives, Times, and Ideas of the Great Economic Thinkers* (6th edition, 1986) by Robert Heilbroner, which helped to better organize my thoughts and writing style. There is so much literature on travel that we had to simply pick and choose the characters we thought best represented the intent of this book. We have noted on the following pages some of the key sources of materials utilized in the book on a chapter-by-chapter basis followed by a section of general references.

## CHAPTER ONE: THE ORIGIN OF TRAVEL

Chapter One, "The Origin of Travel", presents the core element in the development of early travel and sets the stage for describing the adventures of the worldly travelers. For the first part of this section, we found Richard Leakey's book *The Origin of Humankind* extremely useful. The Leakey family is synonymous with an understanding of our early ancestors. To help identify the impact of migration on travel, we also consulted the *Journey of Mankind*, an interactive map created collaboratively with Professor Stephen Oppenheimer in conjunction with the Bradshaw Foundation (Oppenheimer, n.d.).

A book that we depended on for much information on ancient travel in this introductory chapter was *Travel in the Ancient World* by Lionel Casson. This work provides fascinating details about early travel.

Great help for information used in *The Origin of Travel* and for many of the chapters about individual worldly travelers, was the book *The Discovers* by Daniel J. Boorstin. This is a remarkable narrative about many great discoveries, providing insights for better understanding of the contributions of worldly travelers and explorers in terms of their impact on the world.

Much of the background information on the Phoenicians came from *The Phoenicians* by Sabatino Moscasti. For a general history of events and for a better understanding of world history, we consulted the book *Concise History of the World: An Illustrated Timeline* (Revised Edition), as edited by Neil Kagan and published by *National Geographic*. Also helpful in understanding ancient history was the book *The Ancient World: A Social and Cultural History* (Eighth Edition) by D. Brendan Nagle. In addition, we reviewed certain chapters in the book *The Origins of Hospitality and Tourism* by Kevin D. O'Gorman. In addition we utilized the Internet.

# CHAPTER TWO: HERODOTUS, THE ANCIENT WORLDLY TRAVELER

Lionel Casson's book *Travel in the Ancient World* was extremely helpful for the chapter about Herodotus. In addition, Herodotus' book *The Histories*, as edited by Walter Blanco and Jennifer Tolbert Roberts and translated by Walter Blanco, provided important quotations and information. *Herodotus*, by Terrot Reaveley, provided special insights about Herodotus, the traveler, as well as Herodotus, the writer. Grover Ryszard Kapuscinski's *Travels with Herodotus* is an excellent source of information on Herodotus and is written as part of a travel commentary.

*Herodotus, Explorer of the Past*, by J. A. S. Evans, provides useful descriptions into Herodotus' writing style, including his approaches to field interviews, and especially with respect to Herodotus' travels to Egypt. Edited by Peter Derow and Robert Parker, *Herodotus and His World* which also provides good information about Herodotus.

In addition, two articles: 1) "Herodotus: Greek Historian," written by the editors of *Encyclopedia Britannica* and 2) "Herodotus" from the Joukowsky Institute for Archeology at Brown University were very helpful.

*The Story of Philosophy: The Lives and Opinions of the Greater Philosophers* by Will Durant provides some insights into early Greek philosophers like Socrates and Plato as well as the structure and history of early Greece. We also consulted the book *The Ancient World: A Social and Cultural History* by D. Brendan Nagle to better understand the early civilizations of Mesopotamia and Egypt. A useful book for understanding the history of Herodotus' favorite city, Athens, is *The Rise of Athens: The Story of the World's Greatest Civilization* by Anthony Everitt. This book helped us to better understand Herodotus' life in ancient Greece and his love of Athens. The Internet was used in checking time periods and historical information.

## Chapter Three: A Journey with Marco Polo

There is an enormous amount of information about the travels of Marco Polo. Because of the books, articles, and movies, he is probably the best known of the worldly travelers.

While there are 150 different translations of Marco Polo's book, we read and used extensively *The Travels of Marco Polo* as translated by Ronald Latham. We also consulted the book *The Illustrated Edition: The Travels of Marco Polo* as organized by general editor Morris Rossabi. In addition, we found a fine series of articles about Marco Polo written by Mike Edwards, published in *National Geographic's* issues of May 2001, June 2001, and July 2001. This set of articles, with maps and commentary, made the geography of his journeys come alive.

Another fascinating book written about Marco Polo, especially his interactions with Kublai Khan, is *Marco Polo: The Journey that Changed the World* by John Man. The references in this chapter and the chapter on Zheng He about Genghis Khan emanated from our careful reading of the book *Genghis Khan and the Making of the Modern World* by Jack Weatherford. We also found the book *Genghis Khan* by R.P. Lister to be helpful.

*Marco Polo: From Venice to Xanadu* provided a fascinating travelogue about Marco Polo's many adventures throughout his travels. The book *Marco Polo's Silk Road: The Art of the Journey – An Italian at the Court of Kublai Khan* has excellent scholarly commentary and illustrations that make this a must-read for comprehensive information about his travels. The article "Marco Polo" by Fosco Maraini and Edward Peters that appeared in *Encyclopedia Britannica* was also helpful. In obtaining information about countries and about historical incidents, the Internet was highly useful.

# CHAPTER FOUR: IBN BATTUTA, THE WANDERER FROM THE MIDDLE EAST

Extensive information on the travel routes of Ibn Battuta (Battuta is sometimes spelled Battutah) used in this chapter is based on *The Travels of Ibn Battutah* by Ibn Battuta and edited by Tim Mackintosh-Smith. Extremely helpful in understanding Ibn Battuta's travels was the revised edition of *The Adventures of Ibn Battuta, A Muslim Traveler of the 14th Century* by Ross E. Dunn. Also, *The Odyssey of Ibn Battuta: Uncommon Tales of a Medieval Adventurer* by David Waines was also good. Another is *Travels with a Tangerine: A Journey in the Footnotes of Ibn* Battutah by Tim Mackintosh-Smith. A valuable source of research was Chapter 3 in the book *Journeys to the Other Shore* by Roxanne L. Euben. In addition, we found the article "Ibn Battuta, Prince of Travelers" in *National Geographic*, Vol. 180, No. 6, December 1991, pp. 2-49, inclusive of the excellent maps, to be highly valuable.

A difficult part of writing this chapter was in researching Ibn Battuta's journeys. While the chapter attempts to illustrate many of his trips, there is not complete agreement by scholars as to just where he traveled. Our chapter was written to present an overall picture of his travels and does not presume to accurately state the conditions and travel routes taken.

With assistance from Ibn Juzayy, Ibn Battuta's book about his travels was translated in English as *A Gift to Those Who Contemplate the Wonders of Cities and the Marvels of Travelling.* However, it is simply referred to as *The Travels* (or in Arabic: *Rihla*). Even though Ibn Battuta wrote his book in 1355, few people had the opportunity to read it. The book seemed to have simply disappeared but in the nineteenth century; some Frenchmen discovered copies in Constantine, Algeria. It was not until late in the twentieth century that this traveler and his book finally received the attention he richly deserved. Research from the Internet regarding some of the countries visited by Ibn Battuta helped to identify his travel itineraries.

# CHAPTER FIVE: THE SEVEN VOYAGES OF ZHENG HE

Finding information in English on Zheng He was an interesting challenge. While he was one of the greatest admirals of all time, his astounding achievements were initially ignored by most of the world. However, they're now well-known in China and abroad through the publication of Liang Qichao's *Biography of Our Homeland's Great Navigator, Zheng He*. The best single English language information we loved reading about Zheng He came from the book *Zheng He: China and the Oceans in the Early Ming Dynasty, 1405-1433* by Edward L. Dreyer.

Two books by Gavin Menzies, *1434: The Year A Magnificent Chinese Fleet Sailed to Italy and Ignited the Renaissance* and *1421: The Year China Discovered America*, provided interesting insights on the voyages of Zheng He. Another helpful book, *When China Ruled the Seas: The Treasure Fleet of the Dragon Throne, 1405-1433*, by Louise E. Levathes added different perspectives on Zheng He.

Other books of interest about Zheng He include: *Zheng He: The Great Chinese Explorer: A Bilingual Story of Adventure and Discovery (Chinese and English)* by Li Jian, *The Great Voyages of Zheng He: English/ Vietnamese* by Song Nan Zhang and Hao Yu Zhang, and *Zheng He (Discovery)* by Michael Yamashita.

Also, of importance is the excellent article: "China's Great Armada" by Frank Viviano in *National Geographic* Vol. 208, No. 1, pp. 28-53. Another is "The Seven Voyages of Zheng He" which appeared in the *Ancient History Encyclopedia*. For a brief summary of Zheng He, read the article titled "Zheng He" available on the Internet from the *Khan Academy* and, also see the summary on the Internet of the article "Zheng He" which appears in the *Encyclopaedia Britannica*. In addition there are a series of articles and Internet information about Zheng He available from many different sources based on the 600th year celebration of his voyages.

## CHAPTER SIX: CHRISTOPHER COLUMBUS, THE LOST ADMIRAL OF THE OCEAN SEA

There are abundant books, movies, and articles about Christopher Columbus throughout the world. His exploits are well-known and are taught routinely in schools in Europe and the Americas. We particularly enjoyed Columbus as a worldly traveler in the book called *The Discoverers* by Daniel J. Boorstin. We balanced this information with a critical review and well-researched book titled *Christopher Columbus and the Conquest of Paradise* by Kirkpatrick Sale. Also of consequence is *Admiral of the Ocean Sea: A Life of Christopher Columbus* by Samuel E. Morison. His other book, *Christopher Columbus, Mariner,* also provided valuable research.

One book we consider to be a must-read about Christopher Columbus, is *Columbus: The Four Voyages, 1492-1504* by Laurence Bergreen. Not related to the prior book, but having a similar title is another worthwhile book, *The Four Voyages of Christopher Columbus,* written by Christopher Columbus and translated by J. Cohen. More excellent research on Christopher Columbus is *1493: Uncovering the New World Columbus Created* by Charles C. Mann.

We also consulted *History.com Editors* for their updated publication of *Christopher Columbus* (History.com Editors, 2020), as developed and published by A&E Television Networks. Another interesting insight into Christopher Columbus is the article titled "Looks are deceiving: The portraits of Christopher Columbus" by Paul M. Lester (January 1993) in *Visual Anthropology* 5(3-4): 211-227. In addition, we reviewed "Christopher Columbus" which appeared in *History* as updated on October 7, 2020, from the original document dated November 9, 2009. Finally, we noted information on the Internet.

# CHAPTER SEVEN: JEANNE BARET, THE DISGUISED WORLDLY TRAVELER AND BOTANIST

The information about Jeanne Baret is limited partly because she was a woman traveling illegally on a French navy ship. In addition, apparently she left no notes about her travels. For this character in our book, it was necessary to frequently rely on the Internet and piece together a story from the various segments of lore scattered about from the limited sources available.

However, the single best reference about Jeanne Baret's life comes from her biographer Glynis Ridley, who wrote *The Discovery of Jeanne Baret: A Story of Science, the High Seas, and the First Woman to Circumnavigate the Globe*. Glynis Ridley's book also contains admirable information about Jeanne Baret's companion and benefactor Dr. Philibert Commerson. Other sources of information about Dr. Commerson can be found from *Encyclopedia.com*.

Another worthy book is titled *The Secret of Jeanne Baret's: Based on a True Story* by Helen C. Strahinich is a must-read for an added look at Jeanne Baret's life and explorations. Also, John Dunmore's *Monsieur Baret: First Woman Around the World*. The most recent, and a well-researched, book about Jeanne Baret is *In Search of the Woman who Sailed the World* by Danielle Clode (2020).

We also found *Jeanne Baret – Naturalist and 18th Century World Traveler* by Jean Murray an excellent piece. Other important references consulted for this chapter of the book included *The Mariners' Museum and Park* publication titled "The Ages of Exploration" with an article on Jeanne Baret. In addition, note "The Plantswoman Who Dressed As a Boy" by Sandra Knapp in *Nature* 470, 36-37 (February 3, 2011). And, we used the Internet for additional information about Philibert Commerson and Admiral Louis Antoine de Bougainville.

# CHAPTER EIGHT: AN ADVENTUROUS SCIENTIFIC EXPLORATION EXPERIENCE WITH CHARLES DARWIN

The best reference for Charles Darwin's travel in this chapter is, of course, his own book, *The Voyage of the Beagle*. The version of his book utilized most often in this chapter is *The Voyage of the Beagle* with an introduction by H. James Birx, published as part of the "Great Minds Series" by Prometheus Books, Amherst, New York, 2000.

An intriguing read of his various adventures is the well-researched, impressively illustrated, and well written *The Voyage of the Beagle* by James Taylor. This book adds to Charles Darwin's own book by including additional commentary based on personal letters and diaries. With its impressive photos, charts, and illustrations, it truly makes the voyage come alive. In addition, while *The Worldly Travelers* refers only to certain chosen characters, as the Captain of the *Beagle*, Robert FitzRoy was certainly an interesting well-traveled seafarer and aptly described in James Taylor's book.

We found the book *The Young Charles Darwin* by Keith Thomson important to review, written in an interesting format, which filled in many details that had been noted in some of the other readings on Charles Darwin.

A superb commentary on Darwin, especially his travels on the *Beagle,* is contained in "Part Three: Charles Robert Darwin" of the book *South America Called Them* by Victor Wolfgang von Hagen. Further information of interest in describing results from Darwin's travels is his own book is *On the Origin of Species by Means of Natural Selection, or the Preservation of Favoured Races in the Struggle for Life,* better-known simply as *On the Origin of Species.* For even more information about Darwin's life, please see *Charles Darwin* by Janet Browne. Finally, like the other characters in the book, the Internet was helpful.

## CHAPTER NINE: MARK TWAIN, THE INNOCENT WAYFARER

*The Autobiography of Mark Twain*, as edited by Charles Neider, offered us extensive insights into the life and writings of Mark Twain. Also, see *Mark Twain: A Biography* by Albert Paine and *Mark Twain: A Life* by Ron Powers.

Mark Twain loved Bermuda and made eight trips to the Island. It was an important refuge for him. The book: *Twain in Paradise: His Voyages to Bermuda* by Donald Hoffmann offers delightful details of his visits to Bermuda.

An outstanding in-depth examination and study of Mark Twain's travel is contained in *Mark Twain's Travel Literature: The Odyssey of a Mind* by Harold H. Hellwig. A book that caught our attention and which brings a special view of Mark Twain as not only a travel writer but as a tourist is *Mark Twain, Travel Books, and Tourism* by Jeffrey Alan Melton. This explores the depths of travel writing and provides considerable insight into the five books on travel written by Mark Twain.

In addition, Richard Bridgman's book, *Traveling in Mark Twain*, includes some thought-provoking notes about Mark Twain, the traveler and writer. It was useful in helping us to understand the greater intellect of Mark Twain. See also *Mark Twain: His Dangerous Mind, Remarkable Life and Enduring Legacy* by Roy Blount, Jr.; it contains more fascinating insights and aspects of certain events in Mark Twain's life. The Internet was helpful in suggesting other references to peruse.

Finally, Mark Twain's own books on travel provided much of the material for this comparatively short chapter on our worldly traveler. Twain's books included *Following the Equator: A Journey Around the World, The Innocents Abroad, Life on the Mississippi, Roughing It, A Tramp Abroad*, and *Mark Twain's Travel Books and Memoirs.*

# CHAPTER TEN: HEROIC EXPLOITS TO THE FORBIDDEN LAND WITH NAIN SINGH

Nain Singh is not as well-known as our other worldly travelers; yet his contributions to the knowledge of Asia and Tibet in the mid-nineteenth century were unmatched. Researching such a fascinating character was challenging, and an excellent source of important information for this chapter comes from the book titled *The Pundits: British Exploration of Tibet and Central Asia* by Derek Waller. We appreciated the book *Trespassers on the Roof of the World: The Secret Exploration of Tibet* by Peter Hopkirk. As well, an excellent book about the Indian culture is *The Patient Assassin* by Anita Anand. The book titled *Explorers and Discovers of the World*, edited by Daniel B. Baker, provides curious insights as did the book *The Great Explorers*, which was edited by Robin Hanbury-Tenison.

A biography of Nain Singh by Dr. Shekhar Pathak and Dr. Uma Bhatt includes three of his diaries as well as excerpts from articles in the Royal Geographic Society about Nain Singh's travels. It is printed in three volumes titled *Asia ki Peeth Par: Pundit Nain Singh Rawat*. Additional reading to better understand the British Indian Empire's plans for the area where Nain Singh traveled can be found in Robert Johnson's *Spying for Empire: The Great Game in Central and South Asia*. Riaz Dean's book called *Mapping the Great Game: Explorers, Spies and Maps in 19th-century Asia* is a fascinating read. Also, Edmund Smyth's "Obituary: The Pundit Nain Singh" in *Proceedings of the Royal Geographical Society and Monthly Record of Geography* and the article "Nain Singh Rawat, The Spy Explorer by Rina Tripathi are good sources. See also Thomas Montgomerie's "Report of a Route-Survey Made by Pundit, from Nepal to Lhasa, and Thence Through the Upper Valley of the Brahmaputra to Its Source" in *The Journal of the Royal Geographical Society of London* and Henry Trotter's "Account of the Pundit's Journey in Great Tibet From Leh in Ladakh to Lhasa". See also information from the Internet.

## Chapter Eleven: Charles A. Lindbergh: Famous Aviator Becomes an Environmentalist

There are so many books, articles written and movies made about Charles A. Lindbergh. The best book is Charles A. Lindbergh's biography *Lindbergh* by A. Scott Berg. *Lindbergh: Triumph and Tragedy* by Richard Bak was also valuable in our research.

Charles A. Lindbergh's own books – *The Spirit of St. Louis, "WE", Of Flight and Life, The Wartime Journals of Charles A. Lindbergh,* and *Charles A. Lindbergh: Autobiography of Values* – were imperative in researching Lindbergh's historic flight, travels, environmental interests, and life values. We also gained useful insights from the *North to the Orient* by Anne Morrow Lindbergh.

Many articles and speeches by Charles A. Lindbergh are excellent sources of information. His article titled "Is Civilization Progress?" in the July 1964 issue of *Reader's Digest* is an exceptional piece in explaining many of his environmental views. In his article called "Lindbergh & Conservation", published in the *New York Times* on June 23, 1969, Alden Whitman identifies many of Lindbergh's concerns about the wilderness, saving animal species, and other conservation issues.

In addition, other sources include: *The Big Jump: Lindbergh and the Great Atlantic Air Race* by Richard Bak, *Charles Lindbergh and the Spirit of St. Louis* by Dominick A. Pisano and F. Robert van der Linden, *Lindbergh Alone* by Brendan Gill, and *Lindbergh: Flight's Enigmatic Hero* by Von Hardesty. Additional articles of interest include: "Barnstorming with Lindbergh" by Bruce L. Larson in *Minnesota History,* vol. 58, no. 1 (Spring 2002), pp. 2-15. Also, Bruce L. Larson's "Lindbergh's Return to Minnesota" in *Minnesota History,* vol. 42, no. 4 (Winter 1970), pp. 141-152 was worthwhile. See also information from the Internet.

# CHAPTER TWELVE: TRAVELING ON THE WINGS OF AMELIA EARHART, AVIATRIX

This chapter is based on substantial information gathered from a visit to the home where Amelia Earhart grew up in Atchison, Kansas. Some of the materials for the chapter came from a personal collection of newspaper articles about Amelia Earhart beginning in 1987, and movies reviewed about her life. But the lion's share of information is based in *East to Dawn: The Life of Amelia Earhart* by Susan Butler and *The Sound of Wings: The Life of Amelia Earhart* by Mary S. Lovell. We also found of significant interest the book called *Amelia Earhart: The Final Story* written by Vincent V. Loomis with Jeffrey L. Ethell and published by Random House (Loomis and Ethell, 1985). This book makes the strongest case for Amelia Earhart and Fred Noonan being captured by the Japanese and dying in a Japanese prison.

Also of great help were the three books written by Amelia Earhart: *20 Hrs. 40 Min., The Fun of It,* and *Last Flight.* Another source about Amelia Earhart's eventful life is *Letters from Amelia, 1901-1937* by Jean Backus. Mike Campbell wrote a couple of interesting books about Amelia Earhart, especially *Amelia Earhart: The Truth at Last.*

Many books and articles have developed theories of what happened to Amelia Earhart; one is *Amelia Lost: The Life and Disappearance of Amelia Earhart* by Candace Fleming. There is also a worthy book about special events in Amelia Earhart's life titled *"Lady Lindy": The Remarkable life of Amelia Earhart* by C. V. Glines. Another book to review is *Amelia Earhart: The Sky's No Limit* by Lori Van Pelt. For more intimate details about Amelia Earhart, see her sister's book *Amelia Earhart* by Muriel Earhart Morrissey. As well, read *Amelia Earhart: A Biography* by Doris L. Rich. More recently, the Internet has contained considerable information about certain of the details about Amelia Earhart's last flight.

## Chapter Thirteen: Yuri Gagarin, the First Space Cosmonaut/Tourist

The most useful book for this chapter was *The First Manned Spaceflight: Russia's Quest for Space* by Vladimir Suvorov and Alexander Sabelnikov. It's based on the notes of Vladimir Suvorov and his discussions with his nephew, Alexander Sabelnikov. Suvorov was a distinguished chief documentary cinematographer, who eye-witnessed and described, in his top-secret diary, the Soviet space program from 1959-1969, including the events related to Gagarin. Through Suvorov's wife, his private notes were passed on to his nephew, Alexander Sabelnikov. Happily, much of the information gained about the Soviet space program and Yuri Gagarin came from Dr. Edgell's personal friendship and conversations with Alexander Sabelnikov. For a detailed well-written book about Yuri Gagarin, read *Beyond* by Stephen Walker.

A superb book on the early Soviet space program is *The First Soviet Cosmonaut Team* by Colin Burgess and Rex Hall. Another useful reference is *Starman: The Truth Behind the Legend of Yuri Gagarin* by Jamie Doran and Piers Bizony. Also note *Vostok 1: First Human in Space* by Michael D. Cole. Recent new information from the Internet was also helpful.

In addition, please note the book *Yuri Gagarin: The First Man in Space* by Heather Feldman, *Yuri Gagarin, and the Race to Space* by Ben Hubbard, and finally *The Cosmonaut Who Couldn't Stop Smiling: The Life and Legend of Yuri Gagarin* by Andrew L. Jenks.

There are so many first-rate articles about Yuri Gagarin. For example: "Yuri Gagarin's First Speech About His Flight Into Space" printed in *The Atlantic* April 12, 2011, and "Yuri Gagarin: The Journey that Shook the World" by Paul Rincon, *Science Reporter*, BBC News April 10, 2011. Both articles were written to celebrate the 50th anniversary of Yuri Gagarin's flight into space. The article: "Yuri Gagarin: Soviet Cosmonaut", written by the Editors of the Encyclopedia Britannica, adds important information to that cited above.

# GENERAL REFERENCES

(1937). *Pictured left to right: Paul Mantz, Amelia Earhart, Harry Manning, and Fred Noonan posed in front of Earhart's Lockheed 10E Electra prior to taking off from Oakland, California, for Honolulu, Hawaii, March 18, 1937* [Image]. Smithsonian National Air and Space Museum. https://airandspace.si.edu/collection-objects/mantz-paul-earhart-amelia-mary-noonan-fred-manning-harry-lockheed-model-10-e.

(n.d.). *Ibn Battuta* [Image]. Harcourt School. https://www.harcourtschool.com/activity/biographies/battuta/.

(n. d.). *Ibn Battuta's book, Rihla* [Image]. Casa del Libro. https://www.casadellibro.com/libro-a-traves-del-islam/9788420645858/1033316.

Abercrombie, Thomas J. "Ibn Battuta, Prince of Travelers". *National Geographic*, December 1991.

ABiti-Anat, Lilinah. *The History and Culture of the Canaanites and Phoenicians: A History of the Purple People.*

ALL Non-Africans Are Part Neanderthals. (2012). *Living and travel in the earliest of times* [Image]. The Word of Me. https://thewordofme.wordpress.com/2012/01/17/all-non-africans-are-part-neanderthals/.

Alnoaim, Abdulrahman. (2019). *Pyramids of Giza* [Image]. Aesdes. org. http://www.aesdes.org/2019/01/23/aesthetics-exploration-2019-pyramids-of-giza/.

Amelia Earhart. (n.d.). *Amelia Earhart (right) and Neta Snook (left)* [Image]. Time Toast. https://www.timetoast.com/timelines/amelia-earhart--165.

Amelia Earhart Flies Solo Across the Atlantic... (1932). *Article published in the Cleveland News about Amelia Earhart's solo flight across the Atlantic* [Image]. The Cleveland News. https://www.rarenewspapers.com/view/619712.

Amelia Earhart Mystery Could Be Solved at Last. (2018). *Amelia Earhart* [Image]. Today. https://www.today.com/video/amelia-earhart-mystery-could-be-solved-at-last-1180141123509.

Author of the Week – Anne Spencer Lindbergh. (2010). *Charles and Anne Lindbergh* [Image].

Children's Atheneum. http://childrensatheneum.blogspot.com/2010/03/author-of-week-anne-spencer-lindbergh.html.

Aviatrix. (2016). *Amelia Earhart and members of the Ninety-Nines* [Image]. PicsArt. https://picsart.com/blog/post/why-amelia-earhart-was-a-really-big-deal/.

Bak, Richard. *Lindbergh: Triumph and Tragedy.* Dallas, Texas: Taylor Publishing Co., 2000.

Baker, Daniel B. (editor). *Explorers and Discoverers of the World.* Detroit, Michigan: Gale Research Inc., 1993.

Bakker, Egbert J., Irene J. F. De Jong, and Hans Van Wees (editors). *Brill's Companion to Herodotus.* Leiden, The Netherlands: Brill, 2002.

Berg, Scott A. *Lindbergh.* New York, NY: G. P. Putnam's Sons, 1998.

Bergreen, Laurence. *Marco Polo.* New York, NY: Random House Inc., 2007.

Bergreen, Laurence. *Over the Edge of the World.* HarperCollins Publisher, 2003.

Berra, Tim. *Charles Darwin.* Baltimore, Maryland: The Johns Hopkins University Press, 2009.

Biography. (2014*). Marco Polo shortly before his death* [Image]. Biography. https://www.biography.com/explorer/marco-polo.

Biography of Charles Darwin: The Theory of Evolution. (2015). *Charles Robert Darwin, age 31* [Image]. Wiki Didactic. https://edukalife.blogspot. com/2015/07/biography-of-charles-darwin-theory-of.html.

Blanco, Walter, and Jennifer Tolbert Roberts (editors). *Herodotus: The Histories.* New York, NY: W.W. Norton & Company, 1992.

Blount, Jr., *Mark Twain: His Dangerous Mind, Remarkable Life and Enduring Legacy,* Time, Inc., 2015.

Boorstin, Daniel J. *The Discoverers.* New York: Vintage Books, 1985.

Botton, Alain de. *The Art of Travel.* New York: Vintage Books, 2002.

Bowlers, Peter. *Charles Darwin: The Man and His Influence.* Cambridge, Massachusetts: Basil Blackwell Ltd., 1990.

Bridgman, Richard. *Traveling in Mark Twain.* Berkeley, California: University of California Press, 1987.

Burgess, Colin and Hall, Rex (2009). *The First Soviet Cosmonaut Team.* United Kingdom: Chicester.

Burke, John. *Winged Legend: The Story of Amelia Earhart.* New York: Ballantine Books, 1971.

Browne, Janet. *Charles Darwin, Voyaging.* New York: Alfred A. Knopf, 1995.

Burns, Ken, Dayton Duncan, and Geoffrey C. Ward. *Mark Twain: An Illustrated Biography*. New York: Alfred A. Knopf, 2001.

Butler, Susan. *East to Dawn: The Life of Amelia Earhart*. Reading Massachusetts: Addison-Wesley, 1997.

Butler, Richard, and Roslyn Russell (Editors). *Giants of Tourism*. Cambridge, Massachusetts: CABI, 2010.

Byrne, Donn. *Messer Marco Polo*. New York, NY: The Century Co., 1921.

Casson, Lionel. *The Pharaohs*. Chicago, Illinois: Stonehenge, 1981.

Casson, Lionel. *Travel in the Ancient World*. Baltimore, Maryland: The Johns Hopkins University Press, 1994.

Campbell, Mike. *Amelia Earhart: The Truth at Last* (2nd Edition). Sunbury Press, Inc.

Charles Darwin – the man behind the evolution. (2015). *Charles Darwin (pictured on the right) and Professor Henslow (pictured on the left)* [Image]. Mirfaces. https://mirfaces.com/charles-darwin-the-man-behind-the-evolution/.

Charles Darwin – the man behind the evolution. (2015). *Monument to Charles Darwin on the island of San Cristobal* [Image]. https://mirfaces.com/charles-darwin-the-man-behind-the-evolution/.

Charles Lindbergh: An American Aviator. (n.d.). *Charles Lindbergh* [Image]. Charles Lindbergh. http://wwww.charleslindbergh.com/pictures/1927.jpg.

Clemens, Samuel L. *Following the Equator: A Journey Around the World*. Hartford, Connecticut: American Publishing Co., 1897.

_____. *The Innocents Abroad*. Hartford, Connecticut: American Publishing Co., 1869.

_____. *Life on the Mississippi.* Boston, Massachusetts: Charles R. Osgood, 1883.

_____. *More Tramps Abroad.* London, England: Chatto and Windus, 1897.

_____. *Roughing It.* Hartford, Connecticut: American Publishing Co., 1872.

_____. *A Tramp Abroad.* Hartford, Connecticut: American Publishing Co., 1880.

Cole, Michael. *Vostok 1: First Human in Space.* Springfield, New Jersey: Enslow Publishers, 1995.

Cole, Wayne. S. *Charles A. Lindbergh and The Battle Against American Intervention in World War II.* New York: Harcourt Brace Jovanovich, 1974.

Cooper, Robert. *Around the World with Mark Twain.* New York: Arcade Publishing, 2000.

Cousineau, Phil. *The Art of Pilgrimage: The Seeker's Guide to Making Travel Sacred.* Boston, MA: Conari Press, 1998.

Covici, Pascal, Jr. *Mark Twain's Humor: The Image of a World.* Dallas, Texas: Southern Methodist UP, 1962.

Cox, James M. *Mark Twain: The Fate of Humor.* Princeton, New Jersey: Princeton University Press, 1966.

Darwin, Charles. *The Voyage of the Beagle.* Amherst, New York: Prometheus Books, 2000.

Darwin, Charles. *The Origin of Species.* New York, NY: Random House, Inc., 2003

Davidson, Miles H. *Columbus Then and Now: A Life Reexamined.* Norman, Oklahoma: University of Oklahoma Press, 1997.

Davis, Natalie Zemon. *Trickster Travels.* New York: Hill and Wang, 2006.

Dekkak, Mohamed. (2020). *Ibn Battuta's Delhi Escape* [Image]. Mohamed Dekkak. https://dekkak.com/ibn-battutas-delhi-escape/.

Derow, Peter and Robert Parker (editors). *Herodotus and His World.* New York, NY: Oxford University Press, 2003.

Desperado Jack Slade. (2020). *Jack Slade* [Image]. The Senior Voice. https://theseniorvoice.net/desperado-jack-slade/.

Dewald, Carolyn and John Marincola (editors). *The Cambridge Companion to Herodotus.* Cambridge, United Kingdom: Cambridge University Press, 2006.

Dibner, Bern. *Darwin of the Beagle.* New York, NY: Blaisdell Publishing Company, 1964.

Discovery Channel. (n.d.) *Amelia Earhart sharing her knowledge of aviation* [Image]. Pinterest. https://www.pinterest.com/pjlw/amelia-earhart/.

Dolmestch, Carl. *"Our Famous Guest": Mark Twain in Vienna.* Athens, Georgia; University of Georgia Press, 1992.

Doran, Jamie. *Starman: The Truth Behind the Legend of Yuri Gagarin.* London, England: Bloomsbury, 1998.

Dreyer, Edward L. *Zheng He: China and the Oceans in the Early Ming Dynasty, 1405-1433.* New York, NY: Pearson Education, Inc., 2007.

Duffy, James P. *Lindbergh vs. Roosevelt: The Rivalry that Divided America.* New York: MJF Books, 2010.

Dunn, Ross. *The Adventures of Ibn Battuta – the Great Traveler of the 14th Century.* Berkley, California: University of California, 1989.

Durant, Will. *The Story of Philosophy.* New York: Time Incorporated, 1962.

Earhart, Amelia. *20Hrs. 40 Min.* New York, NY: G. P. Putnam's Sons, 1929.

Earhart, Amelia. *The Fun of It.* New York, NY: Brewer, Warren, and Putnam, 1932.

Earhart, Amelia. *Last Flight.* New York, NY: Harcourt Brace and Company, 1937; London, United Kingdom: Harrap, 1938.

Edgell, Sr., David L. "Travel and Tourism, the Language of Peace", *Journal of Hospitality & Tourism*, Volume 12, Number 2, 2014.

Edgell, Sr., David L. *Managing Sustainable Tourism: A Legacy for the Future.* (3rd edition) London: Routledge, 2020.

Edgell, Sr., David L. and Jason R. Swanson, *Tourism Policy and Planning: Yesterday, Today and Tomorrow.* London: Routledge, 2019.

Edwards, Mike. "The Adventures of Marco Polo, Part I". *National Geographic*, May 2001.

Edwards, Mike. "Marco Polo in China, Part II". *National Geographic*, June 2001.

Edwards, Mike. "Marco Polo, Journey Home, Part III". *National Geographic*, July 2001.

Eidsmoe, John. *Columbus & Cortez: Conquerors for Christ.* Green Forest, Arizona: New Leaf Press, 1992.

Eliot, Charles W. (editor). *Lectures on The Harvard Classics.* New York, NY: P. F. Collier & Son Company, 1914.

Emerson, Everett. *Mark Twain: A Literary Life*. Philadelphia: University of Pennsylvania Press, 2000.

Euben, Roxanne L. *Journeys to the Other Shore*. Princeton, New Jersey: Princeton University Press, 2006.

Evans, J. A. S. *Herodotus, Explorer of the Past*. Princeton, New Jersey: Princeton University Press, 1991.

Everett Collection. (n.d.). *Pictured left to right: First Lady Eleanor Roosevelt, Amelia Earhart, Scottish pilot Jim Mollison, his wife, pilot Amy Johnson, President Franklin D. Roosevelt* [Image]. Alamy. https://www.alamy.com/stock-photo-l-r-first-lady-eleanor-roosevelt-amelia-earhart-scottish-pilot-jim-50018434.html.

Fishkin, Shelly Fisher (editor). *A Historical Guide to Mark Twain*. New York: Oxford University Press, 2002.

Francis, Keith. *Charles Darwin and The Origin of Species*. Westport, Connecticut: Greenwood Press, 2007.

Fritze, Ronald H. *Travel Legend and Lore: An Encyclopedia*. Santa Barbara, California: ABC-CLIO, 1998.

Fussell, Paul. *The Norton Book of Travel*. New York, NY: W.W. Norton & Company, 1987

Ganzel, Dewey. *Mark Twain Abroad: The Cruise of the "Quaker City."* Chicago and London: University of Chicago Press, 19698.

Garr, Arnold K. (2018). *The first voyage of Christopher of Columbus* [Image]. Student News Daily. https://www.studentnewsdaily.com/editorials-for-students/columbus-first-voyage/.

Gerbard, Herm. *The Phoenicians*. William Morrow and Company, Inc.

Gibb, H.A.R. *The Travels of Ibn Battuta, Vols. I, II, III.* London, England: Cambridge University Press, 1956.

Gladwell, Malcolm. *Outliers: The Story of Success.* New York, NY: Little, Brown and Company, 2008.

Glover, Terrot R. *Herodotus.* Freeport, New York: Books for Libraries Press, 1924.

Goeldner, Charles R. and J.R. Brent Ritchie. *Tourism: Principles, Practices, Philosophies* (Eleventh Edition). Hoboken, New Jersey: John Wiley & Sons, 2009.

Haddon, Heather. (2012). *Charles Lindbergh Jr.* [Image]. The Wall Street Journal. https://www.wsj.com/articles/SB10001424127887324669104578 205713435130582.

Hanbury-Tenison (editor). *The Great Explorers.* London, England: Thames and Hudson, Ltd., 2010.

Hanes, Elizabeth. (2012). *Amelia Earhart and Fred Noonan* [Image]. History. http://www.history.com/news/what-happened-to-amelia-9-tantalizing-theories-about-the-earhart-disappearance.

Harden, Donald. *The Phoenicians.* Frederick A. Praeger (?) publishing (?), year (?)

Hart, Henry H. *Marco Polo.* Norman, Oklahoma: University of Oklahoma Press, 1976.

Heilbroner, Robert L. *The Worldly Philosophers* (Sixth Edition). New York: Simon & Schuster, Inc., 1986.

Hellwig, Harold H. *Mark Twain's Travel Literature: The Odyssey of a Mind.* Jefferson, North Carolina: McFarland & Company, Inc., 2008.

Herodotus, *The Histories*, Translated by G.C. Macaulay and revised by Donald Lateiner, New York: Barnes & Noble Classics, 2004.

History.com Editors. (2020). *Christopher Columbus*. History.com. https://www.history.com/topics/exploration/christopher-columbus.

HMS Beagle 1:60 Scale, OcCre. (n.d.). *H.M.S. Beagle* [Image]. Historic Ships. https://www.historicships.com/product/hms-beagle-160-scale/.

Hoare, Robert J. *Wings Over the Atlantic*. Boston, Massachusetts: Charles T. Branford Co., 1957.

Hoffmann, Donald. *Mark Twain in Paradise: His Voyages to Bermuda*. Columbia, Missouri: University of Missouri Press, 2006.

Hughes, Glyn. (2019). *Bust of Herodotus and fragment of the text from The Histories VIII on papyrus oxyrhynchus 2099, early 2ⁿᵈ century AD* [Image]. The Hundred Books. http://thehundredbooks.com/herodotus.htm.

Iggulden, Conn. *Genghis: Birth of an Empire*. New York, NY: Bantam Dell, 2007.

Jane, Cecil. *Journals of Christopher Columbus*. London, England: Bonanza Books, 1960.

Johnson, Paul. *Heroes*. New York, NY: HarperCollins Publishers, 2007.

Kalan, Julie. (2014). *Marco Polo at the age of 17, sitting astride between his father and his uncle as they begin their epic journey in Venice* [Image]. Montrealer. https://themontrealeronline.com/2014/08/marco-polo-an-epic-journey/.

Kapuscinski, Ryszard. *Travels with Herodotus*. New York, NY: Alfred A. Knopf, 2007.

Keen, Benjamin. *The Life of Admiral Christopher Columbus.* New Brunswick, New Jersey: Rutgers University Press, 1992.

Kennedy, John F. *Profiles in Courage.* New York, NY: Harper & Brothers, 1956.

Keritner, Richard. (2015). *Charles barnstorming* [Image]. The Nation. https://www.thenation.com/article/archive/may-20-1927-charles-lindbergh-takes-flight-france/.

Keyhoe, Donald E. *Flying with Lindbergh.* New York, NY: Putnam's, 1928.

Kim, Young Min. (2012). *Zheng He's Treasure Fleet* [Image]. Pinterest. https://www.pinterest.com/pin/66709638201600036/.

King, Christopher. (2014). *H.M.S. Beagle* [Image]. Melville House. https://www.mhpbooks.com/digitizing-darwins-library/.

Knauer, Kelly. (2015). *Mark Twain: His Dangerous Mind, Remarkable Life and Enduring Legacy.* New York: Time Home Entertainment, Inc.

Komroff, Manuel. *The Travels of Marco Polo.* New York, NY: The Heritage Press, 1934.

Krulwich, Robert. (2012). *Dr. Philibert Commerson* [Image]. NPR. https://www.pinterest.com/pin/542543086332868932/.

Larner, John. *Marco Polo and the Discovery of the World.* Hong Kong, China: World Print Ltd., 1999.

Latham, Ronald. *The Travels of Marco Polo* (as translated by Ronald Latham). London, England: Penguin Books, 1958.

Leakey, Richard. *The Origin of Humankind.* New York, NY: Basic Books, 1994.

Levathes, Louise. *When China Ruled the Seas: The Treasure Fleet of the Dragon Throne, 1405-1433*. London, Oxford University Press, 1997.

Lindbergh, Anne M. *North to the Orient*. New York, NY: Harcourt, Brace & Co., 1935.

Lindbergh, Charles A. *"WE"*. New York, NY: G.P. Putnam's Sons, 1927

Lindbergh, Charles A. *Of Flight and Life*. New York, NY: Charles Scribner's Sons, 1948.

Lindbergh, Charles A. *The Spirit of St. Louis*. New York, NY: Charles Scribner's Sons, 1953.

Lister, R. P. *Genghis Khan*. New York, NY: Barnes and Noble Books, 1993.

Little Known Facts about Life of a First Man in Space Yuri Gagarin. (n.d.). *Kremlin Wall in Moscow, the location of Yuri Gagarin's ashes* [Image]. English Russia. https://englishrussia.com/2017/03/28/little-known-facts-about-yuri-gagarin/.

Little Known Facts about Life of a First Man in Space Yuri Gagarin. (n.d.). *Yuri Gagarin* [Image]. English Russia. https://englishrussia.com/2017/03/28/little-known-facts-about-yuri-gagarin/.

Little Known Facts about Life of a First Man in Space Yuri Gagarin. (n.d.). *Yuri Gagarin as a six-year-old boy* [Image]. English Russia. https://englishrussia.com/2017/03/28/little-known-facts-about-yuri-gagarin/.

Little Known Facts about Life of a First Man in Space Yuri Gagarin. (n.d.). *Yuri Gagarin (bottom middle) and his siblings – his older brother Valentin (top left), his younger brother Boris (top middle), and his older sister Zoya (right)* [Image]. English Russia. https://englishrussia.com/2017/03/28/little-known-facts-about-yuri-gagarin/.

Little Known Facts about Life of a First Man in Space Yuri Gagarin. (n.d.). *Yuri Gagarin greeting the crowds in celebrating his successful flight* [Image]. English Russia. https://englishrussia.com/2017/03/28/ little-known-facts-about-yuri-gagarin/.

Little Known Facts about Life of a First Man in Space Yuri Gagarin. (n.d.). *Yuri Gagarin in 1954* [Image]. English Russia. https://englishrussia. com/2017/03/28/little-known-facts-about-yuri-gagarin/.

Little Known Facts about Life of a First Man in Space Yuri Gagarin. (n.d.). *Yuri Gagarin (pictured in the center of the first row) and his fellow cosmonaut students training at the Central Flight Medical Commission to be selected to travel into space* [Image]. English Russia. https:// englishrussia.com/2017/03/28/little-known-facts-about-yuri-gagarin/.

Little Known Facts about Life of a First Man in Space Yuri Gagarin. (n.d.). *Yuri Gagarin with his two daughters* [Image]. English Russia. https:// englishrussia.com/2017/03/28/little-known-facts-about-yuri-gagarin/.

Little Known Facts about Life of a First Man in Space Yuri Gagarin. (n.d.). *Yuri Gagarin with his wife Valentina* [Image]. English Russia. https:// englishrussia.com/2017/03/28/little-known-facts-about-yuri-gagarin/.

Loney, John. (n.d.). *Captain Thomas Montgomerie* [Image]. Irvine History Notes. https://irvinehistorynotes.yolasite.com/thomas-george-montgomerie.php.

Loomis, Vincent V. and Jeffrey L. Ethell. (1985). *Amelia Earhart: The Final Story*. Random House: New York City, New York.

Lovell, Mary S. *The Sound of Wings: The Life of Amelia Earhart*. New York, NY: St Martin's Griffin, 1989.

Mackintosh-Smith, Tim. *Travels with a Tangerine*. London, Great Britain: John Murray (Publishers) Ltd., 2001.

Mackintosh-Smith, Tim (editor). *The Travels of Ibn Battuta*. United Kingdom: Macmillan, 2003.

Majid, Anouar. (2013). *Map of the Fertile Crescent* [Image]. Tingis Magazine. https://www.tingismagazine.com/editorials/whence-the-koran/.

Man, John. *Marco Polo: The Journey that Changed the World*. New York: William Morrow, 2009.

Manchester Museum. (2016). *Bust of Herodotus and fragment of the text from "The Histories VIII" on Papyrus Oxyrhynchus 2099, early 2nd century AD* [Image]. Stories from the Museum Floor. https://storiesfromthemuseumfloor.wordpress.com/2016/03/06/how-to-make-a-mummy/.

Maraini, Fosco. (n.d.). *Map depicting the places Marco Polo traveled to* [Image]. Britannica. https://www.britannica.com/biography/Marco-Polo.

Marco Polo and Kublai Khan. (2016). *Kublai Khan presenting the inscribed gold tablet to Niccolò Polo and Maffeo Polo* [Image]. Facts and Details. http://factsanddetails.com/china/cat2/4sub8/entry-5457.html.

Markham, Beryl. (1983). *West with the Night*. New York: North Point Press.

Marin, Xavier. (2015). *Depictions of the ships on which Columbus' crews sailed for the first voyage – the Niña, the Pinta, and the Santa Maria* [Image]. Social Sciences 2nd ESO. http://cienciessocials2n.blogspot.com/2015/03/9-els-descobriments-america-clil.html.

McNamara, Robert. (2019). *Charles Darwin* [Image]. Thought Co. https://www.thoughtco.com/charles-darwin-his-origin-of-the-species-1773841.

Meet Jeanne Baret: The First Woman to Circumnavigate the Globe. (2020). *Jeanne Baret in traditional female attire (pictured on the left) and dressed in male clothing (pictured on the right)* [Image]. Seekapor.com. https://www.seekapor.com/meet-jeanne-baret-the-first-woman-to-circumnavigate-the-globe/.

Melton, Jeffrey Alan. *Mark Twain, Travel Books, and Tourism: The Tide of a Great Popular Movement.* Tuscaloosa, Alabama: The University of Alabama Press, 2002.

Mendelsohn, Jane. *I Was Amelia Earhart.* New York, NY: Alfred A. Knopf, Inc. 1996.

Menzies, Gavin. *142: The Year China Discovered America.* New York, NY: HarperCollins Publishers Inc., 2003.

Menzies, Gavin. *1434: The Year A Magnificent Chinese Fleet Sailed to Italy and Ignited the Renaissance.* New York, NY: HarperCollins Publishers Inc., 2008.

Michelson, Bruce. *Mark Twain on the Loose: A Comic Writer and The American Self.* Amherst, Massachusetts: University of Massachusetts Press, 1995.

Milner, Richard. *Natural History* "Seeing Corals with the Eye of Reason: A Rediscovered Painting Celebrates Charles Darwin's View of Life" (February 2009).

Melton, Jeffrey Alan. *Mark Twain, Travel Books, and Tourism: The Tide of a Great Popular Movement.* Tuscaloosa, Alabama: The University of Alabama Press, 2002.

Mingren, Wu. (2017*). Statue of Herodotus in his hometown of Halicarnassus* [Image]. Ancient Origins. https://www.ancient-origins.net/history/picking-apart-words-herodotus-was-he-father-histories-or-lies-009085

Moody, Oliver. (2018). *Christopher Columbus plants the Spanish flag in the presence of the Taino Indians* [Image]. The Times. https://www.thetimes.co.uk/article/ta-no-tribe-found-by-christopher-columbus-wasn-t-wiped-out-after-all-cdbkfljqb.

Morrison, Samuel E. *Admiral of the Ocean Sea: A life of Christopher Columbus.* Boston, Massachusetts: Little, Brown & Company, 1942.

Morrison, Samuel E. *Christopher Columbus, Mariner.* Boston, Massachusetts: Little, Brown & Company, 1955.

Morrissey, Muriel Earhart. *Amelia Earhart.* Santa Barbara, California: Bellerophon Books, 1992.

Morrissey, Muriel Earhart. *Courage is the Price: The Biography of Amelia Earhart.* McCormick-Armstrong, Pub. Division.

Moscasti, Sabatino. *The Phoenicians.* Manhattan, New York: Rizzoli International Publications, 2000.

Moscati, Sabatino. *The Phoenicians.* London, England: IBTARIS and Company, 2001.

Mosley, Leonard. *Lindbergh: A Biography.* Garden City, New York: Doubleday, 1976.

Nagle, D. Brendan. *The Ancient World: A Social and Cultural History* (Eighth Edition). New York: Pearson, 2014.

Neider, Charles. *The Autobiography of Mark Twain* (as edited by Charles Neider). New York, NY: Harper and Row Publishers, 1990.

Nix, Elizabeth. (2014*). Samuel Clemens, age 15* [Image]. History. https://www.history.com/news/8-things-you-may-not-know-about-mark-twain.

Nordquist, Richard. (2020). Mark Twain [Image]. Thought Co. https://www.thoughtco.com/two-ways-of-seeing-a-river-by-mark-twain-1688773.

Obenzinger, Hilton. *American Palestine: Melville, Twain, and the Holy Land Mania.* Princeton, New Jersey: Princeton University Press, 1999.

O'Gorman, Kevin. *The Origins of Hospitality and Tourism.* Woodeaton, Oxford, United Kingdom: Goodfellow Publishers Limited, 2010.

Olby, Robert. *Charles Darwin*. London: Oxford University Press, 1967.

Oppenheimer, Stephen. (n.d.). *Journey of Mankind* [Interactive Map]. Bradshaw Foundation. Paine, Albert Bigelow, (editor). *Mark Twain's Letters*. New York, NY: Harper and Brothers, 1917.

Pettinato, Tony. (2017). *The Space Race began when the Soviet Union launched Sputnik* [Image]. Genealogy Bank. https://blog.genealogybank. com/on-this-day-space-race-began-as-soviets-launched-sputnik.html.

Pollard, Justin. *Wonders of the Ancient World*. New York: Metro Books, 2008.

Polo, Marco. *The Travels of Marco Polo*. Translated and with an introduction by Robert Latham. London: Penguin Classics, 1958.

Putnam, George Palmer. *Soaring Wings: A Biography of Amelia Earhart*. New York, NY: Harcourt, Brace, 1939.

Reader's Digest. *Mysteries of the Ancient Americas*. Pleasantville, New York: The Reader's Digest Association, Inc., 1986.

Rhapsodyinbooks (2014). *Charles Lindbergh in Nazi Germany with Hermann Göring* [Image]. Legal Legacy. https://legallegacy.wordpress. com/2014/09/11/september-11-1941-charles-lindbergh-excoriates-jews-along-with-fdr-and-the-british-for-trying-to-get-the-u-s-into-wwii/.

Rhapsodyinbooks (2014). Col. *Charles A. Lindbergh tells the House Foreign Affairs Committee that a German air invasion of the United States and the landing of troops is "absolutely impossible"* [Image]. https:// legallegacy.wordpress.com/2014/09/11/september-11-1941-charles-lindbergh-excoriates-jews-along-with-fdr-and-the-british-for-trying-to-get-the-u-s-into-wwii/.

Rich, Doris L. (1989). *Amelia Earhart: A Biography*. Washington, D. C.: Smithsonian Institution Press.

Ridley, Glynis (2010). *The Discovery of Jeanne Baret*. New York: Broadway Paperbacks.

Rodney, Robert M. *Mark Twain Overseas: A Biographical Account of His Voyages, Travels, and Reception in Foreign Lands, 1866-1910*. Washington, D. C.: Three Continents Press, 1993.

Romm, James. *Herodotus*. New Haven, Connecticut: Yale University Press, 1998.

Rossabi, Morris. General Editor. *The Illustrated Edition: The Travels of Marco Polo*. New York: Fall River Press, 2012.

Roth, Anna. (2012). Christopher Columbus bids farewell to the King and Queen as he prepares to leave on his first voyage [Image]. SF Weekly. https://archives.sfweekly.com/foodie/2012/10/08/how-christopher-columbus-changed-the-way-we-eat.

Sale, Kirkpatrick. *Christopher Columbus and the Conquest of Paradise*. London, England: Tauris Parke Paperbacks, 2006.

Saxena, Medha. (2017). *Chinese junk ships commonly used in the thirteenth century* [Image]. The Wire. https://thewire.in/history/ibn-battuta-and-his-times.

Selsam, Millicent. *The Voyage of the Beagle*. New York, NY: Harper & Brothers, 1959.

Sharma, Rahul. (2018*). Marco Polo recounting tales of his travels to Rustichello da Pisa while in prison in 1298* [Image]. Alchetron. https://alchetron.com/Rustichello-da-Pisa.

Shillingsburg, Miriam Jones. *At Home Abroad: Mark Twain in Australasia*. Jackson, Mississippi: University of Mississippi Press, 1988.

Southern, Neta Snook. *I Taught Amelia to Fly*. New York, NY: Vantage Press, 1974.

Strudwick, Helen (General Editor). *The Encyclopedia of Ancient Egypt.* New York: Metro Books, 2006.

Suvorov, Vladimir, and Alexander Sabelnikov. *The First Manned Spaceflight: Russia's Quest for Space.* Commack, New York: Nova Science Publishers, Inc., 1997.

Swapping Skirts for trousers: The Price for a Trip Around the World. (2015). *Map of Jeanne Baret's travels as shown in a map in Admiral Bougainville's book* [Image]. Blog-ical Flask. https://blogicalflask. blogspot.com/.

Swapping Skirts for trousers: The Price for a Trip Around the World. (2015). *The plant discovered by Jeanne Baret, known as bougainvillea* [Image]. Blog-ical Flask. https://blogicalflask.blogspot.com/.

Swapping Skirts for trousers: The Price for a Trip Around the World. (2015). *Plant discovered by Jeanne Baret, later called Solanum baretiae* [Image]. Blog-ictal Flask. https://blogicalflask.blogspot.com/.

Taylor, James. *The Voyage of the Beagle.* Annapolis, Maryland: Naval Institute Press, 2008.

The Bermuda Adventures of Mark Twain. (2011). *Mark Twain in Bermuda* [Image]. Repeating Islands. https://repeatingislands.com/2011/12/02/ the-bermuda-adventures-of-mark-twain/.

The Great Debate: The Annexation of Texas, 1845-1846. (n.d.). *Territorial Acquisitions: 1783 – 1853* [Image]. Weebly. https://texas-annexation. weebly.com/the-opposing-forces.html.

The Man: Yuri Gagarin, the First Cosmonaut. (n.d.). *Yuri Gagarin (left) and Guerman Titov (right), Gagarin's alternate on the Vostok 1 mission* [Image]. Yuriesfera. https://yuriesfera.net/documentos/el-hombre/.

Thomson, Keith. *The Young Charles Darwin.* New York, NY: Yale University Press, 2009.

Topbuzz.com. (n.d.). *Columbus' harmful actions against the natives turns fatal* [Image]. Pinterest. https://www.pinterest.com/pin/848084173564077714/.

TripAdvisor. (2011). *Statue of Admiral Zheng He at Zheng He Treasure Ship Park in Nanjing as he looks out over the shipyards* [Image]. TripAdvisor. https://www.tripadvisor.com/LocationPhotoDirectLink-g294220-d1765570-i42008081-Zheng_He_Treasure_Ship_Park-Nanjing_Jiangsu.html.

Tripathi, Rina. (June 11, 2010): "Nain Singh Rawat", The Spy Explorer. Rina Tripathi's Blog.

Trippe, Juan C. *Charles A. Lindbergh and World Travel.* New York, NY: Wings Club, 1977.

Von Hagen, Victor Wolfgang. *South America Called Them.* New York, NY: Alfred A Knopf, 1945.

Walker, Stephen. *Beyond.* New York, NY: HarperCollins Publishers.

Waller, Derek. *The Pundits.* Lexington, Kentucky: The University Press of Kentucky, 1990.

Wallerstein, Alex. (2014). *Soviet Union spies, Julius, and Ethel Rosenberg* [Image]. Nuclear Secrecy. http://blog.nuclearsecrecy.com/2014/10/17/riddle-julius-rosenberg/.

Weatherford, Jack. *Genghis Khan and the Making of the Modern World.* New York: Three Rivers Press, 2004.

Welland, Dennis. *Mark Twain in England.* Atlantic Highlands, New Jersey: Humanities Press, 1978.

Wellcome Collection. (2018). *Christopher Columbus receiving from Queen Isabel of Spain his nomination as Viceroy of the territories he will discover on his voyages* [Image]. Wikipedia Commons. https://commons.wikimedia. org/wiki/File:Christopher_Columbus_Wellcome_V0044818.jpg.

Whence the Koran? (2018). *Map of the Fertile Crescent* [Image]. Tingis Magazine. https://www.tingismagazine.com/editorials/whence-the-koran/.

Wonham, Henry B. *Mark Twain and the Art of the Tall Tale*. New York, NY: Oxford University Press, 1993.

Zheng He (Cheng Ho) – Chinese Explorer. (2012). *Zheng He is commanding his treasure fleet* [Image]. Epic World History. https:// epicworldhistory.blogspot.com/2012/07/zheng-he-cheng-ho-chinese-explorer.html.

Wellcome Collection. (2018). *Christopher Columbus receiving from Queen Isabel of Spain his nomination as Viceroy of the territories he will discover on his voyages* [Image]. Wikipedia Commons. https://commons.wikimedia. org/wiki/File:Christopher_Columbus_Wellcome_V0044818.jpg.

Whence the Koran? (2018). *Map of the Fertile Crescent* [Image]. Tingis Magazine. https://www.tingismagazine.com/editorials/whence-the-koran/.

Wonham, Henry B. *Mark Twain and the Art of the Tall Tale*. New York, NY: Oxford University Press, 1993.

Zheng He (Cheng Ho) – Chinese Explorer. (2012). *Zheng He is commanding his treasure fleet* [Image]. Epic World History. https:// epicworldhistory.blogspot.com/2012/07/zheng-he-cheng-ho-chinese-explorer.html.

Wellcome Collection. (2018). *Christopher Columbus receiving from Queen Isabel of Spain his nomination as Viceroy of the territories he will discover on his voyages* [Image]. Wikipedia Commons. https://commons.wikimedia. org/wiki/File:Christopher_Columbus_Wellcome_V0044818.jpg.

Whence the Koran? (2018). *Map of the Fertile Crescent* [Image]. Tingis Magazine. https://www.tingismagazine.com/editorials/whence-the-koran/.

Wonham, Henry B. *Mark Twain and the Art of the Tall Tale*. New York, NY: Oxford University Press, 1993.

Zheng He (Cheng Ho) – Chinese Explorer. (2012). *Zheng He is commanding his treasure fleet* [Image]. Epic World History. https://epicworldhistory.blogspot.com/2012/07/zheng-he-cheng-ho-chinese-explorer.html.

Wellcome Collection. (2018). *Christopher Columbus receiving from Queen Isabel of Spain his nomination as Viceroy of the territories he will discover on his voyages* [Image]. Wikipedia Commons. https://commons.wikimedia.org/wiki/File:Christopher_Columbus_Wellcome_V0044818.jpg.

Whence the Koran? (2018). *Map of the Fertile Crescent* [Image]. Tingis Magazine. https://www.tingismagazine.com/editorials/whence-the-koran/.

Wonham, Henry B. *Mark Twain and the Art of the Tall Tale*. New York, NY: Oxford University Press, 1993.

Zheng He (Cheng Ho) – Chinese Explorer. (2012). *Zheng He is commanding his treasure fleet* [Image]. Epic World History. https://epicworldhistory.blogspot.com/2012/07/zheng-he-cheng-ho-chinese-explorer.html.

Wellcome Collection. (2018). Christopher Columbus receiving from Queen Isabel of Spain his nomination as Viceroy of the territories he will discover on his voyages [Image]. Wikipedia Commons. https://commons.wikimedia.org/wiki/File:Christopher_Columbus_Wellcome_V0044818.jpg.

Whence the Koran? (2018). Map of the Fertile Crescent [Image]. Tingis Magazine. https://www.tingismagazine.com/editorials/whence-the-koran/.

Wonham, Henry B. Mark Twain and the Art of the Tall Tale. New York, NY: Oxford University Press, 1993.

Zheng He (Cheng Ho) – Chinese Explorer. (2012). Zheng He is commanding his treasure fleet [Image]. Epic World History. https://epicworldhistory.blogspot.com/2012/07/zheng-he-cheng

NOW IT'S YOUR TURN TO TRAVEL.
WE WISH YOU WELL.